My mind to me a kingdom be a
temple of love, truth and sanctity.

Eamon Melaugh was born on the 4th of July 1933, in Derry City, Northern Ireland. His earliest memories are of the conditions in Derry during the depression years – 'hungry thirties'. In order to contribute to the meagre family income, Eamon had to leave school aged 14 to try and find work. The lack of opportunity for third level education was to be a lasting regret. However, Eamon is a keen reader and has continued his self-education throughout his life. Concentrating on the spiritual reasons for life here on planet Earth. Eamon realises that the most important question in life is, "Where and how will he spend eternity?"

I dedicate this book to my wife, Mary, whom I married in 1956, she has been my one and only girlfriend. Our union has been blessed by our 11 wonderful children.

Mary and Eamon Melaugh and their 11 little darlings

Eamon Melaugh

PATHWAYS TO PARADISE

ETERNITY AWAITS

AUSTIN MACAULEY PUBLISHERS™

LONDON * CAMBRIDGE * NEW YORK * SHARJAH

A CIP catalogue record for this title is available from the British Library.

ISBN 9781528980944 (Paperback)
ISBN 9781528980951 (ePub e-book)

www.austinmacauley.com

First Published (2021)
Austin Macauley Publishers Ltd
25 Canada Square
Canary Wharf
London
E14 5LQ

I wish to thank Joe Mc Allister of Hive Studios for his expertise in all things technological. It would amiss of me not to express my love and gratitude for the patients and forbearance of my wife and children for their encouragement.

Table of Contents

Introduction

There have been countless books written by individuals claiming to have the answers to the complex problems that hinder the spiritual development of mankind; every sort of advice has been offered to those seeking liberation from the struggles of life, and for the seeker there is no definitive solutions in reading words printed on paper. Willie Shakespeare said, *'Words without thought to heaven never go,'* There are those who reject the notion that life has a spiritual dimension, believing that life begins in the womb and ends in the tomb. Those who believe this have made little or no effort to confront the contradiction contained in their belief; the thought that the cosmos and everything therein is the result of chance or fate is truly a bizarre notion. It's patently obvious that there is a guiding intelligence operating throughout the cosmos, without which the cosmos would spin out of control causing chaos and cataclysmic disaster.

The itinerant philosopher, Jesus, who meandered through Palestine two thousand years ago, has left a legacy of spiritual truth if acted upon, and will provide the means and method of spiritual salvation. His message has been manipulated by organised churches around the world and the manipulation has spread confusion. His message was, and is crystal clear. The core of His philosophy was love, pure and simple; to find the true path that will lead to Paradise, love has to be the core reason for all activities.

If every thought conceived was conceived in love, and every word spoken was spoken in love, and every deed performed was performed in love, God would send legions of his angels to surround you and they would feel privileged to be in your company.

Ralph Waldo Emerson has advised us, "If you always do what you have always done you will always get what you have always got," how utterly true.

Liberation from the mundane trivia that is the inevitable consequences of living in secondary causes; liberation from endless trivialities can and will be achieved by the wise and intelligent individual who freely, intelligently, and spiritually accepts that love, and love alone, is the only means of personal liberation. The Beatles got it right when they sang, 'All you need is love,'

There are six questions that must be addressed and satisfactory explanation found (1) Who am I? (2) What am I? (3) Why was I granted life? (4) What, if any, does life impose upon me? (5) What will be my fate when I die? (6) Where and how will I spend eternity? The reason for life in a mortal body of matter is to give the highest human expressions to the divine attributes that God has bequeathed to all of humanity. Place the truth above and beyond every other consideration; or expressed another way, in all situation and circumstances say only what is true, do only what is right—it's as simple or difficult as that. Love and Truth are the twin reasons for all existence and those who seek to give spiritual expression to both are treading the secret path that will most assuredly lead to the gates of paradise. If you sincerely and lovingly seek for Truth and compassion you will be divinely rewarded with an everlasting life of profound peace. Conventional religion cannot of itself provide spiritual liberation; nor can science liberate mankind from the threat that within the cauldron of science we have acquired the ability to end all life forms from planet earth. We live first and foremost in our minds; so, the search for spiritual freedom must begin in the mind. Unfortunately, the mind when used in its negative mode is the root cause of most of the problems that are responsible for all the emotional pain experienced on a regular basis.

Willie Shakespeare again, "The boat that doesn't yield to the rudder will yield to the rocks."

This book is an attempt to providing a spiritual rudder for the rough waters of life. Humanities' greatest need at this turbulent time of mass violence that is rampant around the world is a clear and comprehensive understanding of our moral obligation to each other. There is but one God, and one family of God; we are all spiritually related, which is much stronger than mere family connections, which are in fact the coincidence of mere chance.

Conventional religions preach the false doctrine of hell and the devil; there is no hell and no all-powerful devil; there are demons that we ourselves create in the undisciplined mind. When we entertain thoughts of malice, hate, greed, envy, anger, and deceit, these thoughts are our own created demons. It's this type of negative thought that seriously impedes spiritual development. The mind that wallows in negativity will prevent any and all spiritual progress; the negative mind is your greatest enemy, it has you in a vice like grip at its tender less mercy.

Paradoxically, the mind when used in its positive mode will be the source of spiritual liberation. The mind of mankind has to an overwhelming degree become conditioned by a ceaseless obsession of desiring material things, and when their desires are not realised, frustration and dissatisfaction are the inevitable results; disappointment descends into despair. To end all emotional pain, misery, and indifference caused by spiritual ignorance, accept the spiritual reality that god and you are one and live accordingly.

I will at the end of each chapter interrupt the spiritual dialogue to acquaint the reader with some of my personal experiences of events that are in some instances extremely strange.

Chapter 1

Life

"Without the Way there is no going,
Without the Truth there is no knowing,
Without the Life there is no living."

(Thos. A Kempis)

"The man who lives in the true light and true love has the finest, noblest, and most worthwhile life that ever was or will be, therefore, it cannot but be loved and treasured above any other life." (Theologia Germanica)

Does life have a purpose? If so, how can the purpose be identified? Without this identification life cannot be lived in accordance with whatever obligations that human existence places on each and every individual.

A very brief examination of the cosmos provides convincing evidence that there is a guiding universal intelligence in operation and without this all-pervading intelligence the cosmos would in all likelihood spin out of control and eventually disintegrate. Intelligence is then the means of maintaining order through the whole of creation and if we as individuals are to gain a comprehensive understanding of our position in the grand scheme of life then we must be prepared to conduct an intelligent assessment of what life expects from us. There are many individuals who never have, and will never conduct any meaningful examination of the reason for their existence in human form and what they are supposed to achieve in life.

I had a friend (now deceased), who for forty years had been asking, "What is it all about?" referring to life. He never did receive a satisfactory answer for this reason; he like so many others who ask this mightiest of questions concerning life do not realise they have not reached the necessary psychological level of understanding required to receive an answer.

Life is from God; or to be more precise God is Life. If we start our investigation with this proposition then our inquiry will be speedily rewarded with the most surprising and beautiful results. If you truly desire to know what is life and want to know why you were given life and what life consists of, you take encouragement from the fact that the answers exist, but every individual must raise their level of understanding before they are ready to receive these answers.

Right at the beginning I suggest to you the reader that God who is the supreme architect of life requires from all His children that they give the highest possible human expression to all of His divine attributes. When we, as individuals, freely and lovingly comply with the wishes of God, the right conditions are in place so that we may advance to a higher level of understanding which will allow the individual to give divine expression to the attributes of God.

I will not pursue this matter any further at this juncture as these propositions are comprehensively dealt with in the book. I find it amazing that the millions of individuals refuse to seek, even at a superficial level, explanations as to the reasons for life and from time to time I try to engage other individuals in debate on this most important of all matters. This attempted engagement is always frustrating, not for me, but for the person whom I engage with and the frustration has its origins in ignorance. People everywhere are being defeated by indifference and ignorance, and those who refuse to confront these twin evils must continue to live a life of confusion that must result in dissatisfaction and disappointment. And such a life will inevitably result in a wasted life that is bound to end in disaster, it cannot possibly be otherwise.

I have enquired from a number of individuals what are their opinions of life by asking them this simple question, "What does life mean to you?"

And here are some of the answers,

"A period of consciousness that ends at death." (Journalist)

"Life is something you live." (Politician)

"I don't know." (Market trader)

"Being involved in different activities." (Photographer)

"Life is energy." (Lawyer)

"I haven't thought much about it." (Businessman)

"Life is a preparatory experience for an existence in another dimension." (Taxi driver).

These answers are, I would suggest, typical of the confusion that exists concerning life, its meaning and purpose. Most people are concerned by what they think they should be doing during their lives. The search is never-ending. They seek something that will give meaning to life, what it is that will make life more worthwhile? Many illusions regarding life have been created by ignorance and the task confronting all of mankind is how and where to discover the knowledge that will provide liberation from human folly and all the pain that is the bedfellow of spiritual blindness. There is a way out of confusion and folly, and those with the courage requiring will, after having read this book, will know what is required of them. Many of the propositions in this book will be new and challenging. Don't reject any new knowledge until you have studied the book in its entirety. Let us begin at the only starting place available to the sincere seeker after truth and that is with God. There is only one life; God is life and God is universal and eternal, so life must also be eternal and universal. Life manifests on three levels, there is the spiritual dimension, the intellectual and the physical. If life is God, then God is your foundation, your very being, and if God is not at the very centre of your life you will experience much heartache along the way. God has placed mankind on earth for the purpose of discovering their true identity and to overcome all human problems.

It was the Christ speaking through Jesus who proclaimed the truth concerning mankind's identity when He said, "Ye are the sons of God." Jesus accepted the truth of life, that He and God were one; this is not only the truth of mankind but also all life forms throughout creation. The truth is that God created mankind out of His perfect spiritual substance in His image and likeness— meaning we share all of God's attributes.

There can be no lasting improvement in any life until the truth of our eternal and spiritual relationship to God is accepted and acted upon. The truth of your existence is that the Universal Spirit of God is personalised within you and if you act intelligently on this information you will experience a new life that lives deep within your heart and soul.

'Higher, deeper, innermost, abides Another Life,' [Bhagavad-Gita]

God in His love and goodness for humanity has bestowed all His attributes to every individual. The most important consciousness and the highest expression of consciousness is the Christ Consciousness. Those who have been

16

elevated to this level of understanding experience life in all of its glory and wonderment; Christ Consciousness is available to anyone who is prepared to live life as Jesus lived it.

It is consciousness that produces awareness, intelligence, understanding, intuition and wisdom. Consciousness is universal and pervades all space so everything in creation has to some degree consciousness; there are many degrees in being conscious, but there can be no degrees of consciousness. There is no division in consciousness; it cannot be separated, detached, or removed from anything that exists anywhere in the universe.

Consciousness, like God, never had a beginning, nor will it ever cease to exist, and without it life could not manifest in or out of the body. Consciousness is the only means available whereby we can elevate our lives, or to be more accurate, it is the proper use of consciousness that will lead mankind eventually to spiritual freedom.

Each and every individual must become consciously aware that life is from God and the Consciousness of God is the consciousness in every individual; human existence would be impossible without consciousness. Life means to be consciously aware of your existence in human form, to be aware of your surroundings and activities; your awareness will, if you allow it, let you understand that you are also a spiritual being. To fully understand your place in the universal scheme, as designed by God, it will be necessary for you to raise your consciousness to Christ Consciousness. As this matter is dealt with in more detail later on, we will leave it for now.

Life is subject to the Law of life. When God created the Universe and everything therein He ordained that there should be a Law to govern it. All living things, including mankind, are subject to the Law. To live life as God intended, we need to accept that the Law exists—to understand its mode of operation, what benefits can be gained by adhering to the demands of the Law and what consequences, if any, be there for violation.

Jesus brilliantly and with wonderful simplicity explained the Law when He said, "As ye sow so shall ye reap." This is the Law of Cause and Effect.

Jesus on another occasion had this observation to make regarding the Law, "It is done unto you according to your belief." It is all so wonderfully simple, your thoughts, whatever they are, calls the Law into operation and the quality of your life is determined by the quality of your thinking. The Law is constantly in operation and is always impersonal. It has no faults, but will produce unfavourable results if given wrong direction. The Law is subject to the Word. First there has to be the Word or thought and the Law is automatically set in motion; the Law can only respond according to the direction received from the thought or thoughts.

Let us examine in some detail the reasoning behind the Word and what role it plays in our everyday experiences; according to the evangelist John 1:1-5.

'Before the world was created, the Word already existed (He) was with God, and (He) was the same as God. From the very beginning the Word was with God. Through (Him) God made all things; not one thing in all creation was made without (Him.) The Word was the source of life, and this life brought light to mankind. The light shines in the darkness and the darkness has never put it out,'

John tells us that the Word of God is all-powerful; it is responsible for all creation and everything therein. Further, John goes on to personalise the Word suggesting the Word is in fact a person or being referring to the Word as "he" and "him." In verse 1 John refers to the Word as *'"he" was with God,'* In verse 3 we read, *'through "him" God made all things and not one thing was made without "him",'*

The Word that was in the beginning is the Christ of God. The "He" who was with God in the beginning and was the same as God can be no other than the Christ of God. The Christ is the Universal God individualised in every individual. Christ then is the Word of supreme power and authority. A little later on we will consider the word of power as Christ spoke it through the personality of Jesus.

If your thoughts are negative the Law will respond by producing negative circumstances; conversely if your thoughts are positive you will be rewarded by positive results. For the Law's mode of operation is to produce in the outer physical form whatever direction it has received from the Word. If you violate the Law you will reap exactly what you have sown; violation means negative results, so if you don't like the effect, get to the cause. Think and choose your words carefully; be diligent in your thoughts.

The Old Testament tells us, *'As he thinketh in his heart, he is,'*

We see that the Word is the impetus for calling the Law in to operation and the results are according to the direction received from the Word; the Law is in all circumstances unvarying and cannot in any circumstances be changed or amended. However, the Word that calls the Law into operation can be changed. The Law must, in every situation, comply with the direction it receives from the Word. God created mankind like unto Himself; therefore, each and every individual is the living expression of the Word. The wonderful truth is that you are that very Word, for the Word becomes the thing created. God and His Universal Law is responsible for all of creation and as we have discovered there has to be the involvement of the Word before creation; then every individual is, in fact, the Word. The Law has no inclination of its own and being impersonal must manifest according to the direction it receives from the Word.

The wise and intelligent will form an alliance with the Word and the Law, knowing that with faith they have a formula for securing peace and happiness. If you ask for something and your faith is weak you are sure to be disappointed; your faith has to be strong without a doubt.

Jesus tells us in Mark ch. II ver. 23, *'Have faith in God. I assure you that whoever tells this hill to get up and go and throw itself into the sea and does not doubt in his heart, but believes that which he says will happen. It will be done for him; for this reason I tell you, when you pray and ask for something believe you have received and you will be given whatever you ask for,'*

In this quotation there are guarantees of success and help in every situation no matter how difficult or desperate it is. Any request made to God that is based upon the conviction of success will result in the request being granted. However, Jesus advises us not to doubt, and to pray before making any request. When you have finished praying and having made your request, immediately give thanks to God that your word has been heard and that your request will be granted, don't be impatient and don't doubt your word will not return unto you void. You could pray in the following manner, *"Almighty God I have sent forth my word for (here name your request) in accordance with your divine Law, I lovingly thank you that my word will not return on to me void, but will accomplished that which it was sent forth to achieve."* Do not utter these words lightly; make each word live with sincerity and love and you can be certain that God will respond with love.

You now know that the power of the Law can only be set in motion by the desire of the mind; what the mind decrees will be established in your life. You may not get what you want; if there is conflict in the mind the Law will produce your strongest desire.

The Law is always impersonal, it must however respond to whatever direction it receives from the individual mind. Your word is the seed and the Law is the garden of your immortal soul; without the seed there can be no produce. The seed must first be planted in the soil and when planted there is a waiting period before the flower, fruit or vegetable is produced. If you plant carrot seeds you will get carrots because of the law inherent within the carrot seed. If you desire roses you would be foolish, in the extreme, to plant gooseberries. The law is that you will always get what you plant and you do get your request immediately. When you plant seed in the soil you must wait for the seed to germinate and a further period of time for the plant to grow and reach maturity.

When you desire something and you pray to God, understand that your prayer is the seed. Be sure to choose the right seed; your word is the planting and the Law is the finished produce. You only have to wait, without a doubt in the sure and certain knowledge that your request will be granted. Don't be discouraged if there is a delay in response to your request for help, the work is being done in accordance with your thoughts. Don't doubt, even for a second, for the Law is infallible and you should give continual thanks to God that your word has been heard and will not return unanswered. Jesus, in His knowing, gave to mankind the infallible and immutable Law of Life when He told us that we must receive what is sent forth from the mind.

The Christian Bible contains many promises of God's help for those in need. To receive help, acknowledge God as being the only creator; the source of all power and authority, and in the Son of God. Keep a constant awareness of the spiritual union that exists between you and God and many things will be revealed to you. The macrocosm is spiritually and faithfully reproduced in the microcosm—God being the macrocosm, humanity the microcosm. God is, as you know, first cause. If you desire a life of love, peace and contentment return to first cause, for the divine essence of God is ever seeking individual expression in every person. As individuals, we create all our problems because of our belief in separation from God; a rejection of this false belief is the only guarantee of a life free from all difficulties.

We have established that the mind is subject to the law of cause and effect; when the mind is used with sensitivity and is encouraged to think only positive thoughts life will change in a manner that at this time you cannot comprehend. The effects you experience are caused by the mind; if you don't like the effect then do the wise and intelligent thing by going to the cause, which is the mind. Direct the mind with sensitivity and wisdom that it may become your servant. To stop the mind causing pain and hurt, it's necessary to raise your conscious awareness of why and how things go so badly wrong. Your feelings, emotions and reactions are not the real you; you are, if you so decide, greater than thought, circumstances or events.

Let's return to the Word of power as spoken by Christ through Jesus; the Word of Christ is the Word of Truth and is the most potent Word of all. Therefore, the Word of Christ if accepted by any individual and sent forth with faith will bring forth great spiritual rewards. Every individual should seek freedom from ignorance and folly, for only when we eradicate both can we hope for any spiritual advancement. When you earnestly seek for spiritual liberation and succeed, everything else will be added unto you.

Christ speaking through Jesus proclaimed the universal Truth when He said: 'I and the Father are one,' Send forth this Word of unity, that you and the Father are one and when this spiritual reality is established within your consciousness you stand at the very portal of Paradise. Ask God to make you aware of His Presence; say in your heart, you my beloved Father and I are one and your word will not return unto you void.

Christ proclaimed the truth of unity when He spoke, through Jesus, these words, "I am the Life."

You should sing this hymn of the One Life shared with God and all of humanity; please accept the truth of your eternal existence in and with God. Repeat many times every day with love and humility, *"I am the life,"* knowing that God has created you out of His perfect spiritual substance. Know that you are Life itself and that with the right use of your word the spiritual reality of your union with God will be forever established in your consciousness. The beautiful truth is this, you only have to accept God's wonderful gifts. The great Law of life is ever available to all and will respond to whatever direction it receives. Do not abuse the Law by seeking mere possessions; yes, the Law will grant your desires whatever they may be. Your state of being is the most important aspect of your existence; you should concentrate on your spiritual understanding and seek the kingdom of heaven within you and its right use and everything else will be yours. When you speak the word of truth of your true spiritual identity your word forms a spiritual coalition with the Law and you will know that God and you are one.

The Word to be sent forth is then, *"You my beloved Father and I are one."*

Everyone of intelligence wants to live at peace and contentment with themselves and with everyone else, but doesn't know where or how to find that which they seek. The type of life you live is determined by your habitual thinking. Thoughts determine the quality of life you live and it can't possibly be otherwise. When a true perception of life is found, then and only then will all that pains you be brought to a permanent end. It is the mind that is steeped in the ignorance and confusion that blinds us to the real meaning of life. When the mind is cleansed of ignorance, confusion and illusion life will be clearly seen as an opportunity for the expression of love, wisdom and compassion.

Life has only one source and that source is God. Therefore, God is Life and Life is God. The same Life that lived in Jesus lives in you and me. Life being from God is Universal and we all share in this Life and the life that lives in you is God in you. You are the Life and when you fully accept that God is the Life in you, then you will live Life as opposed to living life. You must accept that you and God are united in Life for all eternity. Your freedom and happiness depends on your willingness to embrace the truth of your unity with God. Of course, if you truly want to be free, you must be prepared and willing to surrender all illusion, inherited opinions and negative thinking.

If your life is filled with negative thinking, if your thoughts are dominated by hate, anger, fear, greed and jealousy you can be sure your life will be one of pain and misery. All our problems stem from our ignorance of what life is and how we are meant to live it. For most individuals the mind has become the great deceiver; a mind deceiving itself, this is the cause of much confusion. Is it any wonder our reasoning is so weak and confused and that trivial events cause so much pain and anger?

God offers to every mind the choice between thinking positive or negative thoughts. If the mind is given negative direction then the outcome must be sadness and regret; alternatively, the mind will produce peace and happiness if given positive direction. The negative mind can do no other than create problems; by its mode of operation it cannot in any circumstances confer contentment. The discontented mind will, you can be sure, heap woe upon heartbreak. To regain mental composure the mind has to be purged of all negativity. The mind purified by love and reason will banish forever all sorrow and sadness, making life more rewarding and worthwhile. When the mind is given intelligent direction, it will delight in being the cause and source of its own improvement; the greatest improvement would be to give the mind over to thoughts of love, honesty, probity and understanding. There is nothing in or out of nature to prevent your mind from harbouring these noble thoughts and giving expression to them. Great thoughts when acted upon become great deeds. You can make real progress if the desire is strong; you have the ability and authority to direct the mind with intelligence. You can, if you so wish, refuse to be influenced by any event, for you are superior to circumstances. It is the limited and stunted mind that causes all our problems, because this type of mind fears to explore new ideas which if adopted would allow mental and spiritual growth.

"A free mind has the power to achieve all things." [Eckhart]

Let love rule the mind and heart that the truth may take hold of your imagination and you will experience lasting peace and contentment. Peace and contentment are the glorious prizes to be gained by those who have their minds under control. The mind that creates the problems is the only instrument for ending them. As the mind becomes purified it becomes more intelligent, its capacity for enjoyment increases. If the mind is mindful of its own progress towards self-awareness it will gain in composure, find liberation and become master of every situation. Use the mind to detect were it needs improving and when the mind discovers weakness, it will use its natural intelligence to correct any flaws. The awakened mind has at its disposal unprejudiced natural intelligence and when this intelligence is employed, it is an invincible means of mind improvement.

To be consciously aware of what is going on in the mind is the only means of ending unhappiness; if the mind is troubled so also is the soul. The quality of your life depends entirely on the condition of the mind. If the mind be at peace your entire being will be in a state of tranquillity. The most important activity that anyone can engage in is to bring to a successful conclusion, all mental folly, and everything that impedes the mind's elevation towards peace and perfection. It is mind conflict, which causes sorrow and sadness. There is genuine satisfaction only when we truly seek to establish the highest moral virtues in our daily intercourse with those we come into contact with. This is the true art of living life as life was intended to be lived.

"What is virtue but repose of mind?" [Thompson]

The truly great individuals of history were those who succeeded in conquering all their negative tendencies. Freedom in the world cannot be secured by overcoming external and unfavourable circumstances alone, but in understanding that the mind is what we allow it to become, friend or foe. If you are unhappy or unsatisfied with your life, you no longer have to endure either; the road to freedom lies before you and the further along the road you travel, the more contentment and peace you will experience. Your fate is not forever fixed; what you decree is your fate. Your life can begin anew; God in His goodness has made you master in your own house. Don't rebel against any situation no matter how adverse and never surrender control over the mind; your ability to think constructive intelligent thoughts is the only means of elevating the mind above all unfavourable circumstances.

The Buddha gave the following excellent advice, "Be a lamp unto yourself."

The true nature of man, which is spiritual, is unchanging; however, the law of evolution requires that man gives spiritual expression to the noblest thoughts and deeds. Then and only then can life in full measure be lived.

Many are ignorant of the presence and purpose of the soul. Without soul, life could not exist; the life that lives in you and me is the conscious expression of the soul. Soul is the Divine Consciousness of God and soul consciousness is the living Presence of God within every person, and when we as individuals give expression to soul consciousness, the life of ignorance and confusion will be ended. Bring your life into the light of your immortal soul, into the light of reason, the light of love; then your judgements will be sound and you will experience a continual improvement in every aspect of life. The only thing that can hold you back from becoming the type of person you most want to be is the undisciplined mind. You will prevail against all adversity when you fill the heart with love and the mind with reason.

In the quest for the real meaning of life many doubts will be encountered; however, when you use your understanding wisely you will overcome any and all obstacles. This overcoming will increase your mental strength providing the required strength to continue on the quest to find the life of continual happiness and permanent peace. It's simply not good enough to possess an active and intelligent mind, it has to be used wisely and positively. The most important thing in any life is how the mind is used. The mind must respond to the direction it receives; if the mind is fed powerful negative impulses it becomes the powerful oppressor and tyrant that will block any advance towards mental and spiritual improvement. Positive thoughts are the solution to all mental problems.

Marcus Aurelius clearly identified the power of the mind for he has written:

'Those who do not observe the movement of their own minds must of necessity be unhappy,'

The more the mind's strength is increased by the exercise of healthy natural thoughts, the greater the benefits it will bestow. You may, in attempting to discipline the mind, have a mental mountain to climb; difficult it may be, but when you reach the mental summit you will see vistas reserved for those courageous souls who have conquered fear, hate, anger and despair. As you look around you from this mountain-top, you will realise that all sorrow and confusion is far below, and having reached this particular elevation you will never again have to descend to the valley of tears and fears.

Until you conquer the mountain of ignorance and confusion, don't despair, for with courage and knowledge you can overcome all the barriers that at times seem insurmountable. God did not create any one of us for failure. With Him at our side, everything is possible and success is divinely guaranteed. Can there be a more reassuring thought than this? Your greatest need is to be true to your genuine self-interest; don't be too concerned by short-term interests of materialism or other personal advantages. Keep the mind focused on being aware of itself and the type of thoughts that are being entertained. If the mind is allowed to wallow in the mire of mundane trivia characterised by casual and negative thoughts then any progress is impossible. The quest for liberation begins in the mind and for the mind to be freed from negative servitude it must be instructed to think thoughts of love, compassion and understanding.

You won't make sense of life until you are able to comprehend who and what you are. To know yourself is of supreme importance, for when you know who and what you are, you have gained the secret of life itself. The truth of your real spiritual identity will set you free from all illusion. You will know that life itself is free and natural and freedom is your natural state. Life is consciousness, awareness and is eternal, never having had a beginning nor will it ever end. Life has produced you the complete person, the spiritual you. It is only when we acquire a clear understanding of our spirituality and accept that life is eternal can we begin to truly live. Because of our false belief in separation from God, who is the only source of life, do we create the problems and conditions we rebel against?

It is your present, false beliefs and borrowed opinions that enslave you. People think they want many things from life and that life should conform to their distorted opinions of it. People continually pander to their material ambitions in the vain hope of achieving worldly success, hoping that things can give them security and bring them happiness. A large house, a beautiful partner, an expensive car or cash in the bank can't make you happy or secure.

People have strange ideas of life, but ideas of life are not life. There are individuals who believe that they can serve and save humanity through some cause. Witness the killing and human destruction perpetrated by fanatics who are serving nationalist or religious causes. Any cause that makes us callous, cruel and that allows us to commit or condone murder is perversion. Perversion, corruption and depravity is rampant in our contemporary society. Paedophilia, drugs and promiscuity are the order of the day and our civilisation is decaying because we have elevated perverted pleasure over common decency. Millions falsely believe that worldly success, if attained, would satisfy the mortal ego and provide lasting pleasure, but the truth is that nothing of this world will provide the self-fulfilment that all decent and intelligent individuals rightly desire. It is our impoverished thinking that causes us to believe that external activities and material acquisitions can provide happiness or contentment.

You must let go of all preconceived ideas. Yes, we live in a material world, but we are spiritual beings first and foremost and as such we are not bound by it. To find the true meaning of life and how to live it we must turn to the source of Life. In truth, you, the real you, are a completely different person to what you believe yourself to be. Your most pressing need at this moment in time is to raise your physiological level of understanding. You are not merely a body with intelligence; you are an indestructible spiritual being, a creation of God. For you to understand and comprehend life you need a power greater than any mental conception. The physical mind or intellectual power is limited to mundane daily activities and can't by themselves bring you the freedom your heart desires.

Cosmic Intelligence

Intellectual ability or the gratification of your desires won't end ignorance or the confusion that causes so much pain. Accept that there is a higher intelligence than your own and it is available to you at all times. It is Cosmic Intelligence, the same intelligence that created your soul, body and mind and it's this intelligence that keeps your body functioning. The truth concerning your life is that you live in the Infinite Mind of Almighty God that fills all space. Know that you will live forever, for the life in you is eternal. It is absurd to think that we can live apart from life. The fact that you live means your living has, therefore, got to be the most obvious and crucial factor in your personal experiences. Life is the Presence of God within you. If God is life then every individual is the individualisation of the Universal Life.

By your awareness of God's in-dwelling presence you bring into sharp focus your higher consciousness. When this happens, you know that life is free and uncomplicated. You are united through all eternity to God, therefore your life cannot be bound by body or limited by mind. If you are to gain freedom you must strive for a clear understanding of your relationship to God. Ego gratification is the main activity of most people. A misspent life seeking thrills, excitement and sex gratification must lead to frustration and failure because this type of life must ignore the presence of God.

Human Folly

There can be little doubt that our civilisation is in a terminal state of decay. On the one hand there is opulence, the acquisition of wealth being the predominant activity of the industrial world. And it has to be said that all too many individuals have acquired more material wealth than they have the moral courage to use intelligently or wisely. In the third world, an innocent child dies every three seconds from starvation or disease directly linked to malnutrition. In the rich capitalist world we pay our farmers billions of dollars not to grow food. Fields are left fallow while millions of children starve to death every year. This crime against our weakest brethren is inexcusable and unforgivable. Our civilisation cannot survive such callous and cruel indifference to the plight of all those innocent victims who have paid with their young lives for our indifference and greed. There must surely be a day of reckoning. Billions of dollars are spent every day purchasing armaments, weapons that are intended to intimidate and kill, while at the same time children are starving to death all over the third world. The monies spent on procuring the means of mass destruction could, if spent wisely, end the pitiless destruction of innocent children who must forfeit their young lives because of callous neglect by capitalist governments.

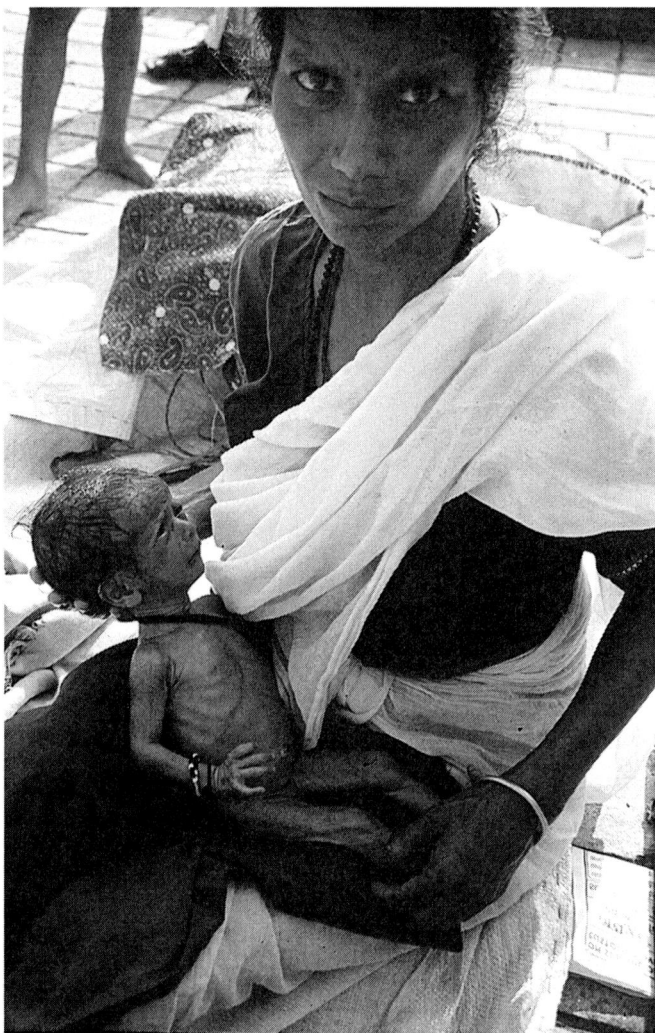

This skeleton child died two days after I took this harrowing photo. Note the sadness in the mother's eyes, she knows that her beautiful child is losing the battle to live.

Famine, hunger and destitution could and should be ended and while they exist, we all know what the consequences will be for the destitute in the third world—death from wilful indifference. While this totally immoral situation is allowed to exist, then we as a species are morally blighted and we can never know peace or happiness. These things happen because we choose to remain ignorant of what life is meant to be. The cardinal reason for life on earth is for the purpose of learning who you are and what you are, certainly not for the passing gratification of the senses. The sooner we learn that we have been placed on earth as essential components in a universal scheme, the architect being God Himself, the sooner we will live life to the full. We have a divine mission in life and you can be certain that you can discover and understand what is expected of you in relation to the universal scheme. When you know and become an active partner with God in His great scheme, then and only then will you find the lasting peace and harmony that your heart and soul desires.

"Just as a candle cannot burn without fire, men cannot live without a spiritual life." [Buddha]

Life Everlasting

Life manifests itself through your consciousness and awareness, and manifests to the exact degree that you are consciously aware of yourself and your relationship to the source of Life. People are complicated, life is not. It is responsive and requires no effort on our part. Your mission in life is to overcome all the illusions of this world.

Jesus said, "I have overcome the world."

You are meant to come to a clear understanding that you are first and foremost an indestructible spiritual being. That you are spirit clothed in a body of flesh and you know that the body will return to dust, while the spiritual you will live forever. In life we desire many things—fortune, fame, power, privilege, respect, good health, expensive car and a beautiful partner or partners. These desires if fulfilled will, we wrongly believe, make us secure and happy. We are made happy only when the soul is freed from all mundane human bondage. Liberation for the soul is liberation also for the outer physical man. The soul if given recognition has the spiritual ability to lift man to the sublime heights of love, peace, harmony and truth. We experience pain in the outer world of materialism and conformity; it's our attachment to outworn beliefs and theories that keeps us enslaved to folly.

A deep spiritual insight into the nature of all things is the true art of living. If your thinking is mechanical, conditional and mundane your life will be dominated by insecurity, and anxiety. To change your life you must return like the Prodigal Son in deepest humility to the Father. No matter how dark or desperate your life has become God will reveal Himself in all His Glory to any true penitent. At some time in every life, when because of the suffering endured by the mind that is full of contradictions, the soul will stir and make known its presence. This stirring of the soul is a crystal-clear message of the need to renounce conventional worldly life and to return to our true spiritual nature. Your soul with its spiritual consciousness is the real you. You exist physically so that the soul may have worldly experiences that can only be achieved while in a human body. When you give yourself over to the spiritual authority of your immortal soul, your soul will respond by taking care of your mind and body, and your soul, mind and body will co-exist in spiritual health and physical harmony. Human activities are for the most part only diversions that cloud our good judgements; when you find true happiness and contentment you won't need diversions. Happiness is from within outwards and never ever from without inwards.

To understand our freedom we must first clearly understand our imprisonment. Only when we are fully aware that we are prisoners of our opinions and reactions can there be any real hope for deliverance. Bondage, when fully understood, can become the means of freedom. Suffering is the inevitable result of being unable or unwilling to see that we are prisoners of pessimistic thoughts and resulting emotional behaviour. Your mind in its negative mode is the prison from which you must escape. So when the mind begins the struggle for freedom, the mind must face the conundrum that it is the problem. The paradox being that mind must be freed from mind. We need to free the mind from mind itself. Only when we become consciously aware that the mind is the problem can the solution be found. The uncontrolled mind is the unobserved mind and the unobserved mind is the cause of all our pain and suffering.

Insist from yourself constant improvement that you may experience inner contentment and spiritual awareness. In every situation and at all times be willing to submit to your finer instincts that you may grow ever more beautifully in character. Liberate your mind from the tyranny of convention; help your mind, by the use of natural intelligence, to protect itself from mass opinions. Allow your mind to cultivate a higher mode of thought than the dangerous mass mind that has imprisoned humanity. Liberation comes through understanding your desires and by becoming aware of the dreadful effects of negative thinking.

What is required is a sustained conscious effort at observing what the mind is thinking and how it induces our moods be they good or evil. No one in the history of mankind is superior to what you may attain. There can be no limits to your potential; you can attain any goal, achieve any ambition, succeed in any quest, conquer all fear, and overcome all obstacles. Know well that you alone are the only one who can reform the mind. Your new birth and new life can only be achieved when you wisely discern that the old life is a shallow contrivance at best, and at worst, bondage. To gain the new life you need only obey reason; let your natural abilities guide you. Learn quickly to pronounce the word no. No, I won't do this stupid thing; no, I won't utter unkind words; no, I won't think silly thoughts. Salvation exists in our unquestioning ability to say no. Never trust to others your happiness or peace of mind; nothing or no one can give you the security you crave. Don't waste time and energy seeking the esteem or approval of others. Seek instead union with wisdom and an understanding of your spiritual relationship to God. Always be prepared to do what reason and intelligence suggests and if convinced by reasoning and intelligence you should be willing to change previously held convictions. The wise and intelligent are those few amongst us who are straining every muscle and sinew in the quest for human perfection and who have fallen in love with their quest for truth.

To know that you have, at last, found the courage and wisdom and you have set sail on the good ship liberty bound for the harbour of truth must be the greatest source of inner contentment. You know that you will experience rough seas, gales may blow you off course, but with God's help you know that you will surely arrive at your chosen port of personal liberty. There is peace of mind, contentment, happiness, joy and liberty only in the truth. The truth of your being is that you are the chosen creation of God. You have been created not for failure, but total success. You have all the right equipment for overcoming any and all obstacles and you can with courage, conviction and perseverance win through against all that might oppose you.

Don't compromise your future peace and inner tranquillity—which will last for eternity—by losing your courage or conviction. When you stumble or fall, as you most certainly will, realise you are being tested by God Himself. Your worthiness, conviction and faith will be tested and sorely tested at times. Don't be disillusioned, angry, resentful or disappointed when events don't or won't go according to your plans. Trials give you the opportunity to prove your worthiness for the virtues you yearn for. When circumstances knock you off balance let the resulting disturbance be a measure of your determination to overcome the cause of your distraction. You will discover that by returning to your quest for inner liberty, your harmony with yourself will increase.

If you work earnestly, secure in the clear understanding that with God as your co-worker you will face every challenge with confidence and eventually you will emerge victorious. And should you have to experience the long dark night of the soul, God will safely see you through to the new dawn of the new day of the new life in the beautiful, new world that is patiently awaiting your new birth. With God you need fear nothing, for there is and never has been any danger in the quest for liberty. Liberty consists in discovering your true spiritual nature and when this is eventually realised you will, at last, be safe. In the outer world of society there is pain, fear, anxiety, and every type of neurosis and in the inner spiritual world there is rest, peace and truth. The only method of escaping all anxieties is to seek refuge in the inner world.

Mankind, in its folly, is ever seeking in the outer world of form and phenomena for that which can only be found within. Freedom means to be independent of regulated society, to be unattached to foolish events, no matter how popular, and of course to be free from all irrational desires and destructive negative emotions. Continue to comply with the necessary functions and duties of society, but without attachment. You should diligently work to attain the victory that truth alone can provide, but work without being anxious about the end result. With sincerity, consistency and union with God, victory is assured.

Life never fails us; it is we who fail, because of the low psychological level at which we operate. To end all emotional fear, envy, greed and all other negative emotions, you must acquire a comprehensive understanding of how and why your mind behaves as it does. Get rid of all pretence; exercise authority over the negative mind and this will allow you to return to your natural self.

You must travel a lonely road; you are unlikely to meet a fellow pilgrim on the way, for certain there is no human organisation in whatever guise to help you on your quest for spiritual liberation. But you are not on your own; God is your constant companion. It is He who is guiding your every step. You have been placed on earth to achieve great things and it is foolish to believe that great achievement is possible without the need for a corresponding effort of mind, soul and spirit. The manner of keeping yourself encouraged is very important. This can best be done by a constant expectation of the dawning of the new day of truth. Cease to care for the trivial matters of day-by-day living; these cares last day by day and rob us of looking at our new life in whole. For life is greater than what we might eat, how we dress, or how others perceive us. If your life is in turmoil it is because you are ruled by your negative thinking. For where there is negative thought, peace of mind or unity cannot exist.

Even in the greatest sinner there is a hidden splendour waiting recognition and liberation. There is in each and every one of us the glorious Presence of God. And awareness of this mighty Presence is the solution to all of mankind's problems. You would do well always to remember that your first and last duty is to your soul and inner well-being.

Our insistence on seeking happiness in the company of others is a mistake repeated with monotonous regularity. The truth is you will never know a single individual who will not, at some time, disappoint you. The secret of living a beautiful life is in doing beautiful things in and with your life. For the beautiful will always attract the beauty. Mankind's greatest tragedy is ignorance and confusion of identity. People see themselves as being bodies and mind only, separate entities living independent lives. The truth is something entirely different, we all live in the Universal Mind of God. All are brothers and sisters whose parent is Almighty God. We are first and foremost spiritual beings temporarily clothed in a material body which will eventually return to mere dust. You are not material dust, you are an indestructible spiritual being and will continue in existence for all eternity. This thought should remove any fear of death, for that which has been created by God in His image and likeness must be eternal.

When you accept, in full, your God-given spiritual image, you will know instinctively that spiritual power and authority are yours also. This acceptance of the spiritual gifts bestowed on you by God Himself is the means of attainment of all spiritual knowledge. You will come to the highest spiritual revelation, which is, man is Spirit and Spirit is God. Everyone and everything exists in the Divine Mind God and nothing can exist outside of Him, the only creator. Your life and living is as permanent as God, for all life is of God. You are in reality an individualisation of the Universal Life of God. Accept this reality and rejoice that God has made this known to you that you may give thanks to God and go on to greater deeds and achievements.

Life is responsive when it is properly understood and life is understood when we recognise and realise that Life lives in and through us. The quality of the life you live is, of course, determined by the conscious effort made to accept that life is eternal and spiritual. Know that God is Life and that God will manifest in and through you, according to your understanding of Him and His Life. It is the Presence of God within you as the Christ that is your true life. There is no life outside of God and there never can be. It is the Universal God individualised in you as the Christ who lives in you and is your life. The more God is allowed to influence your thoughts and actions the greater the degree of Life that will be expressed in you. Your body is but a mass of matter, a medium through which spirit functions. How much attention do we pay to the body? We bathe it, feed it four or five times every day and we dress it in fine clothing; we are always pandering to our bodies in the mistaken belief that we are our bodies. You are learning that you are much more than body, more than mind, greater than the sum total of all the things you mistakenly believe yourself to be.

Our contemporary society is everywhere in conflict with itself. Wars, ethnic cleansing and criminality is rampant worldwide. Moral decay is endemic and the decaying process will continue at an ever-increasing rate. It really is time to leave the asylum, the patients have taken over the institution and ruination is inevitable. If you are content in today's world and have not reached the decision to leave behind all of its follies, conflicts and insanity, your myopic sight will lead you all, with the rest of myopic mankind, to disaster. To cleave to this sad and sordid world is to be part and parcel of the delusion that humanity can, of its own accord, find peace and contentment; the truth is that humanity is drowning in a sea of self-delusion.

Our civilisation cannot continue along the road being trodden by the mass of humanity without dreadful global consequences. God, being the master architect, will ensure that in the end everything must come to a perfect finality. However, between now and humanity's return to sanity and eventually to God there is for so many individuals very painful experiences to be endured. For if we are unprepared to learn through virtue and wisdom then we will have to learn through grief and woe. In the present climate of global instability, it is sheer madness to turn a deaf ear to our hearts and consciences.

Don't get swallowed up in petty self-interest that panders to earthly egos. Strive to become the universal individual that you may know your place in the cosmic scheme of things, and by placing yourself in harmony with spiritual reality you may live life to the full. The first task is to become aware of the reason why you are failing in your endeavour to become the reasonable, rational, wise and sensible person you would like to be. Your belief that worthless goals are somehow important robs you of the opportunity to come to terms with the reasons for your existence in human form. The world and its tinsel have millions mesmerised. Whatever your ambitions, even if everyone is realised beyond your wildest expectation, won't stop your heartache. Being first and foremost a spiritual being, if you gained all of the power and the riches this world has to offer it could not provide one necessity of your immortal soul.

In spite of all attempts to be happy, the life of pain and misery threatens at times to overwhelm each and every one of us. I am of the conviction that we are in danger of being totally swamped by our inability to overcome even trivial problems. There is, however, no need for defeatism; if we can't overcome problems we can most certainly transcend them. In the outer world of form and phenomena every twist and turn of our daily experiences leaves us unfulfilled day after day without the remotest hope that circumstances will change for the better. Now is the time to look carefully and clearly at your life.

The life you truly want is beyond human comprehension. This being the case we should turn completely to God and His loving compassion and allow God to lead us all to the truth. The truth of our present experiences and circumstances is proof enough that we don't understand life and therefore don't, at this time, know what to do with our lives. All of our planning, contrivances, scheming and calculations have not ended the loneliness, pain or misery. Whatever we do only adds to our problems and our frustration grows ever deeper. We require a deeper insight into the reasons for our failure to live a life of contentment.

What is it you most desire from life? Is it merely riches, power or influence? Even if you achieved in abundance everything you think you need, when death comes all of your possessions you must leave behind you. And if you have not made any spiritual advancement you can be sure death will trivialise all your earthly achievements. Only in God alone can there be found true and lasting harmony and happiness. Your life can only change for the better when you decide to remedy all faults and failings. All too many deceive themselves; instead of correcting a fault they pretend it's a virtue. Someone is stubborn and they pretend its strength of character. And so we are reluctant to believe things that may rob us of our false identity.

Man's greatest illusion is the false conviction that he is the person he believes himself to be: a doctor, a dentist, musician, magician, lawyer or labourer. Man is infinitely greater than the sum total of the parts played at. We struggle mentally and emotionally against unfavourable circumstances without ever realising that our mental and emotional crises are the result of our personal negative thoughts and emotions. The mind used in its negative mode is the problem and when the mind is used in this fashion misery and pain must be the outcome. Yet there is available to all the Universal Mind of God that permeates all space and is accessible to all. You don't have to seek for this universal mind, you have yours being in it. To benefit from it, you must first accept that this Mind of God exists and make yourself worthy of receiving guidance, love and wisdom from this astonishing Mind of God. The method of receiving from the universal mind is simplicity itself. Still your outer mind and in periods of mind-silence listen carefully for the quiet voice of God.

The Bible advises, *'Be still and know that I am God'.* Go to any quiet place where you can be on your own. Repeat this prayer for 5 minutes... *"Almighty God you my beloved Father and I are one."*... Listen to what you are saying; when you hear your prayer so does God hear. After five minutes say from your heart... *"Father, Thy Kingdom Come,"* If you engage earnestly in this meditation you will reap great spiritual advantages. Your earthly cares and woes can only be ended when you attain spiritual tranquillity and this will be achieved by the method described. When you reach this blessed state, you become master of your emotions, content in every type of situation, for you are, at last, ready to meet all challenges secure in the knowledge that you are superior to any condition or circumstance.

The path of truth, honesty and duty has to be taken by all sooner or later. And the sooner we begin this inevitable journey the sooner we will arrive at destination liberty. When liberty is won you will become a source of inspiration to all fortunate enough to know you. As a liberated spiritual being you can help others to rise above their problems and to help them on to further spiritual achievements. Nothing in this world can bring you peace or lasting contentment, only total victory over your negative thinking. It is the triumph of principles over expediency that alone can provide you with genuine happiness.

Birth is not the beginning of life, nor is death the end of life. As God is the life that lives in every person then all life is eternal. Life changes from spirit matter to pure spirit, but life can never end. God lives in everything and mankind is the highest spiritual manifestation of the great creator. His living Presence in each and every individual means that all His children will live throughout eternity. As God is eternal, we His children created in His image and Likeness must be eternal also.

As God is spirit, mankind must be spirit also, because we have been created out of God's universal substance. Until now ignorance has clouded your understanding of your oneness with God. Don't allow false belief in division to blind you to the great truth of Life. Everyone exists in universal God, it can't possibly be otherwise. God and mankind are one, this is the rock of truth. The acceptance of this truth means freedom from all mortal conditions. Liberty resides in the creative power of our constructive thoughts and what more constructive thinking can there be, when you think thoughts of love, peace, and goodwill for all of mankind. It's very likely that there are a number of persons whom you hate and that you are not prepared to forgive. Know, that hate has the effect of changing the body structure through chemicalisation. If you think negative thoughts, and none are more negative than hate, you set up a negative chemical reaction in the body and you suffer.

You can see how wise Jesus was when He said, *'Love your enemy,'* Love is the antidote, for it is the only permanent power in the Universe. If you continue to hate, not only do you place your health in peril, but also there can be no spiritual growth. In truth, hatred is the most self-destructive emotion known to man, the most virulent form of active ignorance.

It is folly in the extreme to allow others to upset you. When someone behaves badly towards you don't respond with negative emotions. Another person's bad behaviour, even when it's directed against you, is a problem for the other person. React intelligently; the less love, kindness and consideration there is in a person's life, the more they require it from others. You may respond by thinking how could I possibly love such an objectionable individual, someone consumed by hate and malice. Well, for a start have you not, on occasion, harboured these same emotions? Can you in all honesty criticise another without condemning yourself?

You alone are the sole cause of your emotional condition. All the mental pain you experience is caused by your negative reaction to external events. If anyone causes you pain or anguish know that your psychic awareness needs improving. Destructive emotions can only be destroyed when we realise the pain and misery we cause to ourselves. Be aware of the mind, observe it at work and watch your thoughts and how they generate feelings and emotions. Further observe how the emotions affect your mind and behaviour. Thoughts, feelings and emotions are, not the real you, for you are much greater than these. You are master over every situation if you have the courage to use your intelligence intelligently. The ability you possess. The wisdom to use your innate ability intelligently you also possess; you now possess the knowledge. Nothing can any longer stand in your way except indifference or folly. God has in His Love for you placed you in charge of your life and by so doing has decreed you worthy of His trust. He has created you in His image and likeness. Please take tight hold of this truth, for your spiritual wellbeing depends on your acceptance.

God in His love for you has created you in His image and likeness. Your duty then is to allow this image and likeness of God to manifest in the outer that you may become a light unto a darkened world. By this magnificent act of generosity God has bestowed on you the supreme act of love which is the passkey to all knowledge, wisdom and power. If you really want to live a contented life, you must embrace spiritual love; when you love unconditionally you will live life to its full potential. Each and every one has been endowed by God with the power of thought and our first duty is to think noble thoughts of love, compassion and duty, so that we may find the road that leads to paradise.

As a spiritual being it is your duty, imposed by the Great Creator, to rise above all that is negative and sterile. The secret of a contented life is to live simply, for simplicity is contentment. Your first duty is to create the conditions, which will allow the inner spiritual entity to triumph. To make progress you must choose right in every situation and having made the right choice you must also see it through with conviction. Be willing always to be guided by God, for He can do more than the mind of man is capable of understanding. Learn well and understand clearly that there is no joy or contentment until you perceive yourself as the spiritual offspring of God.

You will not find spiritual refuge in outer worldly affairs. In the world of opinions, you are a mere member of a large chorus, part only of a noisy crowd. The mass mind of the crowd is indifferent to truth, to wisdom, to all that has the power to elevate the mind. You will find joy, peace and contentment only in the spiritual sanctuary of your immortal soul; there you will discover what your destiny is to be. To end your miseries, see your condition as being the result of your opinions, or more accurately, still your mind and its negative patterns of thinking. It is an absurd abuse of natural intelligence to place earthly images over spiritual realities. The truth is no one is content with being what they are, for deep within ourselves we instinctively know that our true home and safety is of another dimension—the inner world of love, humility and compassion.

In truth we create, by our thoughts, the type of experiences we rebel against. Lament all you will against unfavourable conditions and circumstances, but your cares, anxieties and all that causes you pain, you create in the mind. If your mind is in turmoil so must also your circumstances be. Control over your mind means you have control over all things. You may live in the most favourable circumstances—your home may be a castle, you may have wealth untold, you may enjoy the love and respect of all who know you—but if your mind is disturbed you will be miserable. The solution is to correct the mind with intelligence. Purified and loving thoughts are the only means of attaining contentment. There is no other way out of the morass of fear, anger, resentment, or turmoil. Unless and until you achieve mental control of your thoughts your life will continue in the same old, pain-ridden routine.

You may wonder if you have the strength required to make the effort. Your strength will be in proportion to your resolve. The mental resources required for real and lasting change you already possess. The source of all good and all that is vile and reprehensible is within you. To be happy and at peace is perfectly possible and you can attain the heights of spiritual bliss by changing your thoughts from the negative to the spiritually positive. It is only through the knowledge of our failings that we can see the vision of that we wish to attain. With proper vision and the wise use of will power you can penetrate the deepest mysteries of life. Use every moment of the day and every event to discover your true nature and character that you may proclaim the truth. I am who I am and know exactly what is meant.

God identified himself to Moses on Mount Sinai, *"I am, who am."* God being Omnipresent (everywhere present) is present in every atom of every person so any individual can say with supreme spiritual authority, *'I am who I am'*; knowing yourself to be the spiritual image and likeness of God, your creator, you will have attained liberation from limitation. The truth will set you free.

The New Testament has this wonderful advice, *'Prove all things; hold fast that which is good,'* To attain true peace, joy and contentment you must know that you are being directed and sustained by God. Only in this awareness can we find harmony in our daily experiences. The spiritual life will provide you with endless bliss, a peace that cannot be found in the material world, for the spiritual has existed before the material. The truth is, if spiritual consciousness did not exist then the material universe could not exist.

All worldly or human endeavours will sooner or later lead to disappointment. Only that activity which is in harmony with the longing of the soul can save us from all human folly. Only when we have subjugated our recalcitrant mind, that seeks endlessly after excitement and cheap thrills, and replace them with silence and wisdom, can we hope to live a life of harmony. You will of course require determination, stamina and constant encouragement to win through to the end.

Victory will secure a place for you in Paradise and in Paradise all your problems will end forever.

All knowledge and all power are concentrated in your immortal soul. You don't have to seek out holy men, nor do you require direction or help from any man-made organisations or outside sources. You must; however, accept the presence of your immortal soul and listen to its prompting.

Victory is for the Brave

There can be no victory without effort, without defeating doubt and frustration. Yes, you will have dark moments of doubt and despair; all who have travelled the road before you have been tried and tested in many ways. The road is difficult, it has many twists and turn; there are also many traps to tempt the traveller. For the majority the task is too difficult and they give up. Yet, all must return to the spiritual journey and successfully complete it.

This is your earthly mission—to attain a comprehensive understanding of our spiritual relationship to God, and not one person can opt out of this earthly task. Yes, you can postpone this journey; you can foolishly put it off to a future life on earth. You must continue to return to earth until you complete your earthly mission, should that take one thousand earthly lifetimes. The purpose of life is self-realisation and God has placed upon all of us the responsibility not to be defeated by indifference or ignorance from attaining self-realisation. And if we are foolish enough to reject this spiritual duty, we must be prepared to accept the consequences.

You can no longer say you don't know what your mission in life is. You were not placed on earth to be the plaything of fate, neither were you intended to be a slave to your negative emotions. Your life is what you have chosen to make it. It may not be the life you desire. If you truly wish to transform your life you must understand your desires. You become aware of emptiness within you; this emptiness causes you to desire things. Your inner emptiness cannot be satisfied by worldly conquests or cheap thrills. Satisfied desire is only the gateway to yet another desire and another and so it goes on and on. If you lovingly search for your true spiritual self you will find that you are the divine essence of God. Your search for the truth of your existence will lead you to discover that you are a miraculous expression of God's Divine Plan and that you hold a special place in God's intentions for all of humanity. Our petty human imagination cannot conceive of the grandeur of God's Cosmic Plan. We all know that there has to be a more meaningful life to the present chaos and turmoil that are daily experiences; this instinctive reasoning can and should be the spur that induces a desire to seek for the true meaning of life.

Pray earnestly and often every day this simple prayer, *"Almighty God, teach me love, humility and compassion."* This simple prayer has the power to transform your life if you repeat each word slowly and with deep reverence. Of course you must want the thing you request; God will not force anything on you. It is surprisingly wise to see the foolishness of expecting happiness, contentment or inner fulfilment from the routine of work, family or friends. Yes we have obligations, which we must discharge, but our chief obligation is to our true identity, to our inner selves.

Our spiritual poverty causes us to pursue the mundane things of this material world. Things are just that and have no power of their own; they have the false importance we place upon them. If you had everything you desire and more your satisfaction would be short lived. Happiness is not of the exterior world and its material possessions. Joy, love, peace and happiness can only be found in living the spiritual life.

When negative thoughts are banished, the mind by its own inclination improves, and the mind, thus purified, inspires understanding and corrects all human failings. You will be at your most powerful when you liberate the mind from all negativity. When this is achieved you will truly know peace and joy. When you have sincere reverence for life, when you have a clear knowledge of your inner self, and when you have mastered the discipline of self-control, you are at Heaven's gate. By giving glory and honour to God you are at the same time dignifying yourself.

What you have been, what you are now and what you are to become in the future are determined by how you use your mind. The mind that is free from all negative thought will provide you with the contentment and liberty you are seeking. Keep the mind focused on higher thoughts and you will engage in noble deeds, thus ensuring your passage towards the higher life of love. Start now, at this very moment, to put things right. Make the outer world a mirror of your inner world and there can be no outer improvement without inner improvement. If you really desire to be free from cheap excitement, raging passions and the stupidity of callous behaviour, you must elevate your thoughts. There is no other way to improve your life, there never has been and there never will be. When you gain control of your mind you will have control over every thought, word and deed.

Anger, resentment, fear and all other negative emotions will be banished forever. In proportion to the improvement of the mind you will recognise the spiritual power that is located within you. You have been created by nature to be wise, intelligent and understanding. It is your first duty that you live as nature intended. If you continue to live according to the dictates of habit or routine you will not experience any worthwhile change. Spiritual revelations are reserved for those whose minds have been cleansed of all that is petty and pitiful. Your life can be different, but only you can make the change. Take heart from this fact: what has been spiritually accomplished by any individual may also be accomplished by you.

We first and foremost live in our minds, but all too often our minds are full of inherited beliefs, dogmas and outworn theories. Human thoughts are in most cases negative in character and are reactions to fear, doubt and ignorance. How we react to our thoughts determines the quality of life lived. People waste and dissipate their energy in negative reaction to outside events over which they have little or no control. We must clearly understand that the mind has to be guided by wisdom and intuition. If you continue to react mechanically and negatively to life, you will continue to get hurt. You must choose between living life and Living Life.

The life that is spent reacting to emotions is sure to be dominated by anger, fear, resentment, frustration and illusion. If we choose self-delusion instead of self-knowledge, we will never find the purpose and meaning for our existence here on earth. People desperately seek to fill the emptiness within them by seeking security from others as confused and as bewildered as themselves. Know that things or people cannot provide happiness, peace and security.

A contented mind and it alone is the only means of finding happiness. The mind that has discovered contentment is the mind that has been elevated by perception and does everything in conformity with sound reason and behaviour. The good news is that you can become the person you most want to be. Your life will change and your spiritual evolution will begin when you accept that you and the Father are one. When you accept this unity, between God and self, as being the only existing reality, then you will know the Power of God. The Power of God that is inherent within man is dormant until it is realised and recognised, then it becomes active. The active Power of God in the individual elevates him or her above finite, mundane experiences, to a life of peace and bliss, a state of profound peace and lasting contentment that no words can describe. When profound peace is experienced, you will know a love so pure and serene that you will personalise the Presence of reality, for love is the key to the unlocking of all mysteries.

"It is love that asks, that seeks, that knocks, that finds, and that is faithful to what it finds." (Augustine)

Yes, love will find the way no matter how desperate your plight; no matter what ails you, love is the healing balm that all may use to smooth the way. Those wise enough to choose the road of love and to tread it will be led to the Presence of Almighty God. You were placed on planet earth in human form to perfect your humanity by overcoming all negative human emotions and conditions. Spiritual evolution can only begin when the individual perfects his humanity by the method you are now learning. It is our distorted mental reasoning that limits the true expression of Life. You can recover your life by taking stock of where you are and what you have allowed yourself to become. Resolve not to continue along the road trodden by the mass of humanity, the highway of illusion and deception. Leave the shadowy cul-de-sac that ends in a shadowy existence. To be true to our real selves and to become all that we are capable of becoming is the true aim and reason for our existence here on earth.

Life on earth is not the beginning, nor the end of life's experiences. To understand life, we must clearly understand spiritual principles. The first essential is to accept that we have the same creative attributes of the Mind of God. A clear understanding of our Oneness with the Source of Life is the only means of coming to terms with the reason for our existence here on earth. You must get a clear insight of the inner person; the inner is real and substantial and is the power behind the outer.

Life, as it is lived by most individuals, is casual, a series of incidents. Some incidents excite and thrill and give a fleeting sense of happiness; others cause emotional pain and resentment. Thus, we are the victims of chance. It is, of course, not the incidents that cause either excitement or pain, it is our reaction. Emotions are the result of our habitual thinking. All of us have one real desire and that is to find true happiness, to be free from mental and emotional pain and suffering. We have imprisoned ourselves by reacting always in the wrong manner to just about every situation we find ourselves involved in. We jump to automatic conclusions and by so doing we continue along the road of frustration. And yet deep within us we know there has to be a better way. Life can only be understood when we realise our oneness with the source of life.

Consciousness determines the degree of life being expressed. Don't confuse your body, mind, thoughts or your emotions with life, as it should be lived. Your body is merely the focal point through which life on earth manifests. Your body is a material vehicle for your earthly use. Your mind is an instrument at your disposal. You have the choice either to use the mind wisely or foolishly. It is your decision and yours alone whether you use it in its positive or negative mode. But you should know that the mind has to reach the highest that its capable of, and must throw off all that separates it from reason, intelligence and wisdom; only then can life find its true expression in us and through us to all others.

Only through truth can we gain a lasting satisfaction and serene contentment in our lives. All that you could wish to be already exists within you. The search for a satisfactory reason for your life here on earth begins and ends within yourself. All that is to be known is already known by your immortal soul.

The search for a meaningful explanation to life has to be turned inwards. Your consciousness is the point at which you have your experiences, the point at which you express life. To understand Life we must become aware of its source and our relationship to this source. Life should be recognised as a privilege and a wonderful opportunity to give expression to the Truth. Life can only truly express itself when your mind is at peace. Our thoughts are, at any one time, various reactions to fear, worry, doubt, and frustration. Cause and effect is a law we can never hope to escape from and the effects we complain of, we instigate ourselves.

Marcus Aurelius has told us, "All that pains you is yourself."

You have a choice—you can continue to inflict more suffering on yourself or through raised awareness use your suffering to end it. To find your real self you must think anew. You have to put aside our mundane reactions. Your opinions, until now, have not saved you from mental pain. To be free of all suffering it's necessary to raise your physiological level of understanding. The mind has to be tamed and liberated from all illusions, and if you fail to observe the negative activity of your mind you must of necessity be unhappy. The improvement of your mind is the most important task you can, at this time, engage in. The closer you get to liberate the mind from all forms of negativity, the closer you get to freedom. The mind that is free from illusion and negativity can achieve all things.

William Shakespeare has said, "Everything be ready if the mind be so."

You must at all costs end the deception of yourself by yourself. You are the deceiver and the deceived. It's time to stop playing deadly games with yourself. The time has come to put an end to all tendencies that drag us downwards and replace them with the power that leads ever upwards. It is a very consoling fact to know that we have the undoubted ability to elevate our lives by conscious effort. How, you may ask, is it possible to elevate our lives? Where and how do we start? Our conversation should be determined by reason, our acts should be guided by reason and more importantly still, our thoughts should be responsive to absolute reason. If you want freedom, peace, harmony and mental stability, you can have it. But first, you must clearly understand what is stopping you from experiencing the peace and harmony you desire.

You have allowed yourself to be blinded by convention and your thinking has been distorted by your present beliefs. You have accepted inherited beliefs from family, school, acquaintances and religious institutions. You have allowed yourself to become a hollow mental echo chamber.

We are the victims of our own follies; we have mismanaged and misspent our lives chasing after material success. We have adopted the philosophy that elevates the procuring of wealth above all that is decent and moral, when we should be on our knees at the shrine of truth; instead, we are to be found in the market place amongst the moneylenders.

You will never find personal salvation hiding in the multitude of the money grabbers. The material world cannot supply the solutions to the deep morass that our civilisation now finds itself in. Our civilisation is in deep crisis and all present indications are that the crisis will worsen. We are sinking ever deeper into a cesspool of moral, political and every other form of corruption. Wars are rampant, murders commonplace, sexual abuse and child prostitution ever on the increase, the drug problem is escalating out of control. All of the present symptoms and all of the obvious defects are indicators that our civilisation is terminally ill; it can't continue much longer in its present form. There are no signs that the madness can be ended. And yet each and every one of us has the power to change. If we can't change the world, we can change ourselves. Just take a clear look at what is happening all around you, in your street, in your town and country, all around the world.

We have sought power and authority in many things. Power has been sought in wars that have cost millions of lives causing untold physical and mental suffering. Power has been sought by domination of one nation state over another;

by one people over another; by one person over another. In our lust for power we are at times prepared to stoop to genocide, terrorism, and mass murder. Mankind has cynically used fear and terror in the pursuit of power and power has been sought not to end evil, not to do good, but to create more terror and violence. Power is perceived as the means to dominate those we identify as our enemies. It's dreadful to contemplate the degree of terror and madness that only active ignorance can generate.

Rousseau tells us, "The evil done by man falls upon his own head, without making any change in the system of the world."

We have been fighting wars for thousands of years, in the process killing millions of innocent non-combatants, causing untold pain, sorrow and suffering. What have we, as a species, learned from this bloodletting and savagery? The only lesson learned is how to kill more efficiently. In the beginning we used crude cudgels to murder and mutilate each other. Today we have intercontinental ballistic missiles that have the capacity to murder millions in seconds. All violence is the rejection of reason and intelligence.

Emerson, that wise American has told us, "All violence, all that is dreary and repels, is not power, but the absence of power."

There is no problem known to man that can't be resolved by clear thought. Society has taught us to fear, and fear leads to hate, and we fear those we perceive to be different from ourselves. It would seem to be an impossible task to reason mankind from wars and violence. That's because violence begins where and when reasons ends. Life is lived in three worlds, the spiritual, mental and physical. To live a balanced life, we have to be first and foremost a spiritually aware person. When we reason from a spiritual point of view, our judgements will reflect wisdom, compassion and understanding.

The whole basis of your existence is that you are the creation of Almighty God. Man and mankind are creating all the problems that are threatening to overwhelm our civilisation. While we continue to relegate God from of our thoughts and considerations we will pay a dreadful price. You only have to observe what is happening on a global scale for evidence of how things go wrong when we exclude God from our decision making. We must become aware of First Cause, and God is First Cause; indeed the only cause, and we neglect First Cause at our peril. If you allow your mundane mind to determine your thoughts, words and deeds, you are living in secondary causes. And your experiences will be full of confusion and frustration. You will of necessity suffer and your suffering will be screaming a message back at you. Its message will be very clear—something is dreadfully wrong. Frustration increases because you don't understand the cause of your problem. The truth is, you are both cause and effect.

It's not your emotions, whatever they may be, that you have to work on. Your emotions are the result of your unguarded thoughts. If you continue to think negative thoughts you will continue to suffer from negative emotions. If it's self-fulfilment you seek, turn your attention to the only source of fulfilment that is the Presence of God within you. Life without an awareness of God's Presence will, on occasion, provide you with fleeting episodes of cheap thrills and passing sense gratification. The greater your attachment to emotionally induced excitement, the more unsatisfied and unstable your experiences become.

St Augustine knew the secret of a happy life. He has told us, "For a happy life is joy in the Truth."

The truth of your being is that you are an eternal spiritual being. Make the acceptance of this a starting point in your search for liberty and happiness. Know that you can receive nothing of worth from society or any member of society.

Let me quote again from Emerson, "A man contains all that is needful to his government within himself. He is made a law unto himself. All real good or evil that can befall him must be from him. He is not to live to the future as described to him, but to live in the real future by living to the real present. The highest revelation is that God is in every man."

Yes, the Truth is that the Universal God has individualised Himself in you, in me and in everyone ever born. Let this truth saturate your mind, drench your heart and flood your consciousness and God's Presence will be made manifest to you. There is no other way to end the nightmare of violence, fear, anxiety, folly and the stupidity of inhuman behaviour. By now you should have recognised, when, where and how you have gone wrong. You now have at your disposal the knowledge to begin to put things right in your life. But knowledge by itself is not enough; it's the proper use of knowledge that is of supreme importance. The mind that is brim-full of the most esoteric knowledge that remains unused is no better than the most primitive mind.

Amiel had this to say on this subject, "To understand things we must have once been in them and have come out of them, so that first there must be captivity and then deliverance, illusion followed by disillusion, enthusiasm by disappointment. Who is still under the spell and he who never felt the spell, are equally incompetent? We only know well what we have first believed, then judged. To understand we must be free, yet not have been always free."

The life that has been elevated above and beyond the mundane is the life that has accepted the truth that God and mankind are one. Only upon this truth can life be lived that reflects spiritual realities, and this in turn will provide all that the purified heart could wish for. Only in the truth can you hope to resolve all of your present problems and difficulties. Anything short of the truth will inevitably ensure that your life will continue to be a painful experience. No one can give you the truth, it cannot be explained, because the truth goes beyond reason or human understanding.

The truth is beyond mind and greater than all creation. We cannot intellectualise truth for it is greater than the collective finite minds of man. You won't know or understand the truth until you become Truth Itself.

The Buddha has this to say regarding the truth, "The subject on which I meditate is truth. The practice to which I devote myself is truth. The topic of my conversation is truth. My thoughts are always in the truth. For Lo myself has become the truth."

The tragedy for mankind is that the masses of humanity are not as yet ready for the truth and so our global problems will do. You are living in secondary causes, and your experiences will be full of confusion and frustration. You will of necessity suffer and your suffering will be screaming a message back at you; its message will be very clear—something is dreadfully wrong. Frustration increases because you don't understand the cause of your problem. The truth is, you are both cause and effect. St Augustine knew the secret of a happy life, he has told us "For a happy life is joy in the Truth."

Yes the Truth is that the Universal God has individualised Himself in you, in me and in everyone ever born. The truth is beyond mind and greater than all creation. We cannot intellectualise truth for it is greater than the collective finite minds of man. You won't know or understand the truth until you become Truth Itself.

The tragedy for mankind is that the masses of humanity are not as yet ready for the truth and so our global problems will continue to get progressively worse. Don't continue any longer to waste your life chasing after things of this world. Seek diligently for the improvement of your nature and a steady progress towards inner enlightenment, and you will not have wasted your time during this life. Life is too important to be lived either for sense gratification, or in the pursuit of material possessions.

Don't ever surrender your natural freedom to your habitual thoughts and reactions. And don't under any circumstances abandon your free will to passion, prejudice, hate, fear or any other destructive emotion. You must clearly understand that conditions are the creation of your thoughts. You have the power and authority to create your own mental world by the intelligent initiative of positive thinking. You must learn that you have the ability to function as a creative being.

You don't have to be a victim of your nervous negative thinking. The choice that confronts you is this: Do you want a life free of all negative thoughts and emotions or do you wish to continue with mental and emotional pain and suffering? Take heart that there is no problem without a solution. And the solution is always within the problem. If the mind is the problem, then remember that you are greater than your mind; also remember your mind is intended to be your good servant, your best friend and is the only means available, at this time, to make your life here on earth a rewarding experience.

To change the problem-mind, to friend-mind you must give the mind intelligent instructions. Marcus Aurelius, that wise Roman Emperor, had this advice to offer on the use of the mind,

"Those who do not observe the movements of their own minds must of necessity be unhappy." It will profit you immensely to watch the thoughts entering the theatre of your mind and how these unsolicited thoughts cause the mental problems that disturb you. Know that the problem is always within you and accept responsibility for your thoughts and emotions. Balzac, another of our great philosophers and thinkers has this message for us,
"Thought is the key to all treasure." He who has control of his mind has control of everything else. Seneca another colossus of reason said,

"The mind is the master of every kind of fortune; it acts in both ways, being the cause of its own happiness and its own misery."

Your mind is exactly what you make it, friend or foe, liberator or dictator. The autocratic mind will punish you many times every day while it's in control of you. To lead the new life free of pain and suffering you must take responsibility for the mind.

Vivekananda, one of the world's great thinkers advises, "The first lesson, then, is to sit for some time and let the mind run on. The mind is bubbling up all the time. It is like the monkey jumping about. Let the monkey jump as much as he can; you simply watch and wait. Knowledge is power says the proverb, and that is true. Until you know what the mind is doing you cannot control it. Give it full length of the reins; many most hideous thoughts may come into it; you will be astonished that it was possible for you to think such thoughts. But you will find each day the mind's vagaries becoming less and less violent, that each day is becoming calmer until at last it will be under perfect control, but you must patiently practice every day."

When you regain control over your mind, and this can only be done as described above, you will become a very powerful person indeed; you will possess the real and substantial power that only profound peace can provide. I have quoted a few of our great thinkers to convince you of the need of self-examination and to encourage you to make the effort required to regain authority over your life. The great thinkers know the way to salvation for they have been over the course. They have felt the pain of anger, fear, hate and the frustration of being wrong. These individuals were separated by aeons of time: continents, languages, culture, religion and race, but all arrived at the same conclusions concerning life and how it must be lived.

You must establish peace in the mind that is the first requirement, for without peace there can be no harmony, and without harmony there cannot be love, wisdom or compassion. Still the mind becomes aware of God's Presence within you. Use your mind to be consciously aware of Him, the Lord, God Almighty. Make your awareness continual, this is the only means of becoming all that you would want to be.

Within you is a beautiful person and you now know of this other existence within, ever waiting to manifest. This is the real you—the God-created you, the loving you, the compassionate you, the understanding you. Give the real you space to manifest, rein in the outer man and get him under control. Give yourself over to the light of divine knowledge so that your present understanding may be superseded. Be assured that this light will cast out all dark shadows clearing the way for the revelation of God's in-dwelling Presence. It is of the utmost importance that we come to a clear understanding of how we can liberate ourselves from all folly and illusion and come to a spiritual realisation of the truth.

The mission entrusted by God to Jesus was to proclaim the Truth. The Truth, being universal, does not change in any circumstances. It remains constant and does not belong to any individual, group or religious organisation. The Truth cannot be changed or amended; no one can tamper with it and certainly no one can claim that he or she alone is the sole custodian of the Truth.

When Jesus said, "I am the Truth," He proclaimed the Universal Truth. This statement has been mistakenly interpreted as Jesus proclaiming His unique divinity. To be free you need courage, the courage to say only what is true and do only what is right. We need to divest ourselves of all that is false so that perfection may manifest in our lives. Perfection is your natural state. You will have difficulties with the notion that you are perfect. The outer you is very unlikely to be perfect; you probably suffer from all of the defects associated with human nature. But you are not the outer person you think yourself to be. You are something very different indeed; the real you is the spiritual being who has been created by God our Father, and God is your real likeness, this likeness is perfect. You, of course, have opinions concerning yourself and the quality of your life is, to a large extent, determined by these opinions. Your world has been formed by your opinions and beliefs which in most cases have resulted from an unhealthy mixture of ignorance, fear and prejudice.

There is nothing in the affairs of mankind more depressing and terrible than ignorance of our origins and true identity; this ignorance causes all our problems. Wars, ethnic cleansing and all other forms of violence are the direct result of spiritual ignorance concerning our fellow man and our spiritual relationship to each other.

The Power of Love

Without faith and love there can be no meaningful life. Mental and emotional pain is caused by the absence of love. Only when you have sincere and genuine desire to be free from your compulsive desires and your unbridled passions, will you find the courage to change.

Freedom comes from a determined yearning for real change. Past mistakes must be freely admitted; there has to be the conscious surrender of all illusion, negative thinking and instant opinions. There can be no lasting change or freedom without courage, the courage to admit that your life, to this point in time, has been a failure. Millions of individuals will have a beautiful experience.

In Matthew 19: 24 we read, *'But with God all things are possible,'*

It can be done and you, with a constant awareness of God, can do it. Indeed you can't possibly fail because failure for God is impossible. In a world convulsed over power and invariably its misuse, real power has gone almost unnoticed. Real power is power over the outer self. Self-knowledge, self-control and total surrender to the power of the Spirit within leads to a power little understood by society at large. It is your power to take control over your thoughts; if it's real power you seek, start with your thoughts. Your life cannot be right if your thinking is wrong, and negative thinking is the cause of all your problems.

Thoughts Are Things

Thinking makes your day; bad thoughts produce bad days and good thoughts produce good days. Have you ever really thought about the consequences to yourself of your thinking? Yes, thinking makes each day what it is, good or bad, right or wrong, wise or foolish. Nothing is more important to you than the thought process and your awareness of how you are affected by this mental process. Thoughts are things having power—the greater the power of the thought the more power it will generate.

Jesus clearly understood the power of thought when He said, *'All things are possible to him that believeth,'* (Mark 9: 23)

To become a real person the only genuine requirement is to get rid of our negative thoughts and replace them with powerful positive ones. At this point in your life, could you afford to tell anyone your innermost secret thoughts? What goes on in the secrecy of the mind can be so terrible and vile that it can't be told to another person. When you are happy it's because of your happy thoughts. Sadness is the result of sad thoughts.

The Bible has this to say on thought, *'As a man thinkest in his heart so he is,'* And it has this wonderful advice for all of us, *'Be you transformed by the renewing of your mind,'* What this means is, new thinking equals new person.

Problems are caused by distorted thoughts. The ending of all problems, be they mental, emotional or physical can only be found when thinking becomes positive and pure. Thoughts of love and peace when directed outwards to all of humanity will change your life mentally, emotionally and physically. Suffering will end for all time when you fully embrace divine love and peace. You must know thyself and the only starting place for this most important discovery is to become clinically aware of the thought process.

"Everyman has within himself a continent of undiscovered character. Happy is he who proves to be the Columbus of his spirit." (Goethe)

Of all the creatures on earth, man alone has the ability to understand that there is a spiritual dimension to life. Without this ability to comprehend that we are first and foremost spiritual beings we would be no better than the beasts in the fields. We neglect our spirituality at our peril; without it there can be no happiness, peace or contentment. In life your first duty and responsibility is to yourself and your duty is to think constructively and positively. You will only start to live properly and peacefully when you rid the mind of all illusion, folly and ignorance.

The truth is that your life is a combination of consciousness, intelligence and substance. You are these attributes of life. You have a body composed of physical substance, consciousness and intelligence. Now then, the most important question in your life is this, who is this you that has consciousness, intelligence and substance? Only when you can answer this profoundest of all questions satisfactorily, will you know how to live life as God intended it should be lived. Remember Jesus' advice, "Seek and you shall find." If you seek for the true meaning to life with honesty and sincerity and are prepared to go inside your heart, mind and soul, you will be rewarded.

Ask God for help and guidance, but ask in faith and with love and God will respond positively. The Master Jesus gave mankind an assurance of divine help and Jesus would not mislead us about something as important as this. If it's peace and contentment you want, turn to God for only in Him can you experience real serene peace, a peace that is so profound it will elevate every human experience to pure joy.

You now know that it's impossible to experience the true joy of life until you get rid of your habitual negative thoughts and emotions. You will easily recognise the day happiness arrives. It will be that blessed day when you have gone through it without complaining about anything. And you will experience ecstasy the day you have not thought negatively.

Your mind when given wrong directions or allowed unbridled licence will cause you to be nervous, angry, fearful, distrustful, anxious and generally out of sorts with yourself and everyone around you. Truly you and you alone are the author of your troubles. Place the blame on no outside circumstances, you are responsible for the woes that haunt you. For you have the power within yourself to think, act and respond intelligently to every given situation.

Who Am I?

While you remain ignorant of who and what you are, chaos will dominate your life. You will lurch from one emotional crisis to another. It is your negative responses to the outer world that is the cause of all your unhappiness. If your inner spiritual world is right, everything else will be right also. Your acceptance of this truth and your willingness to act intelligently to put first things first is the necessary first step in the new life that is ever waiting for you.

"There are no mysteries out of ourselves. Character is constructed in the midst of the tempests of the world. Our doubts are traitors and make us lose the good we oft might win by fearing to attempt." (Shakespeare)

There can be no rebirth into the bright new life of love, peace and contentment until and unless there is a continuous constructive mental effort to tame and control the thought process. You can never become a true and genuine human being until you are in complete charge of your mind and the thought process itself. It is thoughts of love, healing and peace consciously generated by you and sent forth to all of humanity, that will bring about the new you. If you rule your mind with noble thoughts, your life will be enriched and you will in time experience profound peace. Let me guide you to a self-healing programme of positive meditation. At least once per day find a quiet spot, make yourself comfortable, sit up right in your favourite chair and become consciously aware of the Presence of God within as you breathe in mentally. Say... *"God"*... and as you breathe out mentally say... *"Love"*... sending the thought to all of humanity. Do this for ten minutes with deep concentration and sincerity and your life will unquestionably change beyond your highest expectations.

Your present opinion of life is not life as it could and should be understood. Life is much more important than mere opinions. What you presently think of life is not and never can be the life you truly want to experience. Life, when understood, will be seen to be a true spiritual existence in the conscious presence of the living God within you.

What, you may ask, is my natural self? Well, take a look at the young child; what endears children to us is their spontaneous natural behaviour. The baby is beautiful because it has, as yet, not been contaminated by world opinions.

Jesus said, "Unless you become as little children you cannot enter the Kingdom of Heaven."

Turn to God within you. There you will find the Kingdom of Heaven and it's only in this Kingdom that you will find peace, contentment and true everlasting happiness. The way of salvation is to accept that your life is the expression of God's Life in you. The Life of God in you is the real and substantial life that you must become aware of. When this happens your life and life's experiences will be a joy and a pleasure to you. These facts of life, memorised, won't awaken you out of your spiritual slumbering. Your new knowledge must be put to active and intelligent use.

Facts, no matter how well memorised, won't awaken you to the truth. You must learn and know that you are a spiritual being and that this recognition has to be accorded time and effort to become a conscious reality for you.

Meditate on your oneness with God, in the stillness and quietness of your mind become aware of the still Presence. Don't blindly accept what you've been told. Put your new knowledge to the test of logic and natural intelligence. Never accept any information at face value and never judge new knowledge by what you already believe. Your present beliefs are in many instances the cause of your suffering. Life won't conform to your inherited beliefs or opinions generated in ignorance. If life has so far defeated you, don't despair; accept your experiences as adding to the sum total of your present dissatisfaction inducing an honest desire for change.

Your life is not meant to be limited, either by your negative thinking or by your body. Life is unlimited and when this is recognised and realised you gain total freedom. You are not mind or body alone. God individualised in you as you is the real you. Gaze upon this truth, it is your true nature. Know that you are the chosen vehicle created by God to be the human expression of His Divinity.

If you have been confused, or frustrated by life, don't despair help is ever-present. Life does not deceive you; you have been hurt because of ignorance, indifference and disbelief. All obstacles can and will be overcome by love, wisdom and understanding. Freedom comes when we accept that our problems are caused by the wrong use of the mind. Your mind can only function properly when it is free of negative thoughts and emotions. When you emerge from your false belief in separation from God, you will emerge from mental limitation.

Bring to an end your negative thinking by becoming aware of the damage it does to you. Watch the mind at work. Don't try to stop the negative thoughts, but become aware of them. Observe the emotional damage done to your peace of mind by your unconscious thinking. Every time you think a negative thought you set up in your body and brain negative vibration that in turn cause negative chemical reactions in both mind and body and your mental and physical wellbeing suffers. End your negative thinking and return immediately to the only source of life, which you now know to be God. You also now know that lasting peace can only be found in God. And you now know why and how this conscious union with God produces the conditions all are seeking after.

Man has sought contentment in every type of worldly activity, the acquisition of wealth, goods and property. Contentment has been sought in alcohol, drugs and sex, but none or all of these things can bring you peace of mind and only the mind that has found peace can confer contentment. You will never ever find lasting peace in sense gratification; you must satisfy the longing of your immortal soul. The reality of your existence is that you live and have your being in God, and for this reality to be made manifest in you, it must be firmly established in your consciousness. You are meant to be the focal point for the manifestation of God's consciousness.

Use your thought processes wisely and seek to unite your creative thoughts to the creative power of God and nothing will be impossible to you. The mind of man is a reflection of the infinite mind of God and when this is fully understood, all struggle and turmoil will end. The only condition required for change is a state of constant awareness of the Presence. When you become aware of the Presence, it will become active and the only other requirement of you is patience.

The truth is, there is only God. There is and never can be anyone or anything outside of Him. By the way, this truth should put an end to the absurdity of the existence of the devil. And if there is no devil there can be no hell either. There is only God and it is He who is expressing himself in you now, and you can never be separated from Him. You are the personal expression of God here on earth. To become aware that the Universal God has individualised Himself in you as the Christ, means you are in possession of the secret of Life.

God's plan for you is that His Divine Light will shine in you, His Infinite Love shall be expressed in you and through you to all of humanity, and that through you and others His peace will be established on earth. Through this knowledge and your willingness to help in God's plan for humanity, you will be divinely rewarded. God created you out of His Perfect Universal Substance and He made you in His image and likeness. He has bestowed all of His attributes on you and given you dominion over all things. In doing these things for you, God has bestowed upon you the greatest act of love and generosity. You also now know that God Himself is inviting you to become a co-worker in the service of mankind.

What, you may ask, does God require of me? The answer is really quite simple—to accept the truth of your being and to allow God's attributes to be expressed through you to all His children. His attributes are love, wisdom, compassion, and understanding. Of course there is also consciousness, intelligence, truth and His Substance.

All of the attributes that are of God are applicable to each and every one of us. Your mission in life is to give the highest and noblest expression to all of God's attributes. The best means of doing so is a personal matter for each individual. Some of the things you might consider doing are two periods each day of silent prayer for all of humanity. You could decide to visit the sick or elderly on a regular basis. You could help raise funds for the starving children of the third world. Perhaps you might consider sponsoring a child either in one of the developing countries or fostering a local child. Avail of every opportunity to do something beautiful for those in distress and in time you will become as beautiful as the beautiful thing you do.

Whatever you decide to do, do it quietly, make no public display. What you do secretly for God's sake, but you can be sure that He will reward you openly. If you decide to help humanity in its spiritual quest, know that God Himself will be your partner. It's not necessary to become a preacher or public crusader or to engage in public acts of virtue. In the silence of your heart and mind, radiate thoughts of love, healing and peace, and send these thoughts to all of mankind. While doing so, be aware of the Presence of God within. Your thoughts of love, healing and peace, when charged with an awareness of the Presence, become a very potent force for the good of all humanity. And you will be storing up treasures for yourself in heaven. Great minds, you see, labour for eternity. Let your mind discern everything and encourage it to attain the heights of love, peace and compassion. Then it becomes the vehicle for the expression of the Will of God. By gaining a better understanding of yourself you will better understand the problems of those around you. This will make you more understanding, more considerate; your concern for others will increase. You will be more patient, tactful and thoughtful of others and your relationships will be on a sound footing. Virtues that have long been dormant in you will become active and find manifestation through you enriching every experience you encounter.

The main reasons for your human experiences you now know. You are here on earth to learn lessons that can't be experienced on other planes of consciousness. You have been placed here on earth to find your true spiritual self. The physical body is not you, your mind is not you, your hopes, dreams and desires are not you, your opinions are not you, your beliefs are not you, your possessions are not you, your trade, occupation or profession is not you. Now, when you strip yourself of all these familiar means of identification you are left naked and confused. It is a wretched business to be ignorant of who and what you are. Ignorance is often forgivable but ignorance of self is inexcusable. You have it on Bible authority that God Himself created you out of His Perfect Spiritual Substance in His image and likeness.

Now what this means in relationship to your true identity is this, God in you is who you are; God as you, is what you are. Now these words by themselves express two sentiments or statements which of themselves mean very little. Your true identity has to become a spiritual reality. A mere mental conception or appreciation of what or who you really are is not good enough. To attain this state of 'knowing' you must surrender completely to God. Let God determine your thoughts, guide your actions, control your emotions. Of course, you won't at first be completely successful, you will experience difficulties, trials and tribulations. You will stumble and fall but your greatest glory consists not in never falling but in rising each time you do and continuing on the quest to find reality and truth.

If you examine your life until now, what has it been? The truth is you have been ruled over by an undisciplined mind. Your passions, emotions and mental pain have determined the quality of your life. And because you are governed by a negative mind and all its follies and stupidity, the quality of your life has suffered.

Where has your past life gone? Large periods are now forgotten, the rest is mere memory. How will it be for the remaining time left to you? Will it be the same old thoughtless routine of desires and passions? The need is to become sufficiently honest enough to frankly admit that we really don't know how to live, because we are ignorant of our true identity and our relationship to God and our fellow man.

Yet we are charged by God to discover our true mission in life. We are meant to liberate ourselves from all that binds us to the mortal world of mundane human experiences. It is mindless longing for worldly things—things that are external and in many instances irrelevant that causes our blindness to our spiritual identity. For sure, we all must leave planet earth and in going we must leave our worldly things behind. Death will trivialise all human achievements and if you leave without having completed your spiritual mission it will mean you must return to earth and try again to get it right. Your mission is to discover your place in the Cosmos scheme. This is the real reason for your earthly existence.

Ordinary physical existence without a clear spiritual vision is at best a dream world of illusion and petty make-believe, at worst a nightmare of violence, drugs and alcohol abuse or crime. If you live in a dream world it will end in a prolonged nightmare. Worse still, if you live the nightmare life of crime, it will end in disaster. This is in operation an iron Cosmic Law called Karma. Karma means effort; every thought, word or deed has an effect on us. The greater the negative Karma we have amassed while here on earth the greater the penalty to be paid in the next life on earth. If on the other hand we have amassed a positive Karma, the greater will be our experiences in the future. Jesus put it this way. "What ye sow, so also shall ye reap." As karma is dealt with in some detail in another chapter, I will leave the subject for now.

Christ Consciousness

You and I, as well as everyone else have been placed on earth for a sacred purpose. You would be well advised to clearly understand what exactly this sacred purpose is and then to comply. There is within every individual the Divine Consciousness of God which is divine reality. Absolute consciousness resides within us all.

Consciousness is universal and consciousness produces intelligence, awareness and understanding. While there are no degrees of consciousness there are degrees of being conscious. Your degree of consciousness changes from a waking state to sleep. The important thing to understand about consciousness is that it is from God. Your consciousness, when it becomes absolute, will allow you to clearly understand that your consciousness is of God and is God. You will at some time reach the state of final consciousness. Then you will return to your natural spiritual existence. An awakened consciousness will not be satisfied until it reaches enlightened liberation. The benefit of an enlightened consciousness is that it knows itself to be the point at which God expresses His Divine Will. When the Divine Consciousness of God is allowed to permeate the individual consciousness, limitation ends forever. Total, complete and absolute freedom comes, when we ascend into the Divine Consciousness of God. However, before you can reach such elevated heights of spiritual bliss, you must become consciously aware of the urgent requirement to find a satisfactory explanation for your existence both here on earth and on other planes of consciousness. Consciousness is complete in itself. It cannot be disconnected, removed or severed; consciousness has always existed and will continue to do so. Next to God and Christ, consciousness is the most important thing in your life. Consciousness is the only means of salvation. All problems have their solutions in a clear understanding of consciousness.

You now know that your task is to know yourself, as God knows you; this task can only be accomplished with a conscious effort of consciousness. You must become consciously aware of yourself as a spiritual being, eternal without beginning or end. Your life will only have real meaning and relevance when you know that God can and will express Himself through the particular centre of consciousness that you are.

Life is constantly waiting to express itself in all its love, wisdom and understanding, and this expression depends on consciousness giving direction to intelligence which in turn gives birth to wisdom. When you are willing to be guided by wisdom and intelligence you will come to understand that Life is always seeking its own perfection in and through your consciousness and intelligence. When you fully understand Life, you will receive from Life all of its bounties. Understand clearly that you are Life itself; the Life in you is exactly the same Life in God. And your Life is meant to be the highest possible expression of God. Life Itself is free, uncomplicated and natural. It is people who are complicated and choose to live unnatural lives, and if you need an explanation as to why this is, it is because you live in the past or future; you live in your memory or in your imagination and this is unnatural. You need to live in the ever-present now and in an awareness of the Presence. For the Presence to manifest it has to have stillness in the individual mind. The individual mind has to be clear of all negative thoughts thus creating a clear mental channel for the Presence to express itself in your life. The person, who continually reacts to their negative thoughts, will become conscious of mental pain and emotionally induced suffering.

Hell should be understood, not as a place in which the wicked are punished, rather hell should be recognised as a stunted consciousness in which negative thinking has found favour. Consciousness has to become aware of itself, and of its thought process. The individual consciousness is meant to make the person aware that there is only one Life and that Life is God. The individual consciousness is from God; God's Consciousness permeates through the whole

60

of the Cosmos. And this Universal Creative Power is individualised in you as consciousness.

Jesus said, "The Kingdom of Heaven is within you." Heaven means the highest human experience of God's Consciousness in the individual. Heaven is not a place to be gained, but a reality to be realised. The quality of life is to a large extent decided by how you use your mind and thought process. There is, of course, only one mind—the Universal Mind of God. It is of the utmost importance to us that we understand more of this mind. The Universal Mind has only one mode of operation and that is positive. It knows nothing of hate, anger, fear or any form of negative thinking. The more aware we become of this Perfect Mind and its relationship to our individual mind the more we will understand the power behind creation.

The more aware we become of the power of the Universal Mind and its availability to us as individuals the more we can draw from this Power as an aid in our spiritual journey. In fact, we are the channels designated by the Creative Mind of God for the expression of His Holy Will. God used the mind of Jesus and other great masters to uplift the whole of mankind. You can be sure that God is using human minds for the same purpose even to this present time. For your mind to function at all, necessitates the co-operation of the universal mind of God. The power to use your mind comes directly from the Universal Mind. Our ability to think is strongly suggestive that we share abilities of the Cosmic Mind of God. The ability to overcome all negative thoughts depends on our willingness to recognise that the Creative Mind is truly universal and must permeate our individual minds. We can enter into the highest spiritual realms when we allow the Cosmic Mind to function through our individual mind. When you fully realise that God's Mind and your personal mind are one and the same, you are definitely on the road to spiritual emancipation. From the Universal Mind within, you gain authority over every adverse condition. And the authority of the Universal Mind requires your conscious awareness of its presence. While you continue to live in the personal mind only, you are living in secondary causes.

What you must accept is that you are the instigator of all your thoughts. You are the thinker; you have the choice of what you think and whether your thoughts are negative or positive. In life we must be positive and unafraid, for there is no such thing as failure; failure is only a word in the dictionary. You will have experiences, some you enjoy, others not. See your experiences as stepping-stones as opposed to obstacles. You will know you are gaining in wisdom when you seek to gain knowledge from every experience.

Negativity gets in the way of your wisdom, understanding and sound judgement. To gain final control of the mind it will be necessary for you to halt the thought process. This is given the name meditation and can be of tremendous importance. When you deliberately suspend the thought process and replace it with mind-silence, you are exercising your authority in the most positive manner. Mind silence is the most difficult form of discipline. Your mind has been manipulating you up to this point and won't easily give up its control over you. You will need patience, practice and determination in your quest for mind control. Mind over mind means control over all situations and circumstances. You should be in no doubt that in your quest for freedom you will require persistency and iron-cast resolution. You will wander from the path, old habits will rear their discontented heads, there will, for sure, be fits of depression, dejection and frustration, but you can with persistence prevail against all obstacles.

If you continue to live in a dream world, your existence will be a bitter disappointment for you will realise that the reason for your existence has passed you by. Worse still, if you live the life of drugs or alcohol abuse, if you live your life taking advantage of those around you, if you allow yourself to become a cheat, a perverted liar or criminal, your earthly existence will end in disaster. The iron cosmic law of Karma must be satisfied and every thought, word and deed will ensure either reward or retribution. The greater the negative karma that is amassed while in the human body, the greater the penalty to be paid in the next earthly life; on the other hand, the more positive karma amassed, the greater will be the experiences in the next life on earth.

Everyone has been placed on earth for a sacred spiritual reason; you would be well advised to learn what exactly is the reason for your earthly existence and then to comply. To be clearly conscious of life's mission will be of the greatest comfort to you. To know what God demands of every individual will make life much more interesting, rewarding and is the starting point for the glorious return journey back to perfection and spiritual reality.

You and all of humanity have been wonderfully gifted with all the right spiritual equipment to undertake the journey to the promised land of spiritual freedom. Within you resides the Divine Consciousness of God; which is the route map and compass. You are assured of a safe and interesting journey to your true spiritual home where God is waiting on you with outstretched loving arms. You can succeed, for within you resides the ultimate reality the absolute Consciousness of God; you have the absolute guarantee that with the right desire you can't possibly fail.

Live in the ever-present now, in an awareness of the Presence of God who dwells within your living soul; for the Presence to manifest, there has to be mind-silence. Only in stillness will God make His presence known and only in the 'knowing' of God can there be profound peace and total liberation from all human folly.

THE GREATEST ADVICE EVER GIVEN TO MANKIND WAS DELIVERED BY JESUS:

"SEEK YE FIRST THE KINGDOM OF HEAVEN, AND its RIGHT USE AND EVERYTHING ELSE SHALL BE ADDED ON TO YOU."

"We thank Thee for all those who are now perfect in Thee. We thank Thee that now they are released from their Apprenticeship, and behold Thee face to face, Dwelling forever in light and joy with Thyself." (J. S. Hoyland)

A break from the spiritual narrative.

Chapter 2

Strange Encounters in India

Before I recount my encounter with two 'men' in northern India I had better explain the reasons what I was doing in that exotic country. The story really begins in the year of our Lord 1994. In that year my father, a bespoke tailor by trade, presented me with £1000. And told me enjoy spending it. I have spent my life in a state of constant penury, avoiding destitution, but suffering from uninterrupted financial insufficiency.

At the age of thirteen I left school, barely able to read and write. This lack of a formal education has not got in the way of me penning a one hundred thousand philosophical manuscript on the complexity of life; while the manuscript has not been published, I have had it printed privately and it is available from me. Back to the narrative; I began my working life as a bicycle message boy delivering groceries to middle-class homes. Later I worked in Scotland. I was then sixteen, and I naughtily forged my age to eighteen to qualify for a man's wage. A little latter I was drawn to labouring on building sites in England. And I must confess to being mystified about how the country hasn't sunk in to the Atlantic Ocean because I've dug many deep holes all over the place. In 1956 I married my childhood sweetheart Mary, and we raised eleven wonderful children and fostered fifteen children during the worst of the violence that was rampant throughout Northern Ireland beginning in the late sixties. During these troubled times I was involved in the struggle for civil rights and became a member of a radical socialist political party; these activities made it very difficult for me to find work and consequently I spent long periods on state benefits. My wife and I fostered fifteen children over the years, so the enlarged family consisted of twenty-six in total, fifteen daughters, and eleven sons.

These unusual domestic circumstances meant that my personal disposable financial resources were definitely finite, or in our local parlance, I was always 'skint', or as we say in local parlance again, 'living from hand to mouth,' Money has never been important to me; when I have some money I never know how much, but I know when I don't which is a common enough phenomenon.

So the sudden thrusting by my father of £1000 came as a shock as I had no inkling that this burst of uncharacteristic generosity was ever likely to happen. So in a flash I have the financial ability to fulfil two life-long ambitions, which were to visit a third-world country and to experience a visit into a desert. When I received the cheque I seriously considered donating the cash to a third world 'charity', and would have done so, but for the objection from my father to the idea.

As a child I carried a pre-decimal penny to school every week for 'black babies' in Africa, which ignited an interest in the plight of destitute children in the third world. For the first time in my life I had the financial means to fulfil my ambition to go to Africa. I should mention that I split the £1000, gave my wife half and decided to visit Morocco because it has a desert and is the closest 'third world' country to Ireland. A visit to Morocco could, so-to-speak, kill two birds with one stone. I should again point out that I have been a keen, life-long amateur photographer, and I have two web sites on the net. My desire to visit a third-world country was to give me the opportunity to get exotic photos and I have a life-long political interest in the problems of the destitute in developing countries; I wanted to witness the effects of this dreadful scourge and how it affected those blighted by extreme poverty.

So I set off with my photographic gear and a keen sense of adventure. The only thing I knew about Morocco, apart from its location, was that it is a Muslim, Arabic country and that Bing Crosby and Bob Hope made a Hollywood film in 1942 called *The Road to Morocco*. I confess that I found Morocco fascinating; the scenery, the mountains, and cities, have a very different atmosphere to anything in Europe. Fez would be my favourite Moroccan City, followed by magical Marrakech.

It was in Marrakech that I had what was to become a life changing experience, though at the time I certainly did not recognise the significance of the encounter with a young destitute Moroccan boy. It was a particularly hot afternoon in Djemaa el-Fna, which is a large irregular square in which there is constant and spectacular daylong entertainment. I was enjoying a light lunch at an open-air café when I became aware, out of the corner of my right eye, that a ragged boy of about eight or nine was closely observing me. Initially, I was intrigued by this boy's interest in me; not being the brightest person in the world, it took several minutes to work out that the boy had no interest in me as an individual, but was interested in what I was eating. I came to the conclusion that he was waiting to see if I would leave any food on the plate and he would grab it and make off. When I became aware that the child was hungry, I got up from the table, approached the boy, lifted him over the fence that surrounded the café area, and carried him to my table and made him aware that I intended to provide him with a meal. The waiter who had observed what was happening approached us both and when I informed him that I wanted a meal for the child he became visibly agitated and refused saying, "No food, no food, beggar, beggar."

This reaction shocked and angered me. I slowly got to my feet looked the waiter in the eye and informed him that if the child did not get a meal I would not pay for mine. He left and returned with the owner who was also reluctant to provide a meal. I was outraged and advised him to send for the police as I had no intention of paying for my, by now, consumed meal. I made to leave and informed him that in protest I was refusing to pay. At this point three Germans, who had just sat down at an adjoining table, took umbrage at the attitude of the café owner and also threatened to leave. This act of international solidarity persuaded the café proprietor to relent and he instructed the waiter to serve the boy. I tell you, it was amazing to witness just how much food the child consumed. I arrived at the conclusion that possibly his legs were hollow. When the meal was finished, I took the boy to a clothes' stall and bought him a tee shirt and a pair of shorts, which I made him wear. I then gave him ten dirham which is about £2 in English currency. When I gave him the ten dirham, he ran off, clutching the money in his right hand and his old clothes in the other. I thought to myself *you ungrateful boy*; then I thought that he was, in all likelihood, apprehensive of my intentions. Upon reflection of this incident I decided to clothe and feed a destitute child every day during my stay in Morocco. I returned to Morocco two years later and again fed and clothed destitute children. I would have liked to do more but my money was insufficient to match my intended generosity.

This is how my involvement with 'third world' destitution children began; on my next trip I ventured to Mexico, simply because I spoke a limited amount of almost incomprehensible Spanish. But before I went to Mexico, I suggested to my friends that they give me £5 and I would clothe and feed a destitute child for them. The reaction from my friends was generous and I was able to clothe and feed five children every day. I have also worked with destitute street children in

Egypt, Nepal, and since the year 2000 I have visited India on seventeen occasions and have, [not alone], been responsible for the construction of seventy-two houses in three leper colonies, and five schools for untouchable homeless, street children, who, in the circumstances pertaining to the caste system in India would never see the inside of a school; I should point out that our students receive school meals, clothing, have comprehensive medical and dental care, and now, a mixed gender orphanage for twenty-four children has opened in the city of Dehradun. Thousands have been fed and hundreds clothed. Men and women have been set up in self-employed projects, and what I call crawling cripples, individuals totally unable to walk, have been provided with hand-cranked tricycles. The cost of these machines is £30, a small amount to pay for giving ground-bound cripple mobility.

Now you know how I became involved with 'third world' street children. I will recount two strange meetings I had in India. In the year 2000, I set sail for India, a country that intrigued me having years before read Paul Brunton's strange exploits in India in the early part of the twentieth century. Little did I realise that I would experience strange encounters not all that different from those experienced by Paul Brunton. I arrived in India in mid May 2000 thinking that the temperature would not be too high; I was wrong, the heat was intense. I had expected India to be different from other countries and different it most certainly is. Nothing can prepare the first-time visitor for the amazing variety of experiences that India has to offer. I have to confess that I was appalled at the scale of poverty amongst the 'untouchables' and the attitude of indifference to the plight of those improvised individuals that were everywhere present, and had I the financial means to leave India I would have departed within days, but K L M would not allow it unless I paid the return fare in full. My unalterable determination was at the time, when I get out of this awful country I'll never return. When K L M refused my request for repatriation I left Delhi and travelled to the 'holy city' of Hardwar. Any city built on the banks of the Ganges is deemed to be holy.

Hardwar is a small city and is popular centre for Hindu pilgrims who flock in their thousands to bathe in the holy Ganges believing that their sins as well as their bodies will be cleansed. There is a large number of *shaddus,* 'holy men' or saints; some are completely naked and cover their body with ash from a sacred fire. They do nothing all day long other than give spiritual advice to anyone who is prepared to listen. Hardwar is my favourite city. There is a great vibrancy about the place. Every day, thousands of pilgrims flock to bathe in Mother Ganges. I have taken hundreds of photos in Hardwar. On my first visit to India I spent two days in Hardwar and headed to another holy city called Rishikesh, which is only twenty kilometres north of Hardwar. On my first morning in Rishikesh I was enjoying a cup of chi, (Indian tea), at a street food stall when a holy man pulled up on his new motorbike. I engaged this individual in conversation; he spoke faultless English with an American accent, which encouraged my curiosity. I asked him if there was genuine holy man in the area. To which he replied yes. There was, high up in the mountains, an old man whose age was one hundred and two; I enquired how far up in the mountains he lived and was informed fifty-five minutes by motorbike. I expressed disappointment that it was too far to walk; the biker volunteered to take me as a pillion passenger. I asked how much it would cost and was told fifty rupees or sixty pence. So off we set into the Garhwal Himalayan Mountains, no roads, most of the way, only goat tracks and very steep with deep chasms to our left. I have, during my travels made some dangerous journeys over mountain passes and across deserts in all sorts of vehicles, but this journey was the worst ever; the idiot holy man was determined to frighten me by his reckless speed and dare- devil antics. I was sure we would end up dead at the bottom of the mountain. I cursed my stupidity for setting out on this hare-brained scheme and prayed that my journey would end without tragedy.

When we eventually arrived at the mountain village I was a nervous wreck; my knuckles were bleached white for during the fifty-five minutes having clenched the pillion bar at my back with a vice-like grip so tight, that when we eventually arrived at our destination, I found it difficult to straighten my fingers.

Having dismounted I gave thanks to God and wondered what the return journey would be like. We made our way to the cave of the old holy man; the local inhabitants had built at the entrance to the cave, an ornamental wooden door. My guide suggested that I remain a short distance away as he approached the cave, knocked on the door and called to the old man that he had brought a visitor. When the door opened, there stood a slim man who looked no older than seventy, but was one hundred and two years old. A short conversation took place, then the old man took a long searching look at me; in those few seconds I felt exposed for I felt this holy man could see into my heart and mind. A further short conversation, which did not involve me, and the old man, entered his cave; at this I became despondent, thinking to myself I've made a hair-rising journey for this fleeting encounter. I asked my guide for an explanation of what was happening and was informed that the old man had gone to have a ceremonial bath and we were requested to return in one hour's time. My guide took me on a tour of the village that had sprung up around the holy-man's cave dwelling. We met and talked to some of the villagers for my guide was a frequent visitor to the village and brought many inquisitive individuals to meet the old holy man.

On the completion of our tour, we had lunch and headed off to renew our acquaintance with the holy hermit. For the second time I was to remain a short distance from the cave entrance when the old man responded to the knocking at the door. I was bursting with curiosity wondering what his attitude to me would be. Both men came towards me and to my surprise and consternation the holy man walked past me without a glance; my frustration was increasing by the second and I was annoyed with myself for having undertaking this mission.

At this juncture I decided to sit on a low wall when my guide joined me. I requested an explanation as to what was happening and was informed that the holy man would return in a minute or two. My mind was in turmoil; I did not understand what was happening. The experience was to end on a low wall, I thought that this might be considered disrespectful, but my annoyance was such that protocol didn't seem to be important.

Several minutes past when the holy man appeared in front of me; his hands were behind his back and before I could get to my feet and to my utter astonishment he placed a garland of flowers over my head and unto my shoulders. I was stunned and surprised at this and then he held his left hand over my head and released flower petals that cascaded over me. Then to my amazement he knelt on both knees on the ground and kissed my two feet; at this I immediately thought of Jesus and the washing of the disciples' feet.

In fact, I tried to stop the latter action, but my guide frantically indicated by the use of his hands not to interrupt the action of the holy man. In India the greatest show of affection is to touch the feet of a relative or friend. For a holy man to kiss the feet of a stranger is benediction.

Having kissed my feet the holy man and my guide engaged in a short conversation and the holy man was about to leave when I requested to be photographed with him; he agreed and the photo you can view for yourself. When the old man departed, I suggested to my guide that we go somewhere and have coffee, for I wanted an explanation of the significance of what had just happened. During our coffee break I asked my guide to explain the reasons for the garland of flowers and the kissing of feet. The explanation that I received from my guide, who had over a four-year period of bringing several hundred visitors to the old man, was that I was the only one to receive such a welcome. The fact that the old man deciding to have a 'cleansing' ceremonial bath, the garland of flowers, and the kissing of my two feet, was the greatest honour he had paid to any visitor. When I inquired what the holy man said about me, he told me the following, and I promise you that what I'm about to recount is absolutely true.

The holy man had honoured me with a cleansing ceremonial bath, flowers and kisses because he said, I had been sent to India by God. While the thought that God was personally directing my humanitarian activities was intriguing, I dismissed the notion out of hand. I had only days before my meeting with the holy man tried to escape from the dreadful poverty that was ever-present.

The next morning I left Rishikesh and tried to forget the previous day's experience, but the events later on in the day would prove even stranger. Having left Rishikesh I returned to Hardwar, which is only twenty kilometres distance and spent the day with street children providing clothes and food on an ad-hoc basis. Haridwar is, by Indian standards, a small city built on one bank of the river Ganges; as the river rushes to the sea, Haridwar has been built on the right-hand bank. On the other side of the river is where the improvised homeless live in tents made from black plastic. It was here that I spent the day working with 'untouchable' children. At dusk which would be about 6:30 pm, I decided to call it a day and was resolved to return very early the following day to get early morning photographs as the light can be beautiful at that time of day. I made my way to the dos-house where I stayed, which was on the other side of the river; I had a shower and lay down on the bed to rest before having an evening meal, thinking to myself what the hell am I doing in this poverty stricken country.

And for reasons that I still don't understand the thought that I should cross over again to the other side of the river entered, uninvited, into my mind. I rejected the notion, but the thought became ever stronger. That fact that I could entertain such a preposterous notion caused me to be annoyed at myself. As the thought grew in intensity, I decided to try and rationalise what was going through my mind. If I surrendered to the notion of returning to the other side of the river I thought, *What could I do?* It's dark and possibly risky and therefore stupid. I have long held the view that in all situations I should use my intelligence intelligently and to surrender to this ridiculous notion would be denial of my cherished principle. Not only did the irritating notion remain, but grew in intensity, and became a compulsion that had to be obeyed; in considerable annoyance I relented, and headed across a footbridge to the other side of the river.

The journey over the bridge was spent in mental turmoil; the stupidity of what I was doing was breath-taking—why had I surrendered to an irrational compulsion and why was it that an irrational notion became so powerful that I could not resist it? I thought to myself, this journey is very foolish and possibly dangerous and these thoughts had the effect of making me apprehensive and nervous. Indeed I kept looking over both my shoulder to make sure that I was not being followed.

Just before I reached the end of the bridge I had a decision to make, should I turn right or left? I should point out that on this side of the river, there were only a few lights along the path that ran parallel to the river; I decided to turn right and follow the dimly lit path which led to a road bridge that spanned the river about a half-mile down river. I was very nervous as I had only been in India a few days and was uncertain about the risk of wandering along a dimly lit and deserted path in the dark of night. As I slowly walked towards the road bridge, which was about a half a mile away, I constantly looked behind me to reassure myself that I was not being followed; there wasn't any one on the path in front of me. To my right was the river and to the left was open ground with several hundred black polythene tents in which 'untouchable' families lived without water, toilets or lighting of any sort. I kept thinking to myself this is really foolish and potentially dangerous. Having walked along the path for several hundred meters I noticed to my left that a young girl of about twelve or thirteen was approaching me and she was carrying in her arms a baby of about one year old. I was delighted to see them and approached them with outstretched arms indicating that I wanted to hold the baby; the older child surrendered the baby to me and I thought to myself, *I will come looking for you two tomorrow, take you both across the river, buy you new clothes and take you to a restaurant and get you a nice meal and buy a food parcel for the family.* Then I thought, maybe I won't find them tomorrow so I reached into my left-hand pocket and gave the older girl the contents which would be about two pounds sterling. As I did so a voice from behind said, "May I speak with you." I almost jumped out of my skin with shock, for I heard no approaching sound and was, in spite of my constant vigilance, totally unaware of the presence of this individual. Upon hearing of the individual's request I swung around so fast that I almost lost balance, and was relieved to see that there was only this one person in front of me.

He was a small Indian man, about five foot six inches tall, aged about fifty-six, bald on top and the hair on the sides of his head was well groomed; He was impeccably dressed in a medium brown-striped suit with a matching plain brown shirt and dark brown tie. So astonished was I at this encounter that I blustered somewhat, but recovered my composure and said, "Of course, you may speak with me. What would you like to say?"

His response was, "I have observed you for the past few days and I want you to know that you have a very beautiful soul."

I was, of course, totally unprepared for this compliment. I responded by saying, "Thank you very much, no one has ever said anything as beautiful as that to me before." I was still holding the baby and turned around to give the baby back to the girl whom I assumed to be a sibling sister; I gave the baby a kiss and handed it over and immediately turned around to continue conversing with my complementary acquaintance, only to discover that he had disappeared as mysteriously as he had arrived.

This immediate disappearance was unnerving and I mildly panicked and became frightened; I could not rationalise or even comprehend what was happening to me. I was sure that I had a visitation of some sort and I had seen an apparition, which was not ghostly. What I had experienced was, to me, deeply unsettling and disturbing. Why did this apparition appear to me and for what reason; yes, I was told that I had a very beautiful soul, but I believe all souls being from God are beautiful. I can with ease explain what happened, but I'm unable to understand why it happened. I am, however, convinced that my meeting with the old holy man high up in the Garhwal Himalaya mountains the day before and the apparition in Haridwar were somehow connected.

I left India determined never to return, but three days later while I was uploading to my computer the photos of the destitute street children I became overwhelmed and the tears flooded from my eyes at that moment, when my wife Mary entered my office with a cup of coffee and wanted to know why I was so upset. I replied I've bad news for both of us, I'm going back to India. I have had to reappraise my attitude to the old holy man who said that God had sent me to India.

Bottle feeding a child in India

Truly, Mr Shakespeare was right when he wrote, "There are more things in heaven and earth...than are dreamt of in your philosophy."

What you may want to know is, what has been achieved by my visits?

Seventy-two houses have been built for leper families.

Five Leper Colonies have been provided with toilets and showers.

Five schools have been built for destitute 'untouchable' children, who, in the circumstances pertaining to India would never have seen the inside of a classroom.

A mixed gender orphanage has been provided for street children in Dehradun in the north of India.

Individual transport in the form of hand-cranked tricycles is provided for ground-bound cripples.

Old destitute ladies are provided with sewing machines and training to make them financially self-sufficient.

Suitable individuals are provided with the means of creating self-employment.

Many other initiatives are taking place in the field of medical care and eco-awareness programmes. To all who financially made these achievements possible I offer my consummate gratitude.

House for a Leper family

Chapter 3
Truth

The mundane human mind cannot comprehend the spiritual authority that only truth can confer to humanity. The truth, when spiritually embraced, will raise the individual above and beyond all that is irrelevant and will lead to spiritual knowledge and divine wisdom and finally, to complete liberation.

'We bow unto the Light that burns within every living soul. The Light that is the joy and blessing and peace unending. The light that is wisdom all-knowing, the Light boundless, tide less, space less. Unto that light divine we strive,' (Hindu chant)

"For a happy life is joy in the truth." [Augustine]

There can never be any solution for any of our problems until that blessed day when truth liberates the mind from all forms of irrationality. Confusion and ignorance have a firm grip on the mass of humanity and only a few are wise and courageous enough to search for the remedy that truth alone can provide. To end the nightmare, that is the bedfellow of confusion and ignorance, it's absolutely necessary to have the resolve and courage to know the truth of existence in human form. Only in the truth can a satisfactory explanation for the earthly existence be found. You will, no doubt, experience disappointment and frustration, both of which dissipate energy and cause a resistance to change. But, if you trust in God, your energy level will rise in proportion to any such resistance. You will receive wisdom and strength directly from truth, if truth is sought in love.

Truth of itself, and it alone will supply a dual form of liberty; it will liberate the inner spiritual being, that is the real you, and the outer man from all human failings including fear, anger, resentment, ignorance and uncertainty. The choice is between the ignorance of the multitude, with all the fear and pain that is the bedfellow of ignorance, or the distinguished company of these great souls who have found tranquillity in truth.

The Liberty all seek is not in the formulation of man-made rules, regulation or laws; it resides in the soul of every person. If you truly desire to be free from all human folly you only have to submit to what we have already received from God. Love and compassionate and deeds are the prerogative of truth itself. Truth in all of its wonderment and glory is the beautiful reward for greatness and the greatness required is of a moral and spiritual nature. A person may be a great architect, composer, author, sculptor, doctor, artist; these human qualities are of no spiritual benefit in the quest for the ultimate truth. It is spiritually unimportant to be worldly great; the greatness you should seek for is to live in harmony with God's Divine Law, in order that the truth may manifest in and through you, not only for your own benefit, but that you may help spread spiritual light for the benefit of all of humanity. For truth to manifest you must make yourself a worthy depository and this can only happen when spiritual principles are triumphant over all human considerations.

In truth you are spiritually entitled to every wonderful bounty that God has to offer, but before you can receive the wonderful gifts from God's treasure chest you must make yourself worthy to receive them. Give human expression to spiritual truth; this is the purpose for life on earth. But, to come to a spiritual understanding of truth, it is essential to give full human expression to love and all other spiritual virtues.

The truth to be acquired there has to a profound reverence for life and also for the divine source of life. All have been given dominion over all thought forms, all deeds and all reactions, and only when we assume full responsibility for all thoughts and deeds will the right conditions exist for self-realisation. When God created mankind in His image and likeness, He must have had in mind that His children should live in freedom and abundance. And each of us will live in freedom and live life abundantly only when we place truth over every human consideration.

Take encouragement from the fact that an honest and purified heart possesses the ability to comprehend and rejoice in the truth. God and nature created mankind to be the source of its own satisfaction; all the attributes of God are inherent within every individual and when these wonderful spiritual gifts are used wisely, all human folly will be ended forever. Each and every one of us makes, in reality, the type of world in which we live. If we live the negative life, in the material world we will suffer all the woes and tribulations of the outer world. Conversely if we live the spiritual life of love and understanding and seek to know the truth of life, we will, in time be divinely rewarded.

Those who seek in love and veneration for truth will have such wonderful revelations that at this moment cannot be imagined. It is necessary for the sincere seeker to step out of the common herd of humanity and stand firm on the holy ground of spiritual individuality. Nature calls out to us to be fearless, independent, and noble of spirit and to be of sound judgement. Society with its religions, creeds, dogmas and confused beliefs causes the confusion that is rampant throughout the world today.

You may receive a million explanations of the benefits of truth but an explanation, no matter how eloquent, can never be compared to the reality of truth itself. It is the highest level of intelligence to be actively engaged in constructing strength of character and acquiring the moral fortitude required to reach the heights of virtue and, eventually, truth itself. In the mundane activities of dull routine there is much pain, frustration and short fleeting periods of pleasure frequently induced by alcohol or other substances. Millions are being defeated in their search for love, peace, harmony and understanding because they fail to understand that the outer is the reflection of the inner.

If the inner spiritual life is right so must the outer circumstances be also. No worthwhile life can be constructed upon the mechanical needs of the physical world. What is required is an intense and conscious effort to understand the truth of life itself. Nature in its wisdom has made us strong in spirit; it is, therefore, imperative that we acknowledge spirit and give it due attention, that nature may complete its work in us. It is nature's task to make us complete human beings by freeing each individual from all the burdens associated with mere worldly existence. In spite of its awesome power, nature cannot complete its work in us until we consciously decide to work in harmony with her.

To experience inner contentment and the joy of freedom there must be total submission to spiritual realities. Here we are confronted with the paradox of gaining liberation and freedom by total submission to the higher power of the truth, which is, that God has created every member of humanity in His image and likeness. The truth of our true spiritual identity and this fact alone is the only means available to mankind to end the nightmare of folly and ignorance.

Don't seek to model your life on any individual; the person or persons you think you would like to be, are, if the truth be known, living lives of quiet despair. Contained in every normal mind is the capacity to achieve real and lasting happiness. The mind is set in motion by thought; the fruits of thought are the results of direction given to the mind. There cannot be peace or contentment in any life until the blessed day when the mind is brought under the control of intelligence and will. Intellectual thought alone can't bring any real change in the human condition; intellect has to be supported by wisdom, intuition, reasoning and guided by love. For the truth to manifest, the mind has to be fed a daily diet of love, compassion and understanding and these virtues must be exercised constantly in all situations and circumstances.

Jesus said, "Ye shall know the Truth and the Truth shall set you free." [John 14: 12]

He also assured us that if we ask we shall receive, if we seek we shall find. He was of course referring to truth. What will be the benefit, you may ask; what rewards will you receive if you discover Truth? Well, you will be completely independent of all circumstances; nothing or no one will have any authority over you.

The freedom Jesus spoke of is complete and absolute; it is freedom from all limitation. You will, with the truth, be freed from all your burdens, cares, woes and tribulations. You will be freed from all pain—mental, emotional psychological and physical.

So truth is healing and the truth is that you are the vehicle prepared by the truth for its manifestation in human form. Know that the mighty power and the glory of the truth are waiting on your recognition of its existence within you so that it can manifest through you to all of mankind. To be conscious of the presence of the truth within is to understand the secret of man's unity and oneness with God. Your consciousness when consciously united by you to the universal consciousness that dwells within you is the means of establishing the truth.

The truth, when earnestly sought, will begin to unfold naturally from within, free from suggestion. If you arrive at any conclusions, from without, concerning truth, it will be just that, conclusions of the truth. The truth will manifest from within to the outer, never from the outer to within. No one can give you the truth; it's not in anyone's power to gift the truth to another person. You will not acquire the truth from reading books, attending lectures or any other human activity of the mind or body. The truth cannot be intellectualised. For the truth to manifest, there has to be a purification of all negative thoughts. The heart has to be pure, full of love, compassion and understanding. There are aspects of truth that are obvious—you live and you have consciousness. But do you accept the truth of your life? Your life is eternal because there is only one Life and this Life is God. The truth is that God's Consciousness dwells within you and this Consciousness of God in you will, if you allow it, lead you to the all truth.

It has been written, *'Without courage, there cannot be Truth, and without Truth there can be no other virtue,'* (Scott)

Another great philosopher has said… "To love Truth for Truth's sake is the principle part of human perfection in this world, and the seed of all other virtues."

To be perfect, to be whole, to be complete, we need to live the life of truth. It is God's holy will that the truth shall be made known to all of mankind. Nothing can prevent the will of God from manifesting. His will shall be done. All will come to the truth of the one God existing in every soul as the Christ. Yes, everyone will in time come to know the truth for without the truth there can be no eternal rest or peace. Those who die without coming to the truth must reincarnate on earth, time after time, until truth is found. The 'freedom' mentioned by Jesus in relation to the truth includes freedom from rebirth. Freedom from having to return to earth, in another body, is the greatest freedom of all. When truth manifests and you leave your body at death, you will go to Paradise. Those who are worthy of entering Paradise will never have to return to earth again unless given a spiritual mission.

'My Father's house has many mansions', [John 14; 2], said Jesus.

He was speaking of the different planes of consciousness. This chapter does not permit the opportunity to examine in detail after-death experiences. What you might be interested to know is that Jesus taught His 120 disciples these things in secret. Jesus taught His apostles and disciples that consciousness came from God; that God's Consciousness, being universal, resides in every human consciousness; or more accurately, that all consciousness is of God. You should know that consciousness is something entirely different from intellect. The intellect is an instrument used for the process of thought while consciousness is responsible for all creation. The truth is that God is all and in all for all of eternity. The mighty truth is, that God is universal consciousness, intelligence and substance. There is not one atom in all the universes that is not of God; He fills all space and everything therein.

Paul has told us correctly, "We live and move and have our being in Him."

Now you know, there is only one consciousness, the Infinite Consciousness of God. God who is the creator and you, His manifestation, is one. Jesus came to earth to proclaim the truth and truth is Universal; it never changes. It's the same in all circumstances and for all time. The truth belongs to all. It is not my truth or your truth or even Jesus' truth.

When Jesus said, "I and the Father are one," He proclaimed the Universal Truth.

In Truth, you can say with the same authority… *'The Father and I are one,'* [John 14: 7]

This is the Truth of your being, because there is no other source of life than God. Yet God remains a meaningless notion to countless millions of people because they won't search for God in the only place He can be found, within themselves. Let's examine to see if we can make a statement of truth that can be verified, something that can't be denied. The statement is 'I live,' You know that you live because you are conscious of yourself and your environment. So in absolute surety you can say 'I am,' Nothing or no one can detract from the truth that you exist.

Now let us examine the story about God appearing to Moses on Mount Sinai.

God instructed Moses to lead the Israelites out of Egypt. Moses said to God… *'When I go to the Israelites and say to them the God of your ancestors sent me to you, they will ask me… What is his name? So what can I tell them?'*…

God said… *'I am who I am. This is what you must say to them. The one who is called, I am, has sent me to you,'*

The name of God is the word of power and universal truth. God declared Himself *'I am,'* You can only declare yourself *'I am,'* The *'I am'* in you is the same *'I am'* in God. You and the Father are one. The master Jesus knew this truth; to Him it was a living reality. He was able to do the wonderful things He did because He accepted the Living Presence of God within Him.

Jesus said, *'It's not I who does the work, but the Father who ever remains in me, He does His own work,'* [John 14: 10]

You, or anyone who is prepared to accept that the Living God is present in Spirit will, in time, do the things that Jesus did. If this is the reality of your existence, if God, who is truth, lives in you, then you are the truth. For this reality to become known you must seek deep within yourself and you will know that the truth and your real self are one and the same and if you allow God's Consciousness to lead you, it will lead you to the truth. God lives in you and He will express Himself in you, if you will allow Him to do so. The truth of your living is that you are an indestructible Spiritual Being. You will live forever; nothing can destroy you from perfection you have come to, and to perfection you will, in time, return. If you accept the truth of your being, you will make a quick return to perfection. If you desire to know the truth you may ask, what is the best way to understand and know the truth? You can only come to the truth through diligent recognition and continual realisation that it is God Himself who is working in you. Acknowledge God as being the inspiration in you; say in your heart… *"It is you, my beloved Father, who does the work and I lovingly thank you."* Truth is universal and immortal and when known by the individual, that person will know him or herself as God knows them. The love of God and all His children is a necessary precondition to the unfolding of the truth from within. The truth is from within to the outer man, never from without. Jesus said,

'The kingdom of heaven is within,' [Luke 17:21]

This kingdom is the truth that God as the Christ resides in man.

"The truth makes all things plain." (William Shakespeare)

When you know the truth, you will know that Spirit is your first and only foundation. You will realise that God is the consciousness in you and that you share the one Life of God with every other person in creation. There is no separation anywhere; everything exists in the Mind of God. This is the truth. When you know the truth, you have nothing left to learn; all mysteries will be revealed unto you. Your physical body is only the focal point through which the invisible functions. You cannot see the truth; it cannot be identified by any of the physical senses. It takes a faculty that as yet, you do not understand. I've mentioned it on several occasions; it is the faculty of knowing. The knowing, for certain, of something you never learnt or experienced. It's a knowing from beyond the mind and not dependent on any human authority.

He said, *'A sparrow does not fall but God knows about it.'* And, *'Every hair on your head is counted,'* [Luke 12:6]

This mighty Intelligence found free expression through Jesus because He recognised its existence and realised its power. By the power of this Universal Intelligence all things are possible. It will bring love to the heart, peace to the mind and healing to the body. The truth not only has the power of love, peace and healing, it will provide total freedom upon you. Truth is the central power existing in you and for it to be made known, you must listen. For only in the deepest silence of your soul is the power of Truth realised.

Emerson, the great American thinker, wrote: *'Truth is always present; it only needs to lift the iron lids of the mind's eye to read its oracles,'*

Once we ignite the mind's interest in the truth, it will respond with an insatiable desire to know the truth. The search for truth begins with the mind, but it's an inner vision that will reveal the truth. This inner vision will reveal the truth to be the real you, the spiritual you.

You live in God and He in you. The mighty truth is there can be no separation between the Father and you. And as you enter into the realisation of this unity, you will become consciously aware of the Father residing in you as love, truth and compassion. And when your personal consciousness becomes consciously aware of the Christ Consciousness within then you will know yourself to be the Truth.

The Lord, our God, is the Truth, and since it is God who lives in you, then the Truth is also within you. You should then search and dig in your own garden for that pearl of great price. If you seek the truth it must be for truth's sake and not for any advantage you may gain from it. To be successful in your search, your heart must be full of love, which is the seed of purity and perfection; only when these conditions are established can the truth take hold in you.

You will only fully comprehend and realise the truth when you fully accept the spirituality that you and the Father are one; then the truth will manifest in and through you to all of humanity. Truth, you see, is a sacred trust bequeathed to all of humanity by God and will manifest in any individual when the mind is freed of all that is negative and false. When you free the mind from all forms of malice, all limitation, will end when you allow the mind access to love, compassion, understanding and beauty. Then, and only then does the mind become a suitable vehicle for the expression of God's holy will. And by the power of your individual consciousness you allow the Christ Consciousness to manifest. Christ is complete in God and man and God can only be realised through the conscious awareness of Christ within.

Jesus said, *'With what measure yea mete, it shall be measured to you again,'* [Mark 4: 24]

It is truth that unites all to God, and only through that, can you be with God who is the Truth. And only in the love of God can truth find manifestation.

Christ speaking through Jesus said… *'I am the Life'* [John 14: 6]… Here is the truth stated boldly and simply.

There is only the one Life and each and every individual is in truth Universal Life. The statement *'I am the Life'* must be intellectually accepted, then acted upon. The method you now know.

If you desire the power of truth, the power of love, the power over disease, know that Christ is all power in heaven and on earth. You have been told that the Christ power is within you and you can call upon this power when you clearly recognise its existence and realise your unity with the source of this power.

You have been told that… *'I am'*…is the name of God and… *'I am'*…is the word of power. To meditate, select some place in your home or wherever a place of privacy can be found. Sit on a chair, get your back and neck erect and your feet planted on the ground, hands resting on the thighs. Begin by breathing slowly; as you breathe in mentally say… *'I'*… and as you breathe out mentally say… *'am,'* Make the mental word last as long as the breath. By this method of breathing and by using the word of power *'I am'*, and by a conscious awareness of the presence, remember it's the Christ that breathes, not the body. You now have the formula for reaching deep within yourself to release spiritual energies that will allow truth to manifest and truth will restore mental, emotional and physical equilibrium in you.

You should begin your meditation with this prayer, *"Almighty God, it is you who ever remains in me, you are doing the work for which I lovingly thank you."* I suggest that each meditation should last at least ten minutes. Remember that Christ is the universal creative principle of God; Christ and the Father are one. The truth is God Universal is individualised in you as the Christ. Your acceptance of this spiritual fact and the practice of the meditation periods as described will fill your whole being with spiritual vibrations of the Christ Life; thus, elevating your experiences beyond the physical.

Browning has told us… "I count life just the stuff to try the soul's strength on."

If you are locked into a struggle with yourself against the worst aspects of your character, don't give up on yourself and don't despair. Help is at hand, in fact, is nearer than hands or feet; it is the truth of the Christ Presence.

Give yourself over completely to the truth of your being that it is God Himself who lives in you; when you fully accept this, your mind becomes a vehicle for the expression of God's Divine Will. Before this can happen, the mind must be filled with love and reverence. Only by this means can you be raised above your ordinary mundane existence. If you follow the advice and instructions given, your consciousness will expand and allow the truth to manifest, and by the clearest understanding and the purest love you will know yourself to be the truth incarnate.

Nature calls out to us to be independent, noble of spirit and be of sound judgement. Society with its religious creeds, dogmas and confused beliefs causes the confusion that is rampant throughout the world today. You may receive a million explanations of the benefits of Truth but an explanation, no matter how eloquent, can never be compared to the reality of Truth itself. It is of the highest level of intelligence to be actively engaged in constructing strength of character and acquiring the moral fortitude required to reach the heights of virtue and eventually Truth itself.

In the mundane activities of dull routine there is much pain, frustration and short, fleeting periods of pleasure frequently induced by alcohol or other substances. Millions are being defeated in their search for love, peace, harmony and understanding, because they fail to understand that the outer is the reflection of the inner.

The truth of your being is that God has created you and God did not create you to be a failure; you are meant to live a life of truth, joy, peace and contentment. You were created that the truth should find expression through you to all of creation. For this to manifest, you must rid the mind of all its foolish inclinations and replace them with positive thoughts of Truth. The type of thoughts—*'You my beloved Father and I are one'*, *'Lord God, I live because your infinite life lives in me,'*

These thoughts, if accepted and acted upon, will allow the truth to be realised. The truth cannot be fashioned by your intellect; you cannot by mind power alone create the spiritual conditions required by truth prior to its manifestation. Truth requires that any aspirant must seek for the truth with a deep veneration for truth and a profound love for God. When these conditions are entrenched in the purified heart of the sincere seeker, the Lord God of Truth will reveal all the mysteries and spiritual beauty behind all of creation. Truth is the miracle medicine for all of mankind's illnesses. The truth is that we have become a sick society; the malady grows worse by the hour, and because of our unwillingness to embrace the medicine of Truth mankind is now in a terminal state of spiritual paralysis. Mankind is held captive to the false belief that by creating the right social, economic, political, cultural and educational institutions, universal peace and contentment can be established. The truth is, unless there is a mass conversion to spiritual realities mankind is doomed to slide further into confusion. All religions claim to have the answer to all of humanities problems; yet, in spite of millions of devotees organised religion is incapable of stopping the slide by mankind to disaster.

Chang-tse was right when he said, "Great truths do not take hold of the heart of the masses."

All the while, the Christ of God resides in the soul of every person; the soul is the receptacle and repository of spiritual truth. The universal and the individual are one; only when this unity of God and self is firmly established in your conscious can the Truth find expression in and through you. The only means or method of experiencing the Truth is to accept the truth of your being. You are not a mere mortal being; in reality you are the divine child, a spiritual creation of God. The total acceptance of this spiritual fact will ignite the spark of spiritual inspiration and this will provide not only inspiration but also the human desire and enthusiasm needed to succeed.

Emerson wrote, *'Speak the truth, and all nature and all spirits help you with unexpected furtherance,'*

Start, at this moment in time, to create the conditions, which will allow the truth to manifest. Make the decision to live a modest life dedicated to common decency. Be determined to be faithful to honesty and integrity. And when your dedication becomes stronger than your folly, you will win through to spiritual freedom, profound peace and Truth itself. The only requirement is a change of heart and mind. The ability to attune your mind to Truth lies within the power which God has placed in your hands and when truth manifests in you all circumstances conform to your will. Happiness cannot be found in the mundane world with all its folly and confusion; happiness is found only in the mind that is still and at peace with itself and only the Truth can content the mind. The Truth is, no one can hope to change or elevate their life by habitual thinking and reasoning.

"It is right to yield to the truth." (Horace)

In searching for the Truth you will have to accept, on faith, that the universal truth exists somewhere, and any dedicated and sincere aspirant who is prepared to strive diligently enough can discover it. So faith, dedication and perseverance are the principle requirements in the quest for truth, but there has to be love and passion, understanding and generosity.

"To build up that strength of mind which apprehends and cleaves to great universal truths, is the highest intellectual cultivation." (Channing)

For sure any aspirant who seeks to know the Truth requires an energetic mind, but the mind has to be directed with loving intelligence. And as the mind is made more loving and caring it is also made more intelligent and the capacity for the truth to manifest is greatly increased.

Swedenborg has told us, "Truths, which enters with affection, are reproduced."

The great mass of humanity lives the life of pretence and self-deceit and this leads to frustration and quiet despair; but because there is almost universal confusion, mankind is held in a vice-like grip of ignorance of how to escape to the sanity of the kingdom of heaven within. The Truth is that God provides all space; there is no separation anywhere in the whole of creation. God and you are one; the twin pillars upon which these rocks of truth stand spiritually transparent.

Emerson has told us, "We are very near to greatness: one step and we are safe."

Purify the heart, cleanse the mind and place God and your immortal soul as your first priority and the Truth will be revealed within you and you will be blessed with the wonderful gift of Divine Truth. In the light of Truth, all limitation will permanently end and spiritual visits of unimaginable beauty will be revealed unto you. It was God Almighty who personally breathed the breath of life into you and you can't possibly fail in the quest for Truth. You must, however live your life in harmony with God's universal laws, which you now know. No one can hinder your spiritual progress; if you are sincere, all the forces of nature will, in unseen ways, be of benefit to you. It is the will of God that you should return to Him purified radiating love, humility and spiritual understanding. Know that no one has the ability to frustrate the will of God; it is unchanging and unchangeable, therefore with sincerity and purity you cannot fail.

"There is as esoteric doctrine, each man enters into God so much as God enters into him." (Amiel)

If you give yourself completely to Truth then you can be certain of spiritual rewards, but you must not be impatient; your faith and perseverance will be tested. Where you to enter a race, it is only when you have participated and been victorious can you claim the prize. So it is in the matter of the soul and Truth; to be victorious in the quest for Truth you only have to become as beautiful as God intended you should be, and use your God-granted gifts wisely. If you are weary and jaded; if your life is blighted by folly, fear, anger and negatives emotions, don't despair—you are greater than your present weakness. There is within every person a deeper understanding and a degree of wisdom as yet untapped. To gain access to both, understand that God is the supreme spiritual authority and place your life in His loving arms. If you make the almighty your deepest contemplation, God in the form of Universal Truth will manifest in you.

"To love truth for truth sake is the principle part of human perfection in this world, and the seed of all other virtues." (Locke)

Truth resides in the hearts of enlightened men and women everywhere, and to become an enlightened individual, it's absolutely necessary to become aware that you are a spiritual being. When you become a conscious Son of God, you will be blessed with spiritual love and in spiritual love Truth resides.

"These are not fictions of a visionary imagination, but sober truths spoken by the word of god in scripture and written and engraved in the back of every man's own nature." (Law)

Every aspirant must not only to be prepared to surrender to Truth but must surrender in total love and complete faith. You will manifest Truth upon the acceptance that your individual consciousness is the universal consciousness of Almighty God. Truth is always present and attainable, but won't manifest until the aspirant has placed virtue over all mundane considerations. The conditions that must prevail, you now know to be love, understanding, compassion, generosity and faith. When the mind and consciousness are this purified, your longing for Truth will be rewarded. The light of Truth will be revealed by the Christ of God within you, for Christ means the light of creation that shines in your immortal soul. If Christians were to accept the living presence of God within and live in spiritual love a life dedicated to peace and wisdom the world would, they in a short period of time, become the jewel of all the universes.

"Renouncing the honours at which the world aims, I desire only to know the truth…. And to the maximum of my power I exalt all other men to do the same." (Plato)

"The soul's communication of truth is the highest event in nature and this communication is an influx of the Divine Mind into our mind. Every moment when the individual feels invaded by it is memorable." (Emerson)

The light of Truth shines forth from God by means of the soul. We, in our folly, have imprisoned the soul in the cage of neglect and indifference. While the mass of humanity has forgotten or become callous concerning the soul's presence and its divine mission, the soul is spiritually aware that it is the emissary of Almighty God. The soul's evolution should be recognised as being the reason for earthly existence and is the conscience in every member of humanity.

"Soul is the only reality, and we have forgotten it." (Vivekananda)

"Our indifference to truth is due to our determination to follow our desires. It is of no importance, men say, to know where the truth is, since we know what will give us pleasure." (Vauvenargues)

It is supremely difficult to convince mankind that their physical existence in this world is for the purpose of allowing their immortal soul to become the spiritual means of allowing Truth to manifest. The soul is the only means at our disposal, which will allow the Truth to triumph over all material inclinations and conditions. If you would feed the mind the beautiful diet of positive direction, encourage the mind and consciousness to engage in thoughts that will serve the cause of Truth, and you will be lovingly rewarded by God.

If the life you have lived, until now, is typical of the mass of humanity and if you are struggling for an understanding of your place in creation, wondering if there is an escape route from the confusion and folly of today's world read with care and due attention what the philosopher Law has written.

"Do not let your present and past distress make you feel and acknowledge this twofold great truth: first, that in and of yourself you are nothing but darkness, vanity and misery; second, that of yourself you can no more help yourself to light and comfort, than you can create an angel. People at all times can seem to assent to these two truths, but then it is an assent that has no depth or reality and so is of little or no use. But your condition has opened your heart for a deep and full conviction of these truths. Now give way, I beseech you, to this conviction and hold these two truths in the same degree of certainty as you know two and two to be four and then you are one with the prodigal come to yourself and above half your work is done." (Law)

The sooner the lesson is learnt that emotionally induced excitement and cheap thrills cannot provide mental stability or peace of mind, the sooner will mankind turn to search for lasting and meaningful answers to the problems they face. Truth is indiscernible and cannot be comprehended by mortal mind; the indescribable can only be discerned by the spiritually awakened consciousness.

As the individual spiritually unfolds, the soul will reveal to consciousness the mighty truth that resides in the heart of everyone.

Please accept that truth exists in the consciousness of God and what is established in God's Consciousness is also established in the consciousness of every member of humanity; please don't dissipate your spiritual energy by rejecting this truth. Truth is the only means of attaining true greatness, which will elevate the individual above and beyond grief. Conversely, if you turn away from truth and imitate the deluded mass of humanity your life will be blighted by frustration, and dissatisfaction.

"He who hangs on to the errors of the ignorant multitude must not be counted among the great." (Livcero)

Every day that is not spent in the quest for Truth is a day wasted. For you will come to understand that life is too important to be spent chasing after material possessions or worldly success. In the other side of life, beyond mother earth, there are no financial institutions; no status of wealth or social position; and those who have dedicated the earthly existence to the pursuit of wealth or social position will pay a dreadful price for their folly. For all must die and leave their possessions and reputation behind them. Your life can only have genuine meaning when you know that you are one with Christ of God who is resident within you. The truth is that you are at one with Truth itself though Christ.

"Though we travel the world over to find the beautiful, we must carry it with us or we find it not." (Emerson)

To survive in our tough world without having our humanity being battered, bruised and eventually crushed is possible. However, if you live wisely and modestly and consent only to that which is consistent with the Truth you will not only survive, your life will become the beautiful expression of the spiritual reality. To bring your life into harmony and peace, seek the silent love that dwells within you. Dispense love to friend and foe alike; make love the principle consideration in your worldly affairs, and love will elevate you to the higher spiritual realms where truth abides.

"Man that he does not know what spiritual servitude is and what spiritual liberty is; does not possess the truth that teach this; and without truth spiritual servitude is believed to be freedom and spiritual freedom to be servitude." (Swedenborg)

Spiritual servitude is unquestioning obedience to a religious sect or organisation. These sects or organisations claim to have the key to heaven's gates, but only those who accept the sect's or organisation's dogma and partake in their organised rituals will be admitted to heaven. Spiritual liberty is the acceptance of God's Presence within and living in love and harmony with humanity and nature. Spiritual liberty is the realisation that God resides in the living soul of every individual and that mankind is divine and eternal; this is the truth of existence that leads to genuine spiritual liberty. All else is not liberty but licence. The truth has to be recognised as a spiritual fact of life; it has to be venerated, honoured, respected and loved before it can manifest.

"There is no consolation except in truth alone." (Pascal)

If you have learnt that popular human opinions are worthless and meaningless and are incapable of ending the mechanical lives lived by a confused humanity, you have made a gigantic leap forward in understanding and you are to be congratulated. Mankind has become deluded; this delusion arises because humanity has become indifferent to its own welfare. Fear, violence, anger, anxiety, neuroses of all sorts, obsession with material possessions, obsession with sense gratification and opinions are the self-created obstacles that has blinded humanity to the truth. The philosophy of pleasure at any costs is delusion, for the only genuine pleasure is to be found in solving the mystery of human existence. The frantic pursuit of pleasure is paid for in all the pain, anger and neurosis that is characteristic of modern living. There is a road that leads away from human folly and all the pain that folly inflicts upon us; it is the road of love, truth and spiritual understanding. Let love be your constant companion, ruler and guide, and let truth be your constant ideal. Then, God will become a living reality in your life.

"You have no freedom or power of will to assume any holy temper, or take hold of such degrees of goodness, as you have a mind to have… But you have a true and full freedom of will and choice, either to leave and give up your helpless self to the operation of God on your soul. This is the truth of the freedom of your will." (Law)

Mankind has been overcome by many negative inclinations—illusion, despair, violence, sexual deviation, drugs and alcohol abuse, paedophilia, racialism and others forms of human corruption. While humanity is, at present, in a desperate immoral state for the wise individual, there is no need to despair; by an effort of reason you can find the resolution and the energy required to escape from the clutches of our sick society.

The New Testament has this wonderful advice for those seeking deliverance *'Be not overcome of evil but overcome evil with good,'* (New Testament)

The first requirement is to gain an understanding of the mysteries of existence and pursue this holy crusade with an independent mind with total self-honesty. Keep before you at all times the awareness that there is in reality only God. God is the final reality that all must, at some point in time, realise and the final realisation of God can only be experienced in truth. When the soul communicates the truth to the sincere aspirant, the whole being becomes transformed and becomes spiritual light; this experience is spiritual confirmation of the truth that you and God are one.

Truth is the search for the spiritual light of creation and is the final confirmation of the one life and that each individual is Life and absolutely no one can live apart from life. The whole of humanity belongs to God, all are His children and all must come to the realisation that separation from God is caused by ignorance. Your journey into truth begins with the recognition that God is an in-dwelling presence and is the source of all power and authority. So, the resolution to all human problems is in the recognition of mankind's relationship to the supreme authority of God. Accept that you are the individualisation of Universal Spirit and that you have your being in God. Gaze upon this truth and keep the vision of it before you at all times, for what your inner vision is conscious of, will manifest as an objective reality.

"Without courage there cannot be truth, and without truth there can be no other virtue." [Scott]

The remedy to the confusion that seems to be all-pervasive is to take hold of courage and seek to know the truth. You will, no doubt, experience doubt and frustration, both of which dissipates energy and causes a resistance to change. But, if you trust in God your energy level will rise in proportion to any such resistance. You will receive wisdom and strength directly from truth, if truth is sought in love.

"One truth discovered is immortal, and entitles its author to be so: for, like a new substance in nature, it cannot be destroyed." [Hazlitt]

Truth cannot be experienced until the mind is liberated from limitation and ignorance. Natural intelligence and unprejudiced reason have to be employed to get to the window of spiritual perception. Truth is beyond any human perception and can't be discerned by any human faculty. Yet we instinctively know that truth exists. We perceive it yet it's beyond our power of perception to realise truth. It is perception that provides the thirst to know the truth, perception being a faculty of mind-intelligence; yet, intelligence cannot provide us with the truth. For the truth to manifest, there has to be purity of thought, word and deed. The mind has to be freed from creed, dogma and all other forms of limitation and human authority. Truth, which is God and Life itself, will, if the right mental and spiritual conditions are created, manifest naturally. Spirit alone is the only source of truth and as you are spirit incarnate the truth resides in you. The truth in the midst of you is a mighty power indeed. Allow the truth within to exist in harmony with your awareness of God's presence, which is also within your consciousness. Only in Christ Consciousness can the truth be experienced and in truth you will find peace and the lasting contentment that all are seeking.

"The man himself must become other than he was if he wants to comprehend truth – must become as true as truth itself." [Stringer]

God is all there is seen and unseen; there is no other—this is the truth and God is the truth in manifestation. The spirit of God in the individual will reveal the truth when truth is placed before every other consideration. Consciousness, when raised to the level of Christ Consciousness will allow the truth to manifest and your life will become a very beautiful and rewarding experience. Accept the truth of your being which is that you can never be separated, not even for a second, from God. Accept that every atom of your physical and spiritual being is filled with the Presence of God. Accept that the power, love, consciousness and wisdom of God are within you. Truth, you see, is an active and conscious acceptance of God's Presence within you. Only when you accept that you and the truth are one, will it manifest in and through you. This precious gift from God has to be idolised, loved and venerated; only then can the soul reveal the truth that you and your Creator are one. If you doubt or refuse to believe that you are united to God, then the truth cannot manifest.

Those who are sincere in their quest for truth must understand that without a total commitment to love, their quest must fail. The heart must be kept full of love; this can be accomplished by continually pouring out loving thoughts to all of mankind. For Truth is Love in manifestation; to live in love is to dwell in the truth. Truth resides in every single person and is a mighty spiritual power indeed. When the individual consciousness becomes aware of this power, there must first be love, reason and intelligence to direct its actions.

Truth will bestow upon you the supreme spiritual endowment of enlightenment. And all problems will be at a permanent end. Nothing or no one will be able to harm you. Profound peace will be yours for all eternity. For you will have the mortal senses and emotions forever under control, and you will live eternally in the light of Divine Consciousness.

The truth is always seeking expression through the only means available to it which is consciousness. If you consciously desire, above everything else, to become a channel for the manifestation and expression of truth you must make yourself worthy. Those who seek to become the repository for the expression of truth are the wisest of the wise. The acceptance and expression of love, wisdom and understanding are the only means of becoming spiritually worthy that the truth may manifest in and through the individual.

There is only one means of human improvement and that is from within outwards. Transformation can only begin in the mind. It is the key to all things; it confers upon the individual either pain or contentment. The mind that has been cleansed of all forms of negativity, the negative mind will resist any and all change; it will at first refuse to travel the road to freedom, but will, when tamed, embrace the truth.

The liberated mind will listen intently for the quiet prompting of the soul's presence and in the silence the mind will become ever more active in the quest for conscious union with God. When the mundane thoughts become more refined, more disciplined; when hate is replaced with love; when anger gives way to understanding; when resentment gives way to concern; know that you are on the road to the freedom that only freedom can confer.

Understand that the truth goes beyond mind and is greater even than creation. Truth is Life itself and this Life lives in you and you can never be separated from it, for there is only one life. You are the expression of spiritual truth because God has begotten you. When you firmly accept that God and you are one, when you begin to think and behave accordingly, you make yourself ready for the manifestation of God's Truth.

What is most needed by mankind is not worldly riches, power or popularity, but to become the highest expression of spiritual understanding. If you believe that material things or the achievement of worldly ambitions can bring you peace or contentment you are doomed to bitter disappointment. The outer material world and our mortal senses are but a shadowy reflection of that which is real and substantial. Set your sight, heart, soul and mind on Spiritual love, for love is the Infinite Law of perfection in or out of the human body. And spiritual truth cannot be realised until perfection is attained. Don't think, as most individuals believe, that perfection is impossible. It can be achieved and you are now learning how.

I would remind you again of Jesus' entreaty, "Be ye perfect as your Father in heaven who is perfect."

Yes, perfection is possible if God is at the centre of your daily life. Accept the spiritual truth of your existence. God and you are one; you can never be separated from your Creator. In fact, God and His divine attributes are the only lasting reality in your life.

Truth has individualised itself in your immortal soul, and your consciousness is the means through which the Truth will eventually manifest. The mighty Truth is that you and Almighty God are one, and this has to be completely recognised and realised before the Truth can manifest. Truth is the revelation that will end all ignorance, all confusion, all uncertainty; truth is the knowing that God is all there is, and all of humanity exists in the Infinite Mind of God. It is the living spirit of God within the soul that allows the individual to grow into the living manifestation of the Truth. If you allow the living Spirit of God to influence all decisions and all deeds, keep focused on the Presence, the Truth will enfold from within.

God is incarnate love; therefore, failure is impossible when love is allowed to dominate the mind. With the mind freed from negativity and replaced with love and understanding, your growth into truth is assured. It is God's greatest wish that all His children should come to the truth; that we all may enjoy the wonderful benefits that truth will confer. Whatever condition your life is in, do not despair; if your life is a continuous struggle against emotional crisis, use your suffering wisely to end the pain. Turn completely and confidently to God.

You now know that your spiritual obligation to God, yourself and humanity is to become the living truth. The truth lives in your immortal soul; God Himself has bestowed this wondrous gift upon you. The spirit of God dwells within you and all of humanity. Where the spirit of God dwells so also must the truth of God dwell. Every individual is the living spiritual expression of infinite truth because God resides in every person. You only have to create the right mental and spiritual conditions and the truth will manifest naturally. You can at any time proclaim the truth in mental words. Repeat many times, every day:

"Almighty God, my beloved Father, you have created me out of your perfect spiritual substance, in your image and likeness. Truly Father you and I are one.

I now know that I am the life, the life of infinite love, profound peace, inspired wisdom and perfect health."

While proclaiming this prayer of the truth of your being, be intensely aware of the Presence that is present in every atom and cell of your body and being. The all-important truth can be stated and should be constantly on the lips of every individual.

"I am the life. The Father and I are one. With God all things are possible. The kingdom of heaven is within me. I live and move and have my being in God Almighty. The Lord is my Shepherd; there is nothing I shall want. The imperishable love of God enfolds me. 'The Lord is my light and my salvation.' Lord God you are I Am Who I Am. You are Omnipresent, therefore any individual can proclaim themselves, Who Am I AM."

These are some statements of the universal truth, which you should repeat with great sensitivity, love and hope. If you repeat these short prayers in the manner suggested, the 'Law of the Word' that has been explained in a previous chapter, will be brought into operation and this beneficent law of the word will in time raise your individual consciousness to the level of Universal Consciousness. The truth of your existence is that Christ lives in you and that Christ is the supreme authority, and this authority is available to you when you allow Christ's influence to dominate your life. There cannot be truth without Christ. For the Christ truth to manifest, you have to set yourself exacting standards of moral behaviour.

Spiritual principles should be the corner stone of every consideration. This will ensure that every decision made will reflect the highest degree of morality; you should clearly understand that you would have to reach the peak of personal integrity and honour. Justice and decency must be your mind's constant companion; the mind should, in all circumstances, be encouraged to act in accordance with probity and respect for honesty. The road to truth can be long and hard, lasting many different incarnations, but the journey has to be undertaken by every individual and no one can opt out of it. The wise and intelligent will set out on the road determined to reach destination—freedom.

Those amongst us who love long-distance walking know before setting out that it is necessary to make plans. When the destination has been decided, contingency arrangements have to be made for all foreseeable circumstances. A map of the route to be travelled has to carefully examined and all obstacles have to be studied, and the physical efforts required to overcome all difficulties have to be thoughtfully considered, and so it is on the road to truth. Very careful consideration, indeed, has to be given to many factors. For sure, you can't purchase a route map for this journey; you are very unlikely to find anyone who has successfully been over the route. There are many millions who think they are on the road to spiritual freedom that is truth. Unfortunately for them, they tread the road of human weakness that is mortal limitation. Their sense of separation from God blots out any real progress on the road to infinity. When mortal senses are bound to limited belief, there can be no escape to freedom and peace that is truth. No one can take a single step on the road until they accept that God lives in them; when this truth is recognised and realised, every experience will yield more and more spiritual understanding. When you eventually reach the state of conscious awareness that you and the Father are, in spiritual reality, One, the road to truth and total freedom from human limitation is wide open. Keep the mind full of love, compassion and holy reverence for all that is decent. You see, the road to freedom cannot be measured; there are no physical obstacles to be overcome, only those mental and emotional ones that exist in the doubting mind. Human reasoning is very limited indeed. It is limited to an understanding of human activity and material things. Reason is based exclusively on the mental interpretation of what the five mortal senses observe.

Upon this premise we construct our theories and beliefs and we are bound to suffer the unpleasant experiences that cause so much pain and frustration. Therefore, our limited beliefs become a barrier to the unlimited spiritual understanding that is our divine right. If this were true then all belief that impedes the capacity of spiritual experiences has to be discarded. Truth cannot be reasoned into manifestation, because truth is above and beyond the ability of any mind. However, your capacity to understand reality will expand when you clear the mind of all belief and theories. And yet, the mind is all important in the quest for spiritual liberation; the mind has to arrive at the stage where it can discern everything of critical importance and understand that it has reached the mountain top of spiritual virtue. Only then does it become a worthy receptacle into which the heavenly can descend into the mortal mind.

Mundane thoughts and superficial beliefs make it impossible for the mind to discern the false from that which is true; it is therefore imperative that the mind is spiritually cultivated. The mind that is permitted to wallow in thinly disguised ignorance must remain an impediment to any meaningful spiritual understanding. Doubt, fear, ignorance and aggression will make it impossible for the mind to become the spiritual receptacle into which the Holy Ghost can descend. All mental limitation must be ended, the limitations of false beliefs and outworn ideas. In the place of confusion and limitation a 'knowing' has to be established, the knowing that God lives as the Christ in you. The knowing that God and you are one and that separation exists only in the confused mind. The mind that is willing to express the divine love of the living Christ of God within is the mind freed from all sorrow, all depression, imitation, and limitation. The mind that does not know that it is the cause of its own miseries is unable to comprehend the truth. True freedom is in spiritual liberation, in the clear and certain understanding that you are one with the living God, an inspired knowing that surpasses all human understanding. When you fully recognise and finally realise the source of your own being, you automatically become an instrument for the manifestation of truth to all of humanity.

Freedom of truth will manifest when you become consciously aware of the Universal Consciousness existing in every member of humanity. When your individual consciousness realises its spiritual source, it will proceed to the realisation that the power to overcome all difficulties is available to the mind.

The rock of truth is that there is only God, and separation is a false belief held in the mind that is confused. Separation cannot exist because everything and everyone exists in the universal mind of Almighty God and when this is accepted, truth will manifest. It is the Spirit of God that dwells in every individual and the power of the truth is in this same spirit, and because of this you have access to all spiritual power.

What has happened to mankind is not a mystery; mankind as a whole has indulged in a gross betrayal and disloyalty to spiritual possibilities that are clearly available to all. Mankind in its folly has squandered its finer and nobler inclinations, and in many instances has resorted to self-treachery by placing worldly ambitions over spiritual realities. In most cases it will take Herculean courage and grim determination to admit to the folly of placing material ambition above the search for truth. Everyone wants to be thought of as being exceptional, yet everyone is dragged by desire through the emotional minefield of hate, anger, greed, envy and intolerance. To be genuinely exceptional, the individuals have to set themselves exacting spiritual ambitions and seek to bring these ambitions to fruition.

To experience divine love, truth, freedom and profound peace, we only have to yield to our finer instincts. When we give ourselves over to reason and natural intelligence, we rid ourselves of ignorance and we allow the beautiful person, that we truly are, the opportunity to manifest.

Deep within you shines the spiritual light of God. Let this light shine through you as loving, caring deeds and you will in time be rewarded for the Lord of Truth will send the Holy Ghost to enlighten you concerning all spiritual realities. The Father's house is full of spiritual bounties waiting to be claimed by anyone who is prepared to pay the asking price for the key to the front door. You should, by now, know that you must give yourself over to virtue; in the practice of spiritual virtue you will end all tribulations experienced in the dull routine of mundane life. While you continue to struggle with the effects caused by the ignorant and irrational mind, you must continue to endure pain and emotional punishment. Your suffering can be brought to a permanent end, but only when you yearn for spiritual elevation and a proper and satisfactory explanation for your experiences and for life itself.

The wonderful truth is that within you resides the unlimited creative power of Almighty God. This book is dedicated to helping you gain access to this spiritual power. Your deliverance from spiritual ignorance and confusion is gained through the acceptance of your spiritual divinity. Be firm in your conviction and resolute in you desire to live the life of decency and be spiritually prepared to serve God and mankind and the whole of nature will respond with the utmost generosity.

When you knowingly possess the truth, you have gained a wonderful victory, not only for yourself, but also for the whole of humanity. This possession is for eternity and an eternity of peace, tranquillity and joy; the endless kingdom of love is the reward of truth. We may speak of the truth and intellectually accept the logic of the description of truth, but just as appetite cannot be satisfied by any description of food so the souls longing for truth cannot be satisfied by explanation. The tragedy for the whole of mankind is indifference to the truth of existence, and those few who are interested in finding the truth are confused concerning how or where to begin the quest. When the individual becomes totally dissatisfied with the life of stupidity and resolves to live according to the dictates of reason and intelligence, then, and only then, can the truth be found.

The discovery of truth is the aim and object of life in human form; fortunate and blessed are they who have discovered truth. One of the great obstacles to be overcome is the inability of the individual to see himself as a spiritual being created by God in His image and likeness. When this is realised, the inner, spiritual world would become a reality and all things will be made plain.

It was Jesus who gave us the greatest explanation of truth when He proclaimed, "I and the father are one."

The truth of this statement is that the universal infinite spirit was recognised by Jesus as having individualised itself in Him. The truth is, there is only one source of life, which is God. God being the infinite source of life. We all share life with God, so the truth of existence is you and the father are one. Take hold of this truth; see clearly that God lives in you and is the essence of sanity, reason, intelligence and profound peace. Truth is the spiritual reason for all existence, the only cure for every human problem, a solution for every malady. What changes would take place in the life of every individual if only they would accept they are the spiritual image of Almighty God. Of course, the acceptance has to be reinforced by a constant awareness of God alive within. This acceptance and constant awareness will, in time, bring to an end all struggle, all unnatural craving; it is this that causes fear, confusion and conflict.

Truth won't arrive from any outside source or agency and it won't come as a blinding flash or instant revelation. The reorganisation and realisation of truth is not and cannot be an instantaneous experience. There has to be a stirring of the soul, which allows the spirit of God's presence to be communicated to the outer man. Truth can only be revealed to you through the inner spiritual vision and divine inspiration. You are the individualisation of universal infinite spirit that is of Almighty God. Gaze upon this truth of your true nature that you are spiritual and eternal; let not your gaze be distracted by any other consideration, for what you gaze upon in the inner vision will manifest in the outer. Upon the acceptance of your true spiritual identity the truth will manifest, but the reality of your spirituality must be established in the consciousness. When the truth manifests in the outer, the powers of the Universe become active and all things are then possible.

Individuals, by their indifference to the existence of truth, create all manner of problems including sickness of mind and body. People who believe in the power of evil will pay a terrible price for their ignorance. The truth can never be experienced by anyone who accepts that evil exists; such beliefs are a contradiction of every spiritual law known to exist.

Man, in conscious union with the Christ of God, will manifest truth. In God alone can truth be found. Spiritual perfection will eventually be established when love is fully embraced and allowed to guide thought, word and deed; when this happens, truth is reached and must manifest.

"Man stands in strict connection with a higher fact never yet manifest. There is power over and behind us, and we are the channels for its communications. This open channel to the highest life is the first and last reality, so subtle, so quiet, yet so tenacious, that although I have never expressed the truth, nor the heard the expression of it from any other, I know that the whole truth is for me." [Emerson]

No one can give you the Truth; it's not in anyone's power to gift the Truth to another person. You will not acquire the Truth from reading books, attending lectures or any other human activity of the mind or body. The Truth cannot be intellectualised. For the Truth to manifest, there has to be a purification of all negative thoughts. The mind has to become very sensitive, intelligent and thoughtful, free from all negativity. The heart has to be pure, full of love, compassion and understanding.

God remains a meaningless notion to countless millions of people because they won't search for God in the only place He can be found which is within themselves.

Jesus said, "It's not I who does the work but the Father who ever remains in me, He does His own work."

God lives in you and He will express Himself in you, if you will allow Him to do so. The Truth of your living is that you are an indestructible Spiritual being. You will live forever, nothing can destroy you; from perfection you have come and to perfection you will return.

Without Truth when you leave this earth you must return for another attempt to know the Truth. How, you may ask, is the best way to understand and know the Truth? You can only come to the Truth through diligent recognition and continual realisation that it is God Himself who is working in you. Acknowledge God as being the worker in you, say in your heart, it is you my beloved Father who does the work and I lovingly thank you.

Jesus said, "The Kingdom of Heaven is within."

This Kingdom is the Truth that God as the Christ resides in man. When you know the Truth you have nothing left to learn; all mysteries will be revealed unto you. "The Truth makes all things plain." (William Shakespeare.)

When you know the Truth, you will know that Spirit is your first and only foundation. You will realise that God is the consciousness in you and that you share the one life of God with every other person in creation. There is no separation, anywhere; everything exists in the Mind of God. This is the Truth. Your physical body is only the focal point through which the invisible functions.

You cannot see the Truth; it cannot be identified by any of the physical senses. It takes a faculty, that as yet you do not understand. I've mentioned it on several occasions—it is the faculty of knowing. The knowing, for certain, of something you never learnt or have never experienced. It's a knowing from beyond the mind and not dependent on any human authority. There is Universal Intelligence active through all space and this Universal Intelligence will express itself through the individual consciousness that becomes aware of it and is receptive to it; it is this Intelligence that makes the Truth known to you.

Jesus was very aware of this Universal Intelligence. He said, "A sparrow does not fall but God knows about it." And, "Every hair in your head is counted."

This mighty Intelligence found free expression through Jesus because He recognised its existence and realised its power. By the power of this Universal Intelligence all things are possible. It will bring love to the heart, peace and sensitivity to the mind, and healing to the body. The Truth not only has the power of love, peace and healing, it will provide total freedom upon you. Truth is the central power existing in you and for it to be made known, you must listen. For only in the deepest silence of your soul is the power of Truth realised.

Emerson, the great American thinker, wrote: *'Truth is always present; it only needs to lift the iron lids of the mind's eye to read its oracles,'*

Once we ignite the mind's interest in the Truth, it will respond with an insatiable desire to know the Truth. The search for Truth begins with the mind but it's an inner vision that will reveal the Truth to be the real you, the spiritual you. You live in God and God lives in you. There can be no separation between the Father and you. And as you enter into the realisation of this unity, you will become consciously aware of the Father who resides in you. And when your personal consciousness becomes consciously aware of the Christ Consciousness within you, then you will know yourself to be the Truth.

The Lord, our God is the Truth and it is God who lives in you then the Truth is also within you. You should then search and dig in your own garden for that pearl of great price. If you seek the Truth it must be for Truth's sake and not for any advantage you may gain from it. To be successful in your search, your heart must be full of love. Love is the seed of purity and perfection. and only when these conditions are established can Truth take hold in you. Love is the Light of your life and Truth is your life consumed by love.

Do not allow yourself to be content with inherited faith or passive beliefs. Open up your mind. Become an active enquirer; by all means listen to others, but listen most keenly to the inner voice of intuition. If you live your life dominated by love of God and all His children, your life will be full of light and Truth. Then there will be no more pain, no more sickness, no more suffering. You will rise above any mental emotional or physical problems. Look above and beyond your present difficulties; look to God who rules over-all and see in God that beautiful end to which all your problems will be brought.

You have duties to perform in life, so do your duty without attachment. Don't become bound to mechanical acts you are obliged to perform. One million acts will not nourish your immortal soul. It is your sacred mission to discover the Kingdom of God within you and its right use. The use must be love and service to all of humanity. It is a spiritual imperative placed upon us all by our Creator to love and serve our brothers and sisters.

Browning has told us: "I count life just as stuff to try the soul's strength on."

If you are locked into a struggle with yourself against the worst aspects of your character, don't give up on yourself and don't despair. Help is at hand, in fact, is nearer than hands and feet; it is the Truth of the Christ Presence in you. Remember, your will is independent of your senses. If you consent to be ruled by your passions you are bound to be dreadfully unhappy and unhealthy. On the other hand, if you allow your 'will', free expression, you are on the road to recovery. No experience in any lifetime is more delightful than the spiritual experience of Truth found. To seek the Truth is the sole reason for physical existence here on planet Earth.

"Truth above all, even when upsets and overwhelms us!" [Amiel]

You will receive wisdom and strength directly from the truth, if truth is sought in love. The liberty all seek is not in the formulation of man-made rules, regulation or laws; it resides in the soul of every person.

Truth, in all of its wonderment and glory, is the beautiful reward for greatness. The greatness required is both moral and spiritual. The greatness required is contained in the soul of mankind and the soul's greatness is freely available to those with the wisdom to seek guidance from it. Everyone wants or thinks they want worldly greatness, in the vain expectation that fame will provide recognition, wealth and influence. Were you to gain all these, what benefit would it be to your immortal soul? You will still be the same person. Your mental and emotional problems will still cause you the same degree of frustration. For truth to manifest you must make yourself a worthy repository and this can only happen when spiritual principles have triumphed over all human considerations.

Let the light of spiritual truth illuminate your heart and conscience, that every thought, word and deed reflects divine light; then truth will take hold of your mortal mind and when this happens the divine light of truth will be yours. Before we can experience truth in its spiritual state, we must practice the lower truths. In truth, most individuals live a life of servitude to their undisciplined negative mind. The truth is that in this servile mind dominance has to end, and negativity is to be replaced with noble thoughts of love, compassion and understanding. You must ardently desire to excel in your outer mundane life before you can experience the benefits that your spirit will reward you with.

To give human expression to spiritual Truth is the purpose for life on earth. Every negative experience can become a rich harvest of learning if the right lesson can be learnt; individuals who do not recognise themselves as being spiritual offspring from God will be driven by compulsive desires that, in the end, must lead to despair and failure. The truth is that the pleasure the world gives cannot last. If you find success you will only crave more of the same. In the end nothing matters except the mind living in harmony with the product of harmonious thoughts of wisdom.

Each and every one of us has only one genuine need and that is to become what God intended us to be, a loving and caring person, but that can only happen when we become aware of the truth that we are spiritual and have our being in God. Society with its conflicting beliefs, competing religions, differing dogmas and confused creeds is causing the confusion that is rampant throughout the world; the only remedy for all the confusion and the resulting conflict is the acceptance of the truth.

"Nothing is more delightful than the light of Truth." (Cicero)

It is the highest use of intelligence to be actively engaged in acquiring the moral fortitude necessary to reach the level of virtue that truth demands before it will manifest. You may receive a million explanations of the benefits of truth, but explanations, no matter how eloquent, can never compare to the reality of truth itself. The truth can never ever, under any circumstances, manifest while the individual operates exclusively in the outer world of form and phenomena. Only when the inner spiritual world is right will the outer circumstances be made conducive for the truth to take hold of the heart, mind and soul; then, and only then, is it possible for truth to manifest. No worthwhile life can be constructed upon the mechanical activities in the physical world; what is required is an intense and conscious effort to understand that life has a higher and nobler purpose than sense gratification.

For the truth to manifest it must be accepted; when the truth is recognised and realised then the conditions exist for truth to reveal itself. Let's try a little test to see if the mind is ready to accept that the truth exists. Statement of truth: 'God dwells within you as the Christ. Truth is of God and is God. You are Life itself; you cannot live apart from Life. You are the individualisation of the Universal God. The truth of your living is that God lives in you and is your very life. If you can accept these propositions then it possible for the truth to manifest. Truth will not come in a blinding flash of unsought inspiration; truth will come to the individual who seeks inspiration and is prepared to work hard to overcome all forms of negativity. In spite of its awesome power nature cannot complete its work in us until we consciously decide to work in harmony with her. Spiritual submission to the will of God is the only means available to us that will create the conditions for the manifestation of the truth.

As there is only one consciousness, a single intelligence, and one substance, the truth of your existence is that you and God are one. If you and the Father are one, this unity with God makes your existences spiritually eternal; you are an indestructible spiritual being. You have been created to become a vehicle through which the truth can manifest and flow to the rest of humanity. From the God of truth you have come and to the God of truth you must return. Begin your return now.

"The spirit of a man is the Candle of the Lord, lighted by God, and lighting us to God." (B. Whichcote)

Break from the spiritual narrative.

Chapter 4
Troubled Paramilitary

Some years ago, an ex-paramilitary member of the IRA approached me to confess that his conscience was causing him such torment that he was at the point of suicide, and what prevented him ending his life was a domestic situation in which some of his children were off the rails, and he to his credit he did not want to leave his wife to deal alone with a complicated and deteriorating family situation.

It was a brilliant summer day in early July, the day after my sixty-second birthday. I was out walking through the streets of my hometown, Derry. Walking along the street, a commercial vehicle pulled up beside and the driver offered me a lift. Being an enthusiastic walker it was on the tip of my tongue to refuse this offer and—not for the first time in my life—I instinctively knew that the person in the vehicle was looking for help. So, I reluctantly accepted the offer of a lift and requested to be taken home; during the ten-minute journey I was made aware that my companion was experiencing psychological trauma and was deeply depressed. When we arrived at my home, I invited him in for a cup of coffee. He accepted the offer, and while we drank coffee together he swamped me with details of his problems, which were that he was at the point of suicide as his children were proving difficult. One of his children had a serious congenital health problem, and another teenager was seriously into drugs and had in the recent past attempted suicide—thankfully the attempt was unsuccessful because of the immediate intervention of a police officer, who dived into the river Foyle and most certainly saved the young lady from drowning. Her father, a militant republican, didn't contact the policeman involved to thank him, which was at best shameful and at worst, reprehensible.

It was obvious to me that the ex-paramilitary, having told me of his family problems, was suffering torments of conscience because of his paramilitary activities. I challenged him on this matter and suggested that his conscience was running riot because he had taken part in events that resulted in the deaths of individuals. He agreed with me on this matter and told me he was in the hell of remorse and asked for my advice.

I responded by asking had he been responsible for the deaths of individuals? He responded yes. I asked him how many killings he was responsible for. However, he refused to tell me; I ask him to nod his head in response to two questions, one of which was, had he been involved in the deaths of more than two? He nodded affirmatively. My second question was, were there less than ten? Again he nodded affirmatively. I then requested to know, had he sought help from other sources? He volunteered that he sought help from clerics and from a professional psychologist, which didn't pacify his troubled conscience. His facial expression became extremely sad and in a quiet voice that was an attempt to hide his desperation he said: "Eamon. I'm in hell, can you help me to escape?"

I told him that I can't get him out of hell, it's not in my power, but I can supply him with a moral compass and a roadmap, that if he used wisely, then he would be freed from the fear of hell.

I advised him that if his repentance was sincere and he acted on the advice I was about to offer, he would pay off his karmic debt, thereby pacifying his guilty conscience. He sensed he was on to something important and requested more advice and details of what he had to do? To deliberately take human life is the greatest evil that can be done by mankind; it is cruel and can't be justified in any circumstances. And those who murder must pay a dreadful price for murder is the vilest and evil deed and those who have murdered for whatever reason will be held to account.

Murder, we are informed in the bible, cries out to heaven to be avenged and the murder will face a terrible indictment and a dreadful consequence. There truly is nothing more wicked, immoral and depraved as the deliberate killing of a fellow human being. Murder is evil personified, an advanced type of corruption and a decadent form of inhumanity.

"You are spiritually obliged," I informed him, "to save as many lives that you were responsible for ending."

"How do I do that," was his response?

My answer was. "Every time there is a blood transfusion appeal as a volunteer, if there is an appeal for a bone marrow donor, you volunteer yours, if someone needs a new lung to save his or her life, you volunteer one of yours, if some requires a kidney, you offer one of yours. It's possible to live successfully with one kidney or one lung. On receiving this advice, he immediately became more settled and profusely thanked me for my advice. He wondered why none of the others from whom he sought advice had made these types of suggestions. We said good-bye and off he drove seemingly happy and contented."

There is in this story a serious message for those who foolishly believe that their murderous deeds will never catch up with them.

Whatever happened to the repented ex-paramilitary you ask? Did he ever implement any of the suggestions made by me? Without having any evidence I'm convinced not; I'm sure he returned to Catholicism which foolishly offers salvation on a verbal prayer of contrition; contravening the law of karma.

GOD
'God of all beauty and joy,
Grant unto us that this day we may share with Thee
In the purity of Thy divine passion for beauty;
Make us ambassadors of Thy Kingdom,
In which all things beautiful are forever preserved and perfected,'
(J S Hoyland)

Everything seen and unseen exists in the Mind of God; nothing can exist outside of Him. We are told in the Bible that before God created the Universe a void existed. 'Void', in this context means nothing existed. If this be so, then God had to create everything out of Himself, becoming the things created. Because of our human finite minds, our understanding of God must be incomplete. The mind of God is Infinite, meaning, all-embracing and limitless; the human mind is as stated, finite. It's not the function of the finite mind to comprehend the infinite mind of God. While the human mind is incapable of explaining the totality of our creator, with the intelligent use of mortal mind we can, at least, come to a better understanding of who or what God is, and in order to do that, it will be necessary to answer two pertinent questions concerning self. Do you know who you are? You know your name, your family, your occupation, you will be all too aware of your fears and anxieties, your hopes and aspirations. But you are a great deal more than the sum total of those physical and mental attributes that you accept as being part and parcel of your personality. However, the question of your true identity remains, and it is imperative that the truth of existence is discovered so that spiritual evolution can begin.

Suppose you could come up with a formula of words that would satisfy you, that explained to yourself and others what you believe in, your true identity to be, you would still have to face the question of what you are. Man who does not know himself, so he should not be surprised if he does not know and understand God. It is our crushing ignorance of whom and what God is and our ignorance of our true identity that is at the root of our problems. Active ignorance and its dreadful consequences are the result of living apart from God and the neglect of His Laws. Only when the problem is positively identified can the remedy be put into effect. We will return to this matter later on. For the time being let's return to the fascinating proposition of understanding God. God, of course, cannot be intellectualised for He is above and beyond human comprehension. But don't despair; we possess a higher faculty than intellectual intelligence. We have been blessed with intuition, a wonderful source of unlearnt knowledge, which is always available to us. Let's stick with human knowledge to see how far it will take us in our quest to know and understand more about God and His attributes. We can discuss at length what God's attributes are, but just as we as individuals are greater than those things we identify ourselves as being, so with God He is greater than His collective attributes. But we must find out, for our own satisfaction, exactly what these attributes are and what relevance they have, if any, for us as individuals. It sounds trite to say that God is the sum total of everything seen and unseen and leave it at that, but while this is true, it is supremely important that it can, at least, be substantiated, by human logic and reasoned investigation.

God is referred to in the Bible as *'Spirit,'* In one edition of the Bible, God is referred to as *'A Spirit',* suggesting that there are other spirits in existence; as there is only one God, there can only be one Spirit.

Jesus said: "Hear, O Israel the Lord our God is one Lord."

There is only one Spirit and it is responsible for all that is seen and unseen. Spirit is cause and we, as well as everything else in the Universe are its effects. Spirit covers all aspects of God's Attributes and we should examine them in detail so that we may gain a greater understanding of our creator and how we might become the beautiful person that God intended us to be.

Breath is an attribute of spirit, and breath sustains life in the human body. According to the Bible, *'God created man out of the dust of the earth and into his nostrils He breathed the breath of life and man became a living soul,'* Breath is life in the human body and life lasts only as long as breath enters the physical body; when breath ceases entering the body, physical death occurs. This is not the time to explore this matter. However, we will return to it a little later. Let's examine the other attributes of God, as well as breath there is: Divine Consciousness; Infinite Intelligence; Inspired Wisdom; Profound Peace; Universal Love and Universal Spiritual Substance. Everything created has been created out of this prefect Universal Substance, including human bodies. The perfect creator created you out of His perfect spiritual substance in His image and likeness; perfection is then your natural condition. Why you may ask does the body not manifest perfection? It is the inverted use of the mind that causes all the problems that manifests as disease or illness.

Let's examine the word disease; note that it's composed of two syllables 'dis' and 'ease', which according to most dictionaries means relieve, or alleviate, meaning to finish with. If the mind is continually ill at ease then the physical structure of the body will disintegrate. And disease in some form will inevitably be the predictable consequence of the mind abused by thoughts of hate, anger, envy, greed, and jealousy. The antidote is, or should be obvious, comprehensive love is the only remedy to end all human problems.

"One great thought breathed into a man may generate him." (Channing)

Make God your constant thought and your spiritual regeneration is assured, for God will reward you with a new understanding which will in time result in a life that is full of peace and lasting contentment. The entire root of all your problems is your indifference to the prompting of your immortal soul, which is constantly murmuring to you that God is present within and He is patiently waiting your recognition of His Presence.

Don't waste time trying to get God into your life; God is individualised and personalised in you. You and the father are one. You must however accept this spiritual fact for the Presence to reveal the Truth of your spiritual identity. If you are seeking God, you must search in your consciousness and in your soul. This is the only means; there are no other methods whereby you will experience God. You must accept that you are the child of God; that you live eternally in His Divine Consciousness and that you can never, under any circumstances, be separated from Him. The truth of this, when accepted and acted upon, will result in the manifestation of truth itself.

Of all of God's attributes His love for us has to be the most important. In any life the most important thing has to be love; to live life properly you must love all, even those who hate and despise you. It has been said many times by our greatest thinkers that God is Love and Love is God. Our creator has many attributes, many qualities. God is omnipotent, all powerful; omniscient, all good; and omnipresent, everywhere present and all knowing. Is it any wonder that our tiny finite minds have such difficulty comprehending the Infinite Mind of God? He is Omnipresent, meaning everywhere present.

Paul understood this, for he said: "We live and more have our being in him."

God lives in you, or more accurately you live in God. If this be true then clearly we must share God's qualities and attributes. If we exist in God and He in us, there is no division. There is one complete whole expressed in all, and in these circumstances God's consciousness and all His other attributes exist in each and every one of us. You and I and everyone else must exist in the Consciousness of God. God is personally aware of each one of us existing within Him. If you really and truly desire to change your life completely for the better, you must become aware that it is God who resides within you.

Become aware, consciously aware, of His presence within you, and all that you could ever hope for will come to pass. Now don't pass over this advice lightly. If you desire a life of love, joy and peace, it can only be found in a conscious awareness of God's Presence within. Happiness is the satisfaction of the soul, for in your soul God resides. To be continually aware of the eternal, ever-present, loving God resident within you, is to experience heaven on earth. God is Omniscient meaning all-knowing; there is everywhere present God's Intelligence. Jesus clearly understood this for he has told us: "Every hair of your head is counted."

For God is all knowing and everywhere present. He knows all, sees all, understands all, and remembers all, and he created you in His image and likeness. Startling though it may seem, were you to live the life that God intended you to live, then God's attributes would become active within you. You would come to know all, to see all and understand all. This is exactly what being created in His image and likeness means. God is Omnipotent meaning all-powerful, the Supreme Being, there can be none greater, none more powerful. He stands above everyone and everything, and yet there is the paradox that our Lord God resides in each and every one of us and He has bequeathed to all His Divine qualities. God, by creating mankind in His image and likeness, has endowed mankind with all His qualities and attributes. If mankind would only live in accordance with the law of life every single human problem would be eradicated, in our purified spiritual state we would have dominion over all things. The gift of life with the

110

potential of spiritual power and authority has to be the supreme act of love, the greatest act of generosity. Truly our God is an All-Loving Being. Love, being the chief attribute of God then, is ever-present and eternal. We can become active sons and daughters of God by embracing love in its totality meaning to be devoid of any type of malice.

God, by creating us in His image and likeness has made mankind the recipient of the greatest act of infinite love, and to gain the maximum benefit from this gift we must completely embrace love. We now know that love is the cause of all true manifestation. From the holy font of our Creator, love flows out in a continuous stream that all may bathe in it to become cleansed in body, mind and spirit. We only have to be willing to receive what we have already been given. Have the wisdom to place yourself in the hands of God; allow Him to do what He wishes with you. Allow Him to work out the smallest details of your life. Surrender yourself completely into his loving care and you will find in surrender to God, you gain the complete freedom your heart desires. For only in God and He alone, can happiness, peace and freedom be found. Love has the power and authority to overcome all adversity and will unite body, mind and soul in harmony and peace. But more importantly still is the harmony between God and mankind. It would be quite impossible to overstate the spiritual importance of love. You were created by God to become the complete spiritual expression of love and to share it with all of humanity. The most important thing in life is the willingness to receive the love that God has for you and to share this love with all of humanity. When you are prepared to receive love and to share it, without condition or hesitation, you have discovered the true science of life. If you want to live a life of total freedom, it is as simple or as complicated as unconditional love. God created you to live in peace and harmony; otherwise, He would not have created you in His image and likeness. God lives in you and when you accept that you live in God, then and only then, can you live life to its wonderful potential.

Peace and Contentment

Everyone wants to be happy, to live in peace and contentment, but very few have discovered the secret of how to find these virtues. Most people believe that to be happy you must have things. Happiness is always associated with getting. Ask anyone what would make him or her happy, the answer is always the same. *"If I had...,"* and then they will go on to nominate the object or thing they desire.

111

How foolish we are to believe that mere material things can provide happiness; how slow we are to learn that the only condition that has the authority to provide happiness is a contented mind, and love is the only means of contenting the mind. Happiness, peace and contentment is not in getting, but in letting go, letting go all our negative thinking and replacing it with love. God's love and it alone is the solution to all of our foolishness and folly. Nothing that this world can give will satisfy you. The reason is clear enough if you don't know who and what you are—as long as you remain ignorant of your true self, nothing can satisfy you. Only in the love of God are there the intelligence, the power and the wisdom to end all doubt and uncertainty. In God's love and in it alone resides the ability to become that contented person that God intended us all to be.

Divine Universal Consciousness

One of the most important attributes of God has to be His Divine Consciousness; without consciousness nothing could exist. If nothing could exist without Divine Consciousness then Divine Consciousness is the only eternal reality. Divine Consciousness is at the very centre of mankind's existence. There is a consciousness that pervades all space and everything in space, seen and unseen, and is known as Cosmic Consciousness. You must clearly understand that Cosmic Consciousness exists in every cell of your body, mind and soul. Your consciousness is of the great Cosmic Consciousness and this consciousness, you have received from God. Your consciousness extends beyond all human experiences, all phenomenon, all that is relative through to reality and truth. Your consciousness is in constant communication with Cosmic Consciousness and the impressions we receive from Cosmic Consciousness are not dependent on our human faculties. When you fully and completely understand who and what you are, your consciousness will expand dramatically. Cosmic Consciousness resides within every individual. t is the supreme and ultimate reality. Cosmic Consciousness, being the Consciousness of God has to be the highest spiritual experience possible and blessed is the individual who experiences this overshadowing of the personal consciousness by the Christ Consciousness. Consciousness is and always has been complete and perfect; it is of God and cannot be improved or elevated. Everything that has happened or will ever happen is the result of consciousness; it is the sole motivator of every experience.

Awareness, intelligence, understanding, wisdom and intuition would be impossible without consciousness. Consciousness being Universal fills all space; consequently everything that exists has some level of consciousness. While there are many levels of being conscious there are no degrees of consciousness. God being Universal Consciousness means there can be no separation for anyone or anything in the Universe. When the individual consciousness recognises and realises that it is of God, then the individual consciousness will manifest its full, spiritual potential, which is love, wisdom and understanding. Life's problems can only be overcome when the individual consciousness becomes aware of its divine origins.

God has decreed fundamental immutable laws by which the Cosmos is governed and consciousness is at the core of all experiences and all existence. A clear and precise understanding of the 'Law' must be acquired and when understood, must be adopted, for only by living in total obedience to the Law can life be properly understood and lived as God intended it should be. To be consciously aware that God can only express Himself through your consciousness is of critical importance for you. To know and understand your spiritual relationship to Him who created you in His image and likeness, is the solution to all your problems. Consciousness is the only means available, whereby you are aware of your existence and all experiences throughout life in and out of the physical body. You know that you have a physical existence in a human body and that you live in a material world of form and phenomena. Physical science can explain and satisfy most questions concerning matter and its many manifestations; however, science is unable to resolve the spiritual reasons for the existence of mankind.

The only means for solving the mysteries of life is to embrace the spiritual dimensions of life and to return to the source of life, and the source of lie is God and His Universal Consciousness. It is only when you become consciously aware that your individual consciousness is from God, and without His Universal Consciousness, we all want to know for certain why and how we came into existence; why we were given life, what we are supposed to accomplish in life and what, in fact, is life? There are many perplexing questions and the answers at times seem impossible to find. To understand life it's imperative that we return to fundamental spiritual fact—God is all there is and is the only source of life; then His life lives in every member of humanity, and the acceptance of this spiritual union between God and every individual will, provide the answers to all the questions concerning life, and more importantly still will, in time, confer not only all of God's attributes, but also immortality. You will be you through all eternity; your presence will never cease to exist, but where and how you exist depends on giving loving expression to spiritual love. When that happens, as you must at some time accept this spiritual reality exists, any fear of death will end. What frightens most people about death is the uncertainty of not knowing what will happen to them after so-called death. Many individuals fear the wrath of a vengeful God who will punish them for their wrong doings committed during life on earth; there are of course penalties to be paid for all wrong doings and this is explained in other chapters of this book. Life does not begin at birth, nor does life end at death. Life is eternal and the real you, who is indestructible spirit, will prevail for all time.

God has created you; in him you live and have your being. God's Life is eternal and this makes you an eternal spiritual being. Please be prepared to accept what you have already been given by God Himself. Don't spurn God's loving generosity. There is no division in God; He is whole and complete. There is nothing that is capable of dividing God or separating Him from any part or particle of His creation. God is Universal but He has individualised Himself in all of humanity. There is nothing in or out of the Universe, seen or unseen, that can separate you from God. And the truth of your being is that it is God who is working in you now. God is Infinite Intelligence; God knows everything. Everything that is to be known already exists in the Mind of God. His Infinite Intelligence permeates all space; it not only controls and guides all Universes, but all stars and all planets in all Universes. All heavenly bodies are kept in order and guided by God's Universal Intelligence. This Supreme Intelligence is available to all of humanity and will, if accepted by the individual, direct the course of any life. The individual must allow this guiding intelligence to dominate his or her thought patterns. The thoughts of most individuals are dominated, not by intelligence, but are nervous reactions to fear, hate, anger, resentment and worry. We waste much time and create many problems by trying to remedy the effects, instead of eliminating the cause. The cause of all our pain and anxiety is our ignorance of our true selves. It is only by a clear understanding of our relationship, not only to God, but also to each other that we can end all miseries. Until we reach a clear understanding of ourselves, we should resolve to use our intelligence intelligently. Intelligence must, of necessity, be directed by consciousness, and then it transcends all existing phenomena and form. Both consciousness and intelligence are freely available to all of us. The proper use of consciousness and intelligence will elevate your life experiences to heights that you can't at this time imagine.

William Shakespeare has told us: "There is more in heaven and earth that is thought of in your philosophy."

Consciousness and intelligence are the only means of ending ignorance and doubt and bring about a clear understanding of our true nature. You have an indispensable duty to yourself, to your dignity, decency and honour, to always behave rationally and intelligently.

God Is All There Is

God is Infinite Love, love that is total, complete and unconditional. There can be no lasting happiness, peace or contentment in any life that is not dominated by love. Love is central to life and those who choose to ignore love will experience all of the conditions and circumstances that cause mental, emotional and physical pain. The Infinite Mind of God is dominated by love and this can be proven. God created you out of His Spiritual Substance in His Image and Likeness. He has bestowed all of His attributes upon you and given you domain over all things. You are, you see, the recipient, not only of the greatest act of love, but of generosity also.

God is infinitely great and wondrous as well as meek and lowly and He is expressing Himself in the whole of creation, including each and every one of us. He will manifest according to our realisation of His presence within us. There is no other Being but God, and when you fully accept this, you will shed all false beliefs and will put an end to the belief in Satan and the nonsense of hell. There are religionists and organizations that would have us all believe that God has many negative attributes. For instance, "He is determined to punish all sinners in," "hell fire for all eternity." This type of God has attributes more barbaric than any savage.

Our God is the supreme embodiment of love. Become consciously aware of God within you and when you become consciously united with Him, all limitations, all barriers, all obstacles will disappear. For God has ordained that it is your divine right to accomplish all things.

'With God all things are possible,' (Luke 1: 37)

You are the true temple of God, the temple not made by human hand. Allow yourself to become a channel through which God's love can flow to all of mankind. Take a quantum spiritual leap towards reality; by this simple method recognise that God exists in everyone. For God ever remains within each and every one of us. Your whole duty is to become like unto God, to manifest love, wisdom, understanding and compassion. If you want to live a beautiful life, you must do beautiful things in your life with a pure heart. Now you are beginning to understand what Jesus meant when He said: "God is Spirit and must be worshipped in Spirit." To consciously live in God's presence and to know that the presence lives in you is to worship in Spirit. Because God is the God of Infinite Love, compassion and understanding, it is His Holy Will that peace, love and good will, shall prevail between all peoples. You can become a worker in His vineyard by projecting thoughts of love and peace and goodwill to all. To become an effective worker for the fulfilment of God's Divine Plan, you must be at great peace with yourself. Your mind has to be at ease with itself, free from all negative thoughts. Allow your mind to dwell on thoughts of God's Love, His wisdom, compassion and understanding so that His purpose may be accomplished in you. God created all equal and what anyone has accomplished all may accomplish, for God is no respecter of persons.

If God worked through Jesus, and it's obvious He did, then this statement is true, "You will do even greater things than I if you would only believe."

Our potential ability proves that God will, if we are prepared to co-operate, work through us also. And He would want us all to become as Jesus.

Paul says: "Let the mind be in us that was in Jesus."

A clear indication that what Jesus achieved is possible to you and me. We must think as Jesus thought, and love, as Jesus loved, be as understanding as Jesus understood, be as compassionate as Jesus was compassionate; in short to live as Jesus lived. Yes, if you are prepared to live the life Jesus lived, you will achieve what He achieved. In case this proposition may prove too much for you to accept I would remind you again of Luke 1: 37,

'For with God nothing is impossible,'

The Lord our God is the Infinite Spirit that pervades all space and is responsible for everything seen and unseen. Let the Spirit of God infiltrate your mind. Allow every thought, every word and deed to be dominated by the Loving Presence of God within. No person and no circumstances can prevent you from experiencing the love, peace and joy to be found in the Presence. If your life is in crisis become aware of the Presence that is always present and you will find the peace your heart longs for.

There can be no lasting fulfilment in wordily affairs alone. Wealth, fame, power and prestige, leave those who have succeeded in securing them as unfulfilled as the rest of us. People spend all their lives concerned about what they should be doing. It's not what you do that's important, it's what you were intended to be, and that's the question, *'To be or not to be,'* And to become what God intended you to be is the reason for your present earthly existence. If you fail in this divinely ordained mission, then it will be necessary for you to come back to earth again and again until you comply with this mandate from God.

Spiritual submission will lead to spiritual understanding. Those who do not seek for a spiritual understanding for their existence are wasting their lives. The whole point and objective of life is to come to the Truth. Those who do not aspire to the truth have missed the purpose of life. Don't waste your present earthly life on chasing after fame or fortune; seek to know who and what you are. You have, of course, to live in the world and you will of necessity discharge your worldly obligations, and should fame and fortune come your way use both wisely. Don't on any account allow possessions to possess you. All that you have and think you owe, nature will claim back. Your house, your car and even your body will return to dust. These things have been lent to you temporarily when, as you must die, you will leave them behind. Become a great mind; labour for eternity. God expresses Himself throughout all of creation by means of His conscious awareness and this awareness is the consciousness in every individual.

You exist because God exists and your existence is as permanent as that of God. Your duty to yourself is to make your existence in God as real and relevant to yourself as it is to God. You are very real to God, and because you are important to God, make God as important to you as you are to Him.

You should be aware that it is God who inspires you to do the things that are decent and good. God is ever eager to be of help and will come to your aid if and when requested. An alliance with God will correct any wrong, overcome any obstacle, surmount any problem, remove any difficulty, smooth any path, conquer any fear, and relieve any pain. God is not your best hope, He is your only hope. All that is required of you is to allow God and His perfect intelligence to work in you. God is the consciousness in you and this consciousness is the only spiritual point at which you can contact Him. Your spiritual evolution begins the moment you accept that you and the Father are one. This is the truth and the truth, of your oneness with God, will set you free, to begin your journey into ever-expanding awareness of consciousness. When your spiritual journey begins, you will go on from glory to glory.

From perfection you have come and it's to perfection you will eventually return. Sheer logic demands that we accept that, what is of a perfect mind must also be perfect; perfection is your true natural state.

Jesus said: "Be ye perfect as your Father in Heaven which is perfect."

God has glorified you with His perfect consciousness, intelligence, wisdom, understanding and love. You, the real you, the spiritual you, is perfect; for this perfection to manifest in the outer you must use your intelligence intelligently. If you say only what is true and do only what is right, human perfection would manifest in a short period of time. Focus your attention on God within; give this Presence your permission to do whatever it pleases with you, secure in the sure and certain knowledge that your life will blossom and that you will spiritually prosper. This will take a great deal of courage and trust on your part, but you can be certain God will not fail you. With trust, patience, faith and a conscious awareness of His Presence within, you have found the road to freedom. God will personally rescue you from all wordily grief, pain and adversity. Remember always, God is Life and God's Life lives in you. He is present within you. You could not exist for a second without His presence. This Presence is the only permanent reality and is of vital importance to you. You, the created, and your creator are one. And in the conscious awareness of this union is the open door to ever-lasting freedom.

By yourself you are nothing, and by yourself you will achieve nothing of worth or permanence, but with God you will not fail because it's impossible for God to fail. Say in your heart with love and reverence, *"You my beloved Father and I are one."* When you repeat this statement, be aware that it's the declaration, truth and spiritual reality, and also be aware of the living Presence of God within you. This attitude is the only lasting reality and will elevate you above and beyond all hurt, emotional pain and all worldly conditions; nothing or no one will have any authority over you and you will know that there is no other living being but the Father.

God Is Omnipresent

God alone exists and it is He who inspires you, and with His inspiration comes guaranteed success. The secret of power is within your Consciousness, because the consciousness of God, the Intelligence of God, and the Wisdom of

God will be expressed through you, when you fully accept your oneness with Him who created you like unto Himself. God, who dwells within you, is waiting ever patiently, in love, to reveal Himself, in all of His glory, to you. Before this revelation can be made manifest, you must turn your conscious awareness inward to the Presence that is always present. The Presence you see can only reveal itself in your consciousness. In your oneness with God, confusion, doubt, and misunderstanding will evaporate and you will know your position in the Cosmic Scheme; all mysteries will be revealed. Everything that can be known will be made manifest to you. The invisible will be made visible. Higher Spiritual laws will be revealed to you. For in conscious union with the Father, nature will reveal all her secrets. In the Lord our God there can be no division, you have been individualised because our Universal God has individualised Himself in you. And through this individualization of the Universal, the Father is revealed in you. If God was not resident in you now and always, God could not be Infinite, Omnipresent or Omnipotent. You, your life and your living, prove not only that God exists, but that He is all-powerful. When you recognise that the life that lives in you is God Himself living in your midst, and as you become consciously aware of this truth, your consciousness will become aware of the Universal Power within itself.

This power will manifest in the outer and be expressed as love, compassion, kindness, understanding and consideration. You now know that you already possess these qualities, if you accept that God has bequeathed His spiritual attributes to you; then you must respond by making others aware of the spiritual potential that they also possess. As yet, you don't display this degree of wisdom because your horizons are limited. However, when your consciousness is awakened it will never again remain stationary. The law of an awakened consciousness is always onward, ever upward, constant progress. The Consciousness of God is all-powerful; therefore, seek to make His consciousness your consciousness that you may share in the mighty power of God. Remember in God and Him alone. All things take place, for nothing can exist outside of Him. Your creative powers exist in the Kingdom of Heaven within you and are the active Presence within that is ever seeking expression in the outer. For the inner and outer must become united for you to experience the joys of love and peace.

It has been divinely ordained by God Himself that love and peace shall prevail; His Will for mankind is, what man is capable of becoming, will in the end prevail. Love, peace and harmony for all of mankind has to be God's greatest wish. By freely choosing love and peace you are doing His Will and He will reward you in ways that, at present you can't imagine. In love He begot you and His love for you will continue through all eternity. Reciprocate this love and God will be revealed to you, and in this revelation you will experience joy, harmony and lasting satisfaction with life.

"Love is infallible; it has no errors, for all errors are for want of love." (Lou)

Each and every individual existence is meant to become the highest and noblest expression of God and His Divine attributes. We must acquire a crystal-clear understanding that God is the only existing reality and this spiritual reality exists within your consciousness and when your consciousness becomes aware of itself as being the centre of spiritual reality, then know that God's plan is being accomplished in you.

To be truly at peace means peace profound; you must first accept that God lives in you and is in effect your life. For no one or nothing can exist outside of God, for all expression is of God. Your willingness to accept God as being the only means available for salvation is the first step on the road to liberation. Satisfaction can only be established in your life when you allow God to inspire you to do the good works that nature requires of you.

Jesus came to Earth to proclaim the Universal Truth when he said: "I and the Father are one."

This individual proclamation by Jesus was, in fact, a statement of universal Truth. This universal Truth means that every individual is united for all eternity to God. Take hold of this spiritual reality; recognise its validity, realise its authenticity, and let the actuality of your oneness with God become an accepted fact, and God will reward you in many wonderful ways.

Recognise God as an in-dwelling Presence and as you realise your oneness with your creator, He will respond by making His Presence active in your life. Until this reality takes hold of your consciousness, let your mind and heart rest in the loving care of God. In God's loving care there is total safety; you will be protected from all harm and God Himself will guide you in everything you do.

Your existence in God is eternal and with Him your future through all eternity is assured. What a beautiful prospect—an eternity of love, peace and bliss in union with God. With God as your benefactor, you will be, for all time, free from all confusion and all conflict of heart and mind. While confusion remains, there can be no lasting happiness, for happiness and freedom can only be found in spiritual tranquillity and tranquillity can only be established when the heart is full of love of God and all of mankind.

Unprejudiced natural intelligence nullifies fate and creates the necessary conditions for a speedy return to our natural state of love and secures our position in the spiritual realms. Nature has not confused or hindered you, nor has nature given you the spirit of fear, anger or resentment. All your negative and destructive thoughts you have learnt from the confused and bewildered multitude of a confused humanity.

If you truly want to leave the asylum that is today's world, you can only effectively do so by returning to God and His love. There is no other way, there never has been, nor there ever be an alternative to God; return at once to God that you may bring to an end all that pains you. Your first and last duty is to God and yourself; do then the intelligent thing and return to where you truly belong, in the loving arms of God. Remember always that the antidote to confusion is to accept that God has reproduced in you, all of His attributes, making you heir to all of His creative abilities and the means of gaining access to these attributes is to found only in the acceptance of unconditional love.

If God is without limits, then the same creative principle that resides in God resides within each individual and it can be activated by spiritual love and everything becomes possible. The Infinite Consciousness will overshadow the finite consciousness; when this happens, spiritual power is transferred to the finite consciousness. For the spiritual life to manifest, the mind has to entertain noble and constructive thoughts, and we must pay particular attention to them, that they may make us more kind, considerate and caring individuals. These thoughts are of great importance to us; however, we must go beyond thought into caring deeds. There is an old proverb that states, 'The hand that gives is holier than the lips that pray,' Pay due attention to the message of this old proverb, it has much to teach us.

For most people each and every day is spent making demands from everyone around them. And when these demands are not met, disappointment and frustration are the inevitable results, so each and every day has its sad or bad periods. Don't ever depend on another person for happiness, you most certainly will be disappointed and the disappointment felt will breed frustration. Happiness is to be found only in the mind that is constantly calm and tranquil and this can only be found in living the spiritual life.

Withdraw your attention from the outer world of form and phenomena, for while you live in the outer world alone, there will always be confusion and folly that is rampant in today's world. If your attention is ever fixed on the trivial and mundane incidents that cause you some degree of aggravation, you will never find peace or contentment. The only means of escape from confusion and mystification is to live the life that God Himself has ordained for us.

How foolish we are to attempt the impossible, for without God there can be no peace, contentment, nor happiness. With clear thought and a better understanding, it could be all so beautifully different. The quality of your life must reflect the psychological level at which you allow your mind to operate. Without God's influence and without His love in your heart, your life must remain barren and without any positive meaning or direction. And you will stagger from one crisis to the next. You have allowed yourself to be bound to your opinions, you have acquiesced with your negative thoughts and you should not be surprised at the pain and hurt you heap upon yourself.

Cast aside your opinions; return in love to God and He, in His mercy and goodness, will bless you with love, peace and contentment. Put God to the test. Place your trust in His loving care and you will be divinely rewarded. Your spiritual journey back to perfection and freedom begins with a calculated act of self-surrender into the loving care of God.

God is the supreme power in the Cosmos; in truth there is no other power. The real power of God is contained in His love; as God is eternal, so also is His love. Not only is love eternal, but is also omnipresent. God who is Infinite Love has created all of mankind in His image and then every individual's true identity is love. The expression of unconditional love is then the only means of attaining spiritual perfection, which is necessary for a return to God. It is God and His love for you that sustains life in and out of the body.

To live in the love of God and mankind is to live life free from all human defects and life without human defects is only possible by surrendering to the will and love of God. If you truly desire to know God, to fully realise His existence within you it is imperative that in all situations you give expression to God's chief attribute, which you now know to be unconditional love. There is no other way to experience God, other than by recourse to unconditional love. When you consciously live in the omnipresence of God you will be blessed with Infinite Love, honoured with profound peace, dignified with wisdom and distinguished by Spiritual understanding.

All lives are lived in God; life without God is impossible, and there is no existence for anyone or anything outside of God. To live life as God intended it should be lived, the individual has to be consciously and constantly aware that God lives in every person, or more accurately everyone exists in the Infinite Mind of God. The acceptance of the in-dwelling Presence of God has to become a spiritual reality before life can be lived free from ignorance, confusion and all folly.

Mankind in its dreadful spiritual blindness endlessly seeks after worldly success, in the vain hope of finding lasting peace and happiness. The life that is lived, devoid of spiritual values or ambitions, will inevitably founder on the rocks of despair and frustration. Life cannot be lived until you accept that your reason for life on planet earth, in a human body, is that you may grow into a spiritual likeness of God and manifest all of His wonderful attributes for the benefit of mankind. If you accept this explanation for your existence in a physical body here on earth and act accordingly, your life will change dramatically for the better. Your mission is to grow spiritually into the likeness of Him who created you. Your commitment to God has to be total and complete, no part measure. God in His love for you has bequeathed to you all His attributes in full spiritual measure; all that is of God is yours in full abundance. God expects and is entitled to a full response from you and you now know what is required from you; return to God. This journey is not of time or distance, but is a journey in consciousness, love and supreme intelligence.

God's wonderful attributes, which are within you, must find expression in you and through you, before you can be consciously reunited with God. Those who attempt to live apart from God will, for sure, live a life of misery, confusion and emotional neurosis and the mental instability associated with these human conditions. Your only creative authority is contained in the inner spiritual world of God's spiritual attributes, which are, as you now know, freely available to you.

Deep in your heart, you instinctively know that life is much too important to be wasted on the mere acquisition of wealth or material possessions; it should be said that there is nothing intrinsically wrong in worldly position or wealth, so long as they are relegated to their proper priority in human affairs. Know that it is God who lives in you and this 'knowing' will in time change your life beyond mere human experiences. The Universal Life lives in every person and the individual who becomes aware that all life is from God and is God, that individual will experience God as the in-dwelling Christ. He or she, who lives the Universal Life, lives deep in the Kingdom of Heaven, that Jesus said resides in the soul of every person. God's living presence within you will find expression in the outer when your mind becomes the holy receptacle of virtue from which will flow God's Infinite Love to all of mankind. God in His perfect goodness has for each and every one of His children decreed that we should be the inheritors of His Spiritual treasures, and if God is willing to share these treasures with all individuals then we have the right to expect that God will answer all requests for assistance. Your faith in God should be so complete that you would not consider seeking assistance from any other source.

If your present life is without any real meaning, if you are confused, bewildered or discontented with your present circumstances, there really is only one solution that is guaranteed to bring clarity and hope—turn to God for help and you will be richly rewarded. Confess your spiritual weakness and allow God to influence and guide you; accept His Love in your life that you may live life to its full spiritual potential.

Dwell on the living Presence of God within and in time you will become the perfect human expression of Divine Intelligence, and in so doing you will be fulfilling your spiritual obligation to God, whereas mankind endlessly seeks after worldly success in the vain hope of finding lasting peace and happiness. There is only one source of permanent peace and contentment and that source is in God.

Deep in your heart, you instinctively know that life is much too important to be wasted on the mere acquisition of wealth or material possessions; it should be said that there is nothing intrinsically wrong in worldly position or wealth, so long as they are relegated to their proper priority in human affairs.

You are beginning to understand that there is only one Life, that this 'one Life' is universal, perfect and is the Life of God, and when you are prepared to identify with Life Universal, it will respond by manifesting in you and through you. God is the only solution to all human problems. Mankind is very slow to learn this simple fact and so the problems that, at this time, threaten our civilisation are getting progressively worse.

Philosophy is the pursuit of human knowledge, or wisdom. It is the study of seeming realities and general principles concerning human development. The philosopher is one who studies life as he or she understands it and is based upon human finite concepts and is therefore subject to human error or manipulation There is only one method of attaining an infallible understanding of the Cosmos and mankind's relationship to it, it is by illumination, which is the influx of the Cosmic Mind of God in to the finite mind of man. The benefits of illumination will last for all eternity, in this life-time profound peace, will be a constant companion; every expression and deed will be dominated by inspired wisdom and spiritual love, and the need for further lives in physical form will be ended. Illumination can only be experienced when the individual accepts that they are the individualization of Divine, Infinite intelligence, that God resides in them as love, wisdom, peace and healing power. It is when the individual gives full spiritual expression to the in-dwelling attributes, that God has in His love, bequeathed to all His children, that illumination can manifest.

You now know that there is only 'one life', that God is the only creator of everything seen and unseen; therefore, everything is of God. Without Him, there would be no cosmos, universes, earth and no humanity. Accept the spiritual reality that God has individualised Himself in you as the Christ, that you are the temple of the living God. In this acceptance is freedom from all misery, all uncertainty and all physical and emotional pain. You will be made whole and complete the moment you recognise and realise that you and the Father are one. Accept that you are the Son of God and you will gain the power to elevate your life above all that is mundane and false. Of yourself you can achieve nothing of any lasting worth, but by accepting that it is God who lives and breathes in you, the power to accomplish all things will be placed at your disposal. When the Presence of God fills your consciousness, heart and mind, the sweet fragrance of the spiritual life will be a delight to you. You will be surrounded by divine reality, you will be filled with infinite energy and God will delight you in many wonderful ways.

The more the individual accepts that they are part of the stupendous whole of life, the more the mind becomes filled with a wonderful peace and serenity. All human faults fade into the past and life becomes worth living, because the wholeness of life will manifest in the awakened consciousness and there is nothing in nature that can hinder it.

The acceptance by the individual of the Presence of God within means that person will be blessed with divine, infinite, spiritual love, which will be expressed in every thought and gesture so that humanity will benefit in the most practical way. The great Law of God is contained in the 'Word' of God; the 'Word' is the Presence of the Christ of God in every individual. This is the Truth, and when the truth is experienced, the unending unity of God to all His children will be spiritually understood.

When your spiritual life is right, every other aspect of living will be right also. There can be no worthwhile human existence without a healthy spiritual dimension. The root cause of all human problems is the spiritual ignorance of mankind; there cannot be any real happiness, lasting peace or contentment until the individual trusts their lives to God. In the awareness of the living Presence of the in-dwelling God as the Christ, you are guided and protected. Blessed is the individual who understands and accepts that God is the only source of power and authority and this power and authority is, under strict spiritual circumstances transferred to anyone who lives in the spiritual awareness of their true spiritual relationship to God.

The sooner you learn that the spiritual regulates the physical world, the sooner you will put an end to the folly of sensation and the pleasure-seeking life, that you now know is bound to end in disaster. You are the divine creation of God and your obligation to your inner spiritual essence is to live life in accordance with the known laws of God. When you gain a clear understanding of your spiritual relationship to God, you will quickly learn how to live life and all the burdens you are presently experiencing will be erased. Until that blessed day of spiritual liberation, trust in God. Don't allow discouragement, or dissatisfaction to succeed in defeating you. Do everything in accordance with the highest principles and when you fail, return immediately to the path of reason and personal integrity. If you are in bondage to the worst aspects of your outer, physical nature there is only one means of escape and that is to return to your true identity, which, you now know to be spiritual. When the individual becomes spiritually aware of the inner life, he or she will not allow the outer, physical world to dominate their thoughts and deeds; their exterior obligations and duties will not be allowed to hinder their spiritual advancement.

The New Testament has this to say concerning wisdom: *'Happy is the man that findeth wisdom, and the man that getteth understanding. She is more precious than rubies: and all things thou canst desire are not to be compared unto her,'*

The insistence by God on unconditional love will, no doubt, be difficult, but this difficulty has to be overcome otherwise there can be no spiritual advancement. The greater the difficulty, the more glory in surmounting it.

"Skilful pilots gain their reputation from storms and tempests." [Epicurus]

The thing to do is concentrate your thoughts on God and His wonderful attributes and how you may gain access to your creator's spiritual abilities. The in-dwelling Presence of Almighty God is a spiritual fact of human existence; God dwells in the immortal soul of every individual including you, the reader of these words. Your salvation is in the acceptance that God is the real you, then to live fully in the Presence of God is eternal salvation. You are on planet earth to experience spiritual reality. When this happens, you will manifest perfection, you will be complete in mind, soul and body.

Henry David Thoreau writing on this subject made these interesting observations: *'If men would steadily observe realities only, and not allow themselves to be deluded. Life to compare with such things, as we know, would be like a fairy tale and the Arabian Nights' Entertainment. If we respect only what is inevitable and has a right to be, music and poetry would resound along the streets,'*

By doing everything in your power to please God, and in helping humanity overcome its preoccupation with worldly matters, you will gain access to the wonderful powers of God. If the Presence of God resides within each person as the Christ, then the power and authority of God and Christ must also reside in every person. God and Christ cannot, under any circumstances, be separated from their spiritual attributes or powers, and the truth is neither can any individual. Yes, the wonderful creative power of God resides within the immortal soul of every individual. Acknowledge the existence of your soul, be willing to be guided by it and your life will begin anew.

When the soul is stirred, you will experience a longing for evidence of the existence of God. The contentment all are seeking can only be realised when the soul is acknowledged and allowed to influence all thoughts and inclinations. Any life lived without soul influence will be turbulent, pain ridden, blighted by frustration and eventually chaotic. Acknowledge your true spiritual identity, which is an immortal soul, temporarily housed in a physical body, and God will be your constant companion, and with God your life will become a blessed experience of contentment that will last through out eternity.

We have been placed on planet earth to experience spiritual self-fulfilment and this can only happen if God is central to every thought, word and deed. Many mysteries will be revealed when you allow God's will to be expressed through you to all of humanity. Call to mind the Presence of God many times every day; prayer is the best way of bringing the Presence to mind, and when aware of the Presence ask God to influence you every moment of every day, that your remaining days may be joyous.

Almighty God is the only creator and we are spiritually obliged to acknowledge this and to accept that we, His children, must live the life of love, compassion and spiritual understanding. If you desire to become a genuine spiritual being, the only thing to accomplish this most beautiful of all human obligations is to give the highest human expression to the divine attributes that God Himself has bequeathed to you. These attributes are love, goodness, kindness, consideration, generosity, compassion and understanding. These attributes are the stepping stones that will definitely lead to the gates of Paradise.

"When you thus cease to be finite, you become one with the Infinite. In the reduction of your soul to its simplest self, its divine essence, you realise this Union, this Identity." [Plotinus]

Break from the spiritual narrative.

Chapter 5

A Visit to Heaven and Hell

'Everyone wants to go to heaven; however, nobody wants to die,'

Most individuals who believe in an after-life, would like to think that they will spend eternity of profound peace and bliss in heaven and the wicked will be incarcerated for all eternity in hell. This is the popular belief of most individuals. Personally, I don't subscribe to either of these views.

Conviction based on a prolonged investigation suggests that no one enters heaven; the reason for this belief is based on the statement of Jesus when he advised his disciples: "I go to prepare a place for you; for where I go you cannot enter."

Jesus' disciples had spent three years with him and received private tuition in all matters spiritual. Why then were they unfit to enter heaven? If the chosen disciples of Jesus could not enter heaven, what type of life is any individual supposed to live to qualify for entry?

It is my personal belief that every human being will in time spiritually qualify for admission to heaven; this however can only happen when individuals live the type of life that Jesus lived. The acceptance of the doctrine of reincarnation and living according to its precepts will provide the explanation of why the overwhelming majority of humanity cannot leave earth at death and gain entry to heaven. If the disciples of Jesus were deemed unfit to gain entry to heaven, then there has to be little or no realistic expectation that any of us, myself included, will on leaving earth gain entry to heaven.

Reincarnation will provide multiple opportunities for everyone to live a spiritual life that is dominated by compassionate deeds, unconditional love, and spiritual truth; this type of life demands the abandonment of malice, hate, meanness, envy, greed, and hatred. These spiritually destructive inclinations must be conquered and replaced by the intelligent use of intelligence.

According to the Bible, *'God is omnipotent, omniscient, and omnipresent,'* Omnipresent means everywhere present; there is not a millimetre of space in the whole of the Cosmos that is not God occupied. If this were true where is the space to accommodate hell?

Hell is the invention of the churches; according to church doctrine the wicked are dispatched to hell on death to suffer eternally the flames of hell. It's unimaginable if we look at how God is described in the Bible as being omniscient, which means supremely good. If hell exists then God is neither omnipresent nor omniscient; by believing in hell and everlasting physical punishment we diminish God. What then happens to the rogue and rascal, the cruel and the callous? Jesus informs us that His Father House had many mansions, meaning different abodes for the different lives lived by the individual members of humanity. Those who have lived good and noble lives will be rewarded with a pleasant abode in the spiritual world. The wicked will be obliged to live in unpleasant and dire circumstances, a purgatory, a place of atonement; there will be overwhelming remorse by those who lived a life filled with hate, anger, and those who lived a life of immoral perversion. Those who have lived the life of thoughtless and worthless deeds will spend a length of time in a very unpleasant abode. It is for those who have mis-spent their time on planet earth. How could I have allowed myself to be so spiritually deluded, to have lived a life of abject spiritual stupidity? We all must go before a spiritual council composed of high spiritual being to be confronted with the deeds performed and the deeds left unperformed.

Faced with spiritual reality before the council, there can be no hiding of any of the details of the life no matter how unpleasant and embarrassing. Exposure will be full and painful. At the end of the proceedings, the consequences of the mis-spent life will be made clear. The consequences will be unpleasant to hear and bear. The denunciation will be severe and unpleasant; the individual will be informed that they must return to earth in another attempt to live the life of spirituality.

Before reincarnating into a different human body, the quality of the new life to be lived will depend on the efforts in the past life. Those who were rich and financially powerful and were totally indifferent to the suffering and plight of their fellow human beings and the dreadful destitution endured by the poor in the 'third world' will find themselves living in the same degree of poverty that they were indifferent to in their previous life.

Height of compassion

Jesus was absolutely right when he proclaimed: "As you sow so also shall ye reap."

This is the golden Law of karma. All may use this wonderful law to enrich and enhance their lives and propel their spiritual journey to the point when it will end the cycle of reincarnation. When a life has been lived in moral purity and service to all of humanity, when a life has been lived without hate, malice, envy, greed, and resentment, then when death comes, as it must, the purified individual will enter not heaven, but paradise.

If and when paradise is the attained, there is no longer any requirement to reincarnate to earthly existence; your earthly apprenticeship has successfully ended. You will continue with a new mission in the spiritual world; you will be spiritually charged to serve mankind on a higher plane. You may be appointed as an angel-guide to an individual living on planet earth, or you could be appointed as a healing being or given some other spiritual mission. Eventually when you have perfected your spirituality you will enter heaven.

Let me now acquaint you with my experience in heaven and hell.

The year England adopted the decimal system of currency replacing pounds, shilling and pence I purchased a second-hand book costing five-shilling on the subject of self-hypnotism; I wanted to acquire the ability to hypnotise myself, so that I could carry out an experiment under its influence, which was to visit hell and heaven in that order.

I studied the method of self-hypnosis suggested in the book and practiced the technique recommended. My experiment lasted for approximately six weeks. At the end of this time, I was able to induce a profound self-hypnotic state. I was now ready to begin my experiment, and on a Friday evening, shortly after nine o'clock, I informed my wife that I was retiring for the night; this surprised her and she enquired if I was feeling all right? I assured that I was, but felt sleepy and headed for the bedroom and began to introduce a deep relaxed state. This procedure takes about eight or ten minutes. It involves deep breathing and specialist meditation.

This procedure introduces a calm and sedated feeling of profound peace and harmony. The mind becomes receptive to any intelligent proposition, which introduces a heightened response to any suggestion made.

When I felt secure and positive, I mentally uttered the desire to enter hell. I immediately found myself in a place of deplorable depression and it was an appalling experience; such was the awful vision that greeted me that I became extremely sad and depressed for those incarcerated there. I felt genuine remorse for the desperate misery of those pitiful creatures that are forced to endure the hurt, aggravation and the hopelessness of a protracted period of self-humiliation and unending remorse.

In the hell that I experienced, there were many miniature volcanic structures, the size and shape of traffic cones spewing intermittent yellow and orange flames and foul smelling sulphurous smoke which spread far and wide; there was a low haunting droning sound of the collective moaning of the distressed inmates of this dreadful place and the misery that pervades everywhere. In this place of utter desolation there is no physical pain; there is monumental emotional self-inflicted recrimination. Those in this dreadful place and their suffering now realise that they have mis-spent their time on earth chasing after illusionary and worthless worldly gains. If every human desire was satisfied in full, there would be no lasting satisfaction. The only lasting satisfaction is the reward for living in love for God, everyone and everything in creation.

We all wonder if there is life beyond physical death, and if so what we can expect to experience? Am I destined for heaven or hell? Is the question everyone asks of themselves at some point in their lives? It's very likely that the individual in most cases will convince themselves that they are destined to go to heaven, at least that is the hoped-for outcome. The thought of ending up in hell is too dreadful to contemplate.

I personally do not believe in hell; there is, however, for those who have lived a life of tyranny, crime, and indifference, the fact there will be a severe price to be paid. The individual who has lived a life of hate, deceit, or violence will be punished. A life of deceit, corruption or treachery will earn for those who lived the life of social irresponsibility, a harsh spiritual reality. Culpable individual will be forced to endure very unpleasant circumstances; indeed those who find themselves in this situation will be full of self-recrimination, remorse and regret. They will wonder how they could have been so utterly stupid.

Eventually, after a prolonged period of remorse and personal recrimination, they will be released from bondage and will reincarnate back on earth. The quality of their new life will be exclusively determined by their deeds in their previous earthly existence. 'What goes around comes around', is a remarkable truism.

Back to the narrative, when I had my fill of the horror and revulsion of hell, I made a hasty retreat by mentally making the wish to visit heaven. Immediately as I expressed the desire to leave hell for heaven, I found myself on top of a small cotton wool-type cloud. This was astonishing and totally unexpected. I was alone in this vast space of conventional sky; there were many small white clouds and blue sky, the white and blue were not the conventional hues of these two colours. There was a very beautiful soft luminance that had the effect of adding a feeling of profound peace and tranquillity. While the serenity was very potent, I wondered where all the residents of heaven were? There was total absence of any being, angel, saint, or other spiritual entity's; this absence was unnerving. There was no sign of Jesus, His mother, apostles, the prophets, popes or the presence of any individual. There was one astonishing article present in heaven so bizarre that I was totally confused by its presence; it was a Second World War artillery field gun, the type used in those twenty-one-gun salutes. I was totally unprepared for this strange phenomenon; heaven was a vast empty space except for this one incongruous instrument of violence. There was a peculiarity about this instrument of violence which was that growing around its contours in exquisite beauty was green ivy and small lily of the valley flowers; the gun in spite of the vulgarity normally associated with violence had become a thing of delicate beauty and I thought to myself that *the most beautiful thing was that this weapon will never again be used in the cause of death and destruction.*

I was totally unprepared and was therefore, unsettled by the experience of heaven devoid of even a single spiritual entity; lost for any rational explanation of this strange phenomenon of a deserted heaven. *Finally,* I thought to myself, *if this is heaven, then God must be present.* W-A-N-G. Immediately, there was an instantaneous silent explosion of a beautiful and dramatic enhancement of radiant light and colour. At a stroke, all confusion and disappointment was replaced with wonderment and awe; this stunning sensation was further enhanced by the awareness of the sensation that I could sense the light and its very pleasant effects on the whole of my being.

It's highly unlike that I will ever experience such a phenomenal sense of peace and well-being ever again. Stretching to infinity. shafts of luminosity glowed with incandescent brilliance. These shafts of golden-coloured light passed through my body. I became aware that this awesome, dazzling light was shining through my back and exiting by my chest; obviously then, the light was directly behind me. I decided to turn one hundred and eighty to degrees to ascertain what was the cause of this spectacular phenomenon and instinctively knew that the cause would be more spectacular than its effect.

Slowly and expectantly at the same time, not daring to speculate on what to expect, when I made the turn I was confronted by a small disc of dazzling light, a sun of intensive light that was so powerful that I instinctively knew under normal circumstances I wouldn't be able to stare into this degree of light, for the disc of light was a thousand times brighter than our solar sun.

Yet, staring into this light caused no adverse effect on the eyes, when the realisation that staring in to this amount or light or brightness should be impossible. I concluded that this disc of brilliant light was the creator. What else could it be? Then I thought of the Bible's definition that 'God is Light', and who am I to take exception to this definition?

This story will, I have no doubt, be dismissed by a large number of individuals as the ranting of an overactive imagination; fanciful, but definitely the out-pouring of a deluded or disturbed mind. And I can understand this negative response, but I would retaliate by reminding the reader that I conceived the notion and patiently practiced the technique of self-hypnosis before I undertook my mission, and what I experienced was and remains totally convincing to me.

Jesus commenting about heaven made this amazing statement, "No one has gone to heaven except the son of man who came down again." Now then, what are we to make of this statement? It seems obvious to me that heaven is not attainable, until or unless there has been a sustained and conscientious effort to know and spiritually understand our relationship to and with God. A life of casual goodness or moral piety is not good enough to gain entry to paradise, you must be able to verbally state with conviction two truths concerning your true spiritually identity: 'who am I and what am I?' Of all of the important questions encountered during earthly existence, none are more important than these. Unless and until this mystery is satisfactorily resolved, a satisfying life of spiritual authenticity cannot be lived, nor can a life of satisfaction be experienced. Fate can't and therefore, won't supply the solutions that absolute truth demands from all of us.

Human existence in a body of gross matter here on planet earth provides the genuine thinker with, if sought, spiritual knowledge and wisdom. However, the greater and more profound the knowledge gained demands that the intelligent recipient will strive to become as great and as profound as the message or messages contained in the new knowledge. Those who continue to try to construct a meaningful life on the illusory foundations of worldly activities or mundane experiences will be doomed to bitter disappointment. Chasing after temporary and futile human excitement and fleeting pleasures must, as they will, end in bitter disappointment. The reason for human existence here on earth is to allow each and every individual to fulfil a divine mission entrusted to humanity by God. The search for spiritual fulfilment and the road that must be travelled begins in the inner realms of self, within each individual and there alone can be found the inspiration and stimulation. The truth is that each and every individual has written into his or her soul the truth of his or her spiritual identity.

The naked truth is that there are no organisations, be they religious or secular, spiritually equipped to help; religious leaders are as confused as humanity. No one can solve your problems for you. Problems have been, whether you accept it or not, self-created; your confusion is self-inflicted. Self-deception is unbridled, worldly ambitions are self-created and self-defeating. Ultimately, this will lead to frustration and eventually to hopeless despair; people are being defeated by naïve and distorted views of life.

All too many individuals demand impractical events of life, great wealth, power, and respect when we should be enthusiastically seeking to understand spiritual love, the principles of passives, and profound peace, compassion and truth are the liberators we reject to our great cost and peril.

Human being has been mechanically conditioned to accept the status-quo. I want to make every individual dissatisfied with being a mere mechanical follower of the confused heard of bewildered humanity. End the struggle to be something other than you are; God created you and the perfect creator cannot create imperfection. If imperfect thoughts are entertained, the inevitable consequences must be rob ourselves of perfection; this is a dreadful deception perpetrated by ourselves on ourselves.

This article has been written in the hope that it may be of some benefit to those few individuals who are seeking for answers to life's mystifying questions. I would point out that the word mystery in biblical terms means a revealed secret. All that must be known is contained in the soul of every individual and is ever-waiting on the call for revelation. The Divine Truth is that God has spiritually equipped every member of humanity with the sure and certain truth of his or her existence, with clear thought and the acceptance that all life is a profound and beautiful gift that will lead to spiritual salvation. All can make the same statement, with the same authority and certainty, that was made by Jesus, 'I and the Father are One,' God is omnipresent and occupies all space. He dwells in every atom and cell of every person. When you can recognise God existing in every person and everything, and recognise every person and everything existing in God, you stand at the portal of Paradise. Your spiritual mission is to give the highest human expression to the divine attributes that God has bequeathed to all of mankind.

Chapter 6

Christ

"When joys have lost their bloom and breath,
And life itself is vapid,
Why, as we reach the Falls of death,
Feel we its tide more rapid?" (Thomas Campbell)

John, one of the twelve apostles, disciple and friend of Jesus. Of the four evangelists, John was the most devoted and spiritual. In John's own words, we are informed that the Christ Principle spoke through the personality of Jesus. John tells us that the Word of God is all-powerful; that it is responsible for all creation and everything therein. Further John goes on to personalise the Word suggesting that the Word is in fact a person or being referring to the Word as "he" and "him." In verse 1 John refers to the Word as, '"He" was with God,' In verse 3 we read, 'Through "him" God made all things, and not one thing was made without "him",'

'Before the world was created, the Word already existed (he) was with God, and (he) was the same as God. From the very beginning the Word was with God. Through (him) God made all things; not one thing in all creation was made without (him.) The Word was the source of life, and this life brought light to mankind. The light shines in the darkness, and the darkness has never put it out,'

The Truth is, Christ is neither a person nor an individual, but is the all-powerful creative principle of God. Notice in the above quotation from the Bible the words he and him are in brackets, and are intended to suggest that Christ was or became human through Jesus. Christ is as stated as the Universal Creative, Principle of God, and being universal he must reside in every individual.

God is passive, Christ is the active spiritual principle of the Father, and the Holy Ghost is the descending consciousness of God to any person who has liberated themselves from spiritual deception.

In a few seconds and in a couple of sentences you have placed before you the Universal Truth of the relationship between God and Christ. God is the passive phase of Divinity; Christ is the creative and active phase of the same Divinity. Please, don't judge this new information on what you currently believe; neither should you passively accept this proposition. Neither accept nor reject this information; put it to the test of logic. The rest of the information in this premise will help you to make an informed and valued judgement.

Upon hearing the word Christ just about everyone instinctively thinks of Jesus. We have been led to believe that Christ was the individual called Jesus. The Christian churches would have us believe that Jesus was uniquely the Son of God. In fact, that he was alone God Incarnate. That Jesus was the one great exception set above the whole of humanity. There has been a great deal of argument and controversy concerning Jesus and his mission on earth and it's not my intention to enter into controversy in order to be controversial. In order to understand who or what Christ is, it's necessary to clearly understand what bond, connection or link existed between God, Christ and Jesus.

Jesus was unquestionably the greatest man who ever lived and he in his earthly mission was to reveal the Truth of what was is possible when we allow God to dominate every thoughts, words and deeds. Jesus' mission was to proclaim the truth that God and man are one. The Universal God has individualised Himself in each and every one of us. That we are dual in nature; in our human form we are still spiritual. Jesus showed us that to understand our relationship to God we must accept that we are first and foremost spiritual beings. Jesus' acceptance of the Christ Principle was, and still is the only way to a clear understanding and knowledge of our oneness to God.

God individualised Himself in Jesus and Jesus knew God lived in Him and was His very life. Christ is the personal expression of God in you. God being Universal, has individualised himself in you as the Christ. It is of importance to you that you understand clearly the relationship between God, Christ and you. Jesus said a number of things we should at this point, consider. "Of myself I can do nothing it's the Father who ever remains within me, he does the work," and, "I have only to ask and legions will be sent to help." "Why threaten to persecute me when I say I am the Son of God, do not your scriptures say that ye are the Sons of God."

To fully understand what is meant by the term Christ, it's necessary to examine this relationship between Christ and Jesus. It has to be said that Jesus was a man, but what a man He was, divinely ordained by God to become the complete divine expression in man. Jesus admitted that by himself he could do nothing and it was God who worked through Him. He was saying, in fact, that he was an instrument of God. On another occasion he told us that he required help from other spiritual beings. For he said, as previously quoted, "I have only to ask and legions will be sent to help me." If Jesus needed help from the legions mentioned then his powers were to some degree limited. Again, he said, "I am the Son of God, ye are the Sons of God." Jesus is clearly indicating that what was true of him was true for all of us.

On yet another occasion when he had healed the sick, he advised them to sin no more, least a worst thing should befall them. Two points about this advice from Jesus, first the healing was of a conditional or temporary nature and dependent on the recipient's changing their life-styles. It would seem that good health is to be found in living the good life; secondly, that the power and authority of Jesus had limitations when others were involved. Jesus, the sublime master, the greatest prophet, ever came to earth to complete the mission started by Moses before him. Moses' mission was to proclaim God Universal. Jesus' mission was to proclaim God individualised in mankind: "The I am God." God individualised in each and every one of us is the enduring Truth for all of mankind.

Jesus saw this clearly and proclaimed, "I and the Father are one." And, the basis of his acceptance of this and a sustained conscious awareness of God's presence within him, allowed Jesus to do the wonderful things he did. Jesus did not ask us to believe in him, but in Him who sent him. Jesus said, "Truly I tell you, he who listens to my word and believes in Him who sent me, has Eternal Life," Jesus, to his everlasting glory revealed the Father in the Son. God will be fully revealed in you, when you fully realise the presence that is God within. God's presence is within, as the Christ. If you believe Jesus to be exclusively the Christ, your reasoning is at fault, for Christ is God in you and is all power in heaven and on earth. Christ is universal and resides in every human being who ever lived. He belongs to the whole of humanity and in His love for us He is ever-waiting on our recognition of His presence within each and every one of us.

The Christian churches would have us believe that Jesus alone, and only he, can claim the title Christ. Christ is the personal expression of God within mankind and dwells in you and everyone else. Christ is the Divine Life that lives in each and every one of us. Without Christ, life would be impossible. You can only understand Christ when you recognise the Christ in all personalities. You must not think of the personality of Jesus, the man, nor when you consider Christ imagine the personality of Jesus, for this will blind you to the Christ Principle within you.

The Bible tells us, *'The Word was in the beginning and that Word was with God, that very Word that was God and that Word was made flesh,'* The Word that was made flesh in the beginning is the Christ. Christ has been in the world from the beginning and did not first appear two thousand years ago.

Christ has not left us. He resides in every individual and is central to human existence. It is imperative that we have a crystal-clear understanding of the Christ Principle and our relationship to it. There is nothing more important to you than, that you should recognise and realise your oneness with the Christ. When this awareness takes hold of you, you are in the Presence of the Father and you will express God's Love for all. Not only will you be blessed by this love, that is of God, but all others whom come into contact with you will also feel the power of Christ' love.

Your Christ power will put an end to all adverse circumstances, to any and all unpleasant conditions. You will raise above all mundane circumstances; nothing or no one will have power or dominion over you. Nothing can affect the Christ in you, and when you accept your oneness with Christ you will be above and beyond all that pains you. Christ is all power in the universe and through Christ, you transcend all your problems and establish the true meaning to life. If you are at this time in spiritual darkness, don't despair; plant in your consciousness the idea of your oneness with the Christ. Keep the idea of this union alive and like the seed planted in the dark earth this unity between the life in the seed and the life in the dark earth bring forth the image and likeness inherent in the seed; so will the seed of Christ planted in your consciousness, spring forth as the life of God within you. You need only to be aware, constantly aware, of the presence for it to manifest in you. A state of continual awareness is the only condition required. This degree of awareness will create all the conditions necessary for the eventual manifestation in your life of the Christ. The continual awareness will of its own accord purify the mind of all-negative emotions and sinful deeds. The human mind must reach the highest pinnacle of perfection, only then does it become a worthy receptacle for the influx of the Divine. All saints, mystics, avatars, and all saviours throughout history achieved what they did because they accepted the presence of Christ within themselves. You can, by using this method, be at all times consciously aware of the Presence within. You may also achieve what they did; you only need to exercise the same degree of commitment.

What you gaze upon, you bring forth. Get your sights on God from Him alone, and His presence within you will manifest. Of yourself you are nothing; it is the power of God within that is the only reality. The greatest obstacle to the realisation of God within is ignorance of the Christ in you. Life if lived without the awareness of your oneness with God has to be a reflection of your habitual thoughts and it is these mundane thoughts which cause all the problems you complain of. You can, if you wish, continue to waste your time and create more frustration by vainly trying to remedy the effects instead of eradicating the cause.

Jesus gives us this wonderful advice, "Seek ye first the kingdom of heaven and its right use and everything else shall be added into you."

The kingdom of heaven is the Christ presence within you. When you find this kingdom, everything else is yours. Happiness, peace, joy and all that you could hope and wish for will come to pass. We waste our lives chasing after material possessions that we know will not bring us the things we greatly desire. In our heart of hearts, we want peace of mind. We want to be loved, admired, respected and appreciated by everyone around us; all these things will materialise naturally when we give first priority to First Cause. Christ then must become first priority. The creative principle will become active within you, when for the love of God and Christ, you decide to live the life of love, compassion and spiritual understanding. With the Christ principle active within you, all things, all will be possible. Christ is the consciousness of God manifesting in you and all of mankind. And the Christ is ever active in you and never more so than when you are aware of his presence. The spiritual light in you is the Christ of God in you. Spiritually, you stand or fall. Based either on the acceptance or rejection of this proposition., you need only look into your own heart and mind to see the need of accepting the truth of God and man united in love, peace and happiness through the continual awareness of Christ within. Only with Christ can you bring any worthwhile meaning to your life. Without Christ at the very centre of your life you will continue to suffer from anger, fear, frustration and all the other forms of mental upheaval.

With Christ in your consciousness and heart you are superior to circumstances. Nothing in or out of this world can harm you. In Psalm 27, we read, *'The Lord is my light and my salvation, whom shall I fear? The Lord is the strength of my life; of whom shall I be afraid,'* With god as the Christ in you and your continual awareness of this presence is the open door to freedom. Accept the Christ into your life and you will know when the realisation is strong in your consciousness, that there is a freedom beyond human comprehension. Christ is at work in you now; accept and realise this truth so that the truth can manifest in your life now. The Christ consciousness will reveal God the creator and you his creation as one. You will know that God himself lives and breathes in you, and you will express God's presence as love, compassion, understanding and healing to all.

For you to overcome all problems by yourself whatever they may be would mean conflict and struggle with no guarantee of success. With Christ there is no need to struggle, or strain, you will not have to strive, for you will not have to overcome anything; you will transcend everything. In the book of *Job,* we read, *'Make the almighty himself your treasure and the almighty shall be a joy to you,'* Realise the Christ in you is omnipotent, omnipresent and omniscient, and you don't have to wait until sometime in the future, for some sort of indefinable benefits. The Bible has this to say, *'As long as he sought the Lord, God made him to prosper,'* Christ is beyond your mortal concepts; your limited mental faculties won't allow you to know the Christ. Let your mortal senses be still and in silent conscious awareness, Christ will take possession of your soul, your consciousness, heart and mind. People everywhere want immortality. The very wealthy can have their dead bodies deep-frozen in the hope that in some future time science will make it possible to inject the body with life. Fortunes are being made by pharmaceutical companies peddling all sort of creams and potions to slow down the ageing process of the human skin. There are financial rewards untold, waiting for the person who can put an end to death. People fear death; they are terrified of the unknown, or dread being punished by a vengeful God for their sins. There is nothing more dreadful than ignorance and the more active the ignorance, the more dreadful the consequences.

You must clearly understand that Christ within you is the Power that controls and gives direction to your life. With Christ you will overcome all obstacles, clear any hurdles, dismantle any barriers, overcome any hindrances, and nothing will be impossible to you. Not only will Christ make clear the way, but Christ will clear the way. If you play your part, Christ will, most assuredly, discharge His Divine obligation to you. Nothing in the Universe is more certain than that. Accept that you belong to Christ and Christ to God and act accordingly. The great creative power within you is the Christ of God. You now know that the Christ is the Word of God; the Word that was God, and the Word was made flesh. The Word of God dwells within you as the Christ. Christ is all power in heaven and on earth. This Power resides in you and this power can be developed in you by recognising its existence and by becoming aware of the presence of Christ within you.

Christ knows all that is to be known; there can be no mysteries that are not revealed to Christ, because Christ is your true spiritual identity and when the Christ consciousness unfolds within, all will be revealed to you. Cleanse the mind and become still and silent and in the quietude of mind, and purity of thought, and the Truth of Christ will unfold in you. Your heart must be at peace, full of love and compassion. The mind has to be free of hate, anger and all negative thoughts, before the Christ consciousness can manifest. There is nothing more important than you have the clearest picture possible of your relationship to God through Christ. The Christ is the Spirit of God in you. Remember, spirit is the collective attributes of Almighty God. Christ, when fully realised means these attributes manifesting in you and through you to all of mankind. Jesus proved that Christ could manifest in the flesh the glory of God. And Jesus told us, "You will do even greater things if you would only believe." With Christ there are no limits to your abilities; everything will be possible to you. However, there has to be in place the necessary understanding, love and wisdom, so that you use your new powers in the service of humanity and not for any narrow personal reasons. Make a conscious decision to allow the spirit of almighty God, the Christ in you to be your only guide, and watch your life change to what it could and should be. If you fully accept that it is the Christ that dwells in you, this acceptance will unfold a higher understanding and so shall the Christ manifest in you according to your level of awareness and understanding.

You are on earth to gain a clear understanding of who and what you are, to learn that you are an immortal spiritual being. Your awareness has to be raised beyond your physical experiences, and above and beyond your human activities. In pursuit of that which is real and substantial, you must clearly demonstrate self-mastery in the positive use of your mind and its thoughts. You must also be prepared to trust the unseen. In love, give your trust to God and in Him, through the Christ in you, your trust will be spiritually rewarded. Say in your heart, *"It's you, my beloved Father who is ever guiding me."* Use your time here on earth wisely and intelligently, constantly seek to improve your inner awareness. Be prepared to become spiritually submissive and yet keep an open and receptive mind. You are meant to learn while here on earth that body or mortal mind does not limit life. Life is completely free when we live the Christ life. You are meant to clearly understand that it is God who lives in you and He is your very existence. Christ is the only source of Life drawn from the Christ source so that your life may be complete and whole. Life alone lives and all of our troubles stem from the mistaken concept of ourselves being separated from God, who is the only possible source of Life. If we don't learn these truths while here on earth then it will be necessary for us to return, after physical death, in another body to continue the search for the truth of our being. To overcome all difficulties that exist in our search for ourselves we should give ourselves over completely to Christ. In our conscious union with Christ there is always growth. This growth is silent, it won't make the faintest whisper. It will, however make its presence felt to the mind that is similarly silent and receptive. Wait in love, with hope, trust and expectancy and the presence of Christ within will be revealed unto you. Be consciously aware of the Christ for in reality, He and you are one. Only through the awareness of Christ will you grow into the truth, and in the truth you will be set free from all worldly woes and tribulations.

Realise in healing that the Christ Power permeates every cell in the human body and if you can make the person, in need of help aware of the Christ presence within, healing will take place. Clearly understand that the presence is always present and will become a healing power when you are conscious of the presence within you. You can send thoughts of love and healing charged with an awareness of the Presence. If you act in love and a heightened awareness of the Presence you will become a healer of all conditions. To become a healer, you must know who does the healing and you must know how to use the healing power. In all healing, not some, Christ does the work.

You must have a loving reverence for the presence. It's all so wonderfully simple—'God in the midst of you is mighty,' When you wish to help someone in distress, find somewhere quiet, still the mind, think of the person or persons you know needs help, then become aware of the presence. Know that the healing force is pouring through you and is being received by the patient or patients. Before beginning a healing say, *"It is you, my beloved Father, who is doing the work for which I lovingly thank you, in anticipation for the healing."* Say in your heart, *"Father, I lovingly thank you for what you are, infinite love, compassion and understanding."* You will notice in this healing method there is no begging to God; there is no mention of disease or sickness. It is inconsistent to ask the God of infinite love and compassion to heal a disease. Disease is the effect of using the mind in its negative mode. With a constant awareness of the presence of Christ within, nothing will be impossible to you, for Christ is all power in heaven and on earth; this power is the Love of God, for all spiritual power is contained in love. Let Christ dwell in your heart and your heart will become full of love, wisdom, compassion, and peace will flood through your mind and the wisdom of Christ will enfold you, and life will become a whole new experience full of joy and peace. You will, at last, realise the eternal Christ of God resides in your immortal soul. It is the power of Christ that resides within every member of humanity that will establish health of body and peace of mind and more importantly, still you will know yourself to be the eternal son of Almighty God. All things are possible to any individual who becomes the Son of God and if this were to be your experience you will be amazed at the things that become possible to you. The in-dwelling presence of Christ recognised and realised, all limitation will end and nothing will be impossible. In Christ you will truly know divine love; you will experience peace that surpasses all human understanding. Love, peace, health and happiness are your divine inheritance and when you accept that the Presence, of God Universal, has individualised Himself as the Christ in you, God will personally present you with your Divine inheritance.

When the Consciousness of Christ manifests you will know and understand that you are a spiritual being housed in a physical body. Your body is not you, for human bodies are created out of matter, which has many a manifestation, but has no power or authority of its own. Power resides within you, for God created you in his image and likeness; free yourself from all burdens by recognition of the truth that what is God's is also yours. The spiritual you has unlimited powers that emanate from God Himself, but until you live Life as God intended, you will not be allowed to have access to these powers. When you place Christ awareness first in your order of priorities you will become a much more loving and considerate parson. Your thoughts will be more refined, your words, more understanding, and your deeds will reflect your new nature. For Christ consciousness will cleanse the mind of negative thoughts and folly. Christ's presence will bestow the greatest blessing of life upon you; love peace and contentment will be yours to a degree, you cannot at this time imagine.

Mankind is at this moment in time, behaving more and more irrationally. Human behaviour is degenerating into every type of perversion; hate, anger, ignorance and stupidity, is the daily diet of mankind. Is it any wonder that our civilisation is on the brink of collapse? Mankind cannot continue to ignore God, Christ and spiritual realities, for the consequences have been clearly spelt out, by biblical prophets. While the mass of humanity is on the road to disaster, there exists, for the wise and intelligent, the opportunity to avoid the adversity that is sure to overtake mankind. Christ the only begotten Son of God, is Universal and resides in every individual and through Christ, all have access to all of God's attributes. Were you to live the Christ life, it would be a life of profound peace and contentment. You would have access to all of God's other wonderful attributes: healing power, prophecy and other spiritual powers. In Christ alone resides everlasting contentment; only in Christ will you find the security that no amount of human activity can provide.

So the choice facing each and every one of us is this: do we continue to tread the road that we know from history and personal experience but that cannot provide the quality of life we desire. Or do we return to, Christ and Truth that we know will bring to a permanent end all human problems. By constant awareness of the Christ within you, you will come to a realisation of yourself as the spiritual Son of God and your life will change accordingly, as Jesus said; "I am the life." And when you fully realise that there is only one Life, then and only then. can you begin to live Life as God intended you should. But this realisation is reserved only for those who live the Christ Life. When you accept the truth of your oneness with God, through the Christ, your true spiritual state will manifest and your immortal soul will rejoice; your mind will be at peace; your body will manifest perfect health and your mortal consciousness will be overshadowed by Christ Consciousness. These are but the few of the many benefits that are to be gained by acceptance of the Presence of the Christ who dwells in the human soul of every individual. You know that God is divine love and to comply with your spiritual obligation to God and mankind, you must give expression to love in its purest form. As a spiritual being you and God are one. The truth is that God and you are united for eternity in love, wisdom and peace. This reality will only manifest when you recognise the presence of Christ within you.

Your real worth is determined by the value you place on your spiritual identity and on the state of your relationship to God. It is of supreme importance that you clearly understand that God has chosen you as a vehicle for the expression of his divine will, which is that you express Infinite Life. Have the courage and faith to place your trust in Christ that in Him you may overcome all obstacles, doubts and confusion. Refuse to allow presently held beliefs and opinions to hinder your search for truth and freedom, for spiritual freedom belongs not to mortal mind, but to your immortal soul. Trust in God and through the Christ you will be guided and inspired to know the truth for your earthly experiences, for you will only gain control over your life by spiritual knowledge and its proper use. Have done with petty self-interest and place your spiritual well-being first in your order of priorities, end the quest for ego gratification, put a stop to the foolish notion that cheap thrills and excitement can provide contentment or lasting peace of mind.

The unknown can never be known until you trust the unseen.

"Great men are they who know that the spiritual is stronger than any material force." (Emerson)

The truly great individuals of history were those few who recognised their oneness with God and behaved accordingly. You should follow their wonderful example and turn your attention to the Christ who dwells in your soul. For without a spiritual understanding of your true identity your world will be dominated by the illusion of form and phenomena. Your thoughts and reactions will be dominated by every trivial incident. If you continue to live in the outer physical world of phenomena, just about every event will cause negative emotional reactions. This is the inevitable price that must be paid by those, who spend their time living in the world of secondary causes. As the spiritual world lies beyond the myopic sight of the human eye, humanity continues to stumble from crisis to crisis. How sad it is, for with a little spiritual insight it could be so wonderfully different. It is the law that each and every life must reflect the psychological level at which the individual mind operates. The mind that is constantly aware of the presence of Christ will radiate love, compassion and understanding to all. And the mind that radiates such thoughts is operating at the highest psychological level; this will confer greatness upon the individual wise enough to recognise Christ as being all power in the Universe. To live a life free of pain and hurt Christ must influence every thought, word and deed; for its thoughts, words and deeds of the mundane mind that causes all the daily problems that on occasions threaten to overwhelm us.

When you finally realise that you and God are one, all doubt, all fear, all confusion, and all pain will end forever; new vistas will be revealed to you raising your vision beyond mere human activities, and you will understand that humanity is the one family of God. Mankind's agony is caused by the false belief in separation from God. The truth is that no one can ever be separated from God. If this could happen, then God could not be omnipresent and therefore not universal. God being omnipresent is consciously aware of every individual and His Consciousness is in each individual as the Christ is in the immortal soul of every person.

The task facing each and every individual is exactly the same; the individual consciousness has to be united with the Universal Consciousness of God, and you now know that the Christ within you is the Universal Consciousness of Almighty God. Allow the Christ Consciousness to become active within you, that the radiant light of God may shine through you to all of humanity. You will never understand yourself, until you understand God and you will never understand God until you realise that He exists within you as the Christ. Ask God to allow you to know Him better, to love Him more and to do His will always. This is the formula for advancement; ask god for help, but ask in faith, knowing, in your heart, that God will respond. If you have total belief that God will answer your plea, your prayer is answered before you utter a word. Before you ask God for anything become aware of the Presence of Christ within you and your request will be granted. Be patient and do not allow doubt to enter your mind. Your absolute conviction that God will answer your prayer is the absolute guarantee that God will respond in your favour.

All our earthly problems, whatever they may be can only be ended when we clearly see that we are living life unnaturally; life lived without a strong spiritual dimension must be one of disappointment and failure. There is a certain method of avoiding all the problems encountered by each of us; accept that the Consciousness of God resides in you as the Christ within you. Union with God through the acceptance of the living presence of Christ is really very simple; we only have to allow God's holy will expression in and through you. Give your life over completely to spiritual reality that you are first and foremost a spiritual being and you will feel the beneficial influences within your heart and soul, allowing you to enjoy peace and contentment. Only in Christ can you overcome all your difficulties, because Christ is power of God in you and this Presence is in essence the spiritual source of your existence. The dominion of all power resides in Christ and as Christ resides in you, power in all of its potential, resides in your heart when it has been Christ purified. The great spiritual powers of God are individualised in you as the Christ is awaiting expression through you; begin now to give expression to these powers so that they may grow in strength within you. Love is power, compassion is power, understanding is power, forgiveness is power. Exercise these powers for the love of God, and you are for certain, on the high road to freedom. When you accept that Christ is the living essence of God and that Christ lives in you then the word of God will be expressed in and through you. You will become the living witness to the truth that God and man are eternally united in Christ. And when you allow Christ to flood your heart and mind you will become aware of a spiritual awakening, allowing you a clear understanding of the creative powers that are, at this time, dormant within you. Christ has been described as the only Son of God, this being so, Christ has to be the only existent reality, and everything that exists does so because of Him. By your conscious acceptance of the in-dwelling Christ you become one with reality. You will experience a new birth into the kingdom of heaven.

The truly great men of history sought, above everything, spiritual liberation and divine freedom, but they realised that the human mind was incapable of penetrating into the spiritual realms. So they sought within their hearts for God, the only place where He can be found, and eventually they discovered that man and God are united in Christ. You are the spiritual image of Almighty God and if you wish this image to be reflected in the outer then turn completely to the living presence of Christ within you. If you would only recognise and realise it is the spirit of Christ that lives in you and the Christ is omnipotent, omnipresent and omniscient, your life would be a wondrous, beautiful and everlasting blessing. And when the Presence manifests in the outer, you become the inheritor of tremendous spiritual powers and of benefit to all of mankind. The acceptance of the truth of your oneness with God through Christ will allow the soul to rejoice and you will be blessed with the wisdom of Christ. Your mind will be at peace, your body will manifest perfect health and your consciousness will reflect Divine Reality. These are but a few of the many spiritual and mortal benefits to be gained when you turn completely to the Presence of Christ who dwells in your immortal soul. However, it is only when the aspirant is prepared to give the noblest expression to the highest human values can he or she expect God to become active in their lives.

Our afflictions must continue while we continue to ignore God or to violate His Laws; the Law, when properly understood and intelligently applied will raise mankind to spiritual levels that few can, at this moment in time, comprehend. God, recognised and realised will become active within you and the means chosen by God for His spiritual involvement is the Christ in you. But you must give constant attention to the Presence of Christ within. The conditions required for the manifestation of Christ are, a permanent end to negative thinking, and all mundane human inclinations. When thinking becomes positive and when your motivation is dominated by love, then you're on the road to freedom and human perfection.

Your real worth is determined by the value you place on your spiritual identity and your understanding of your relationship to God. The wisdom to accept that God and you are one will allow the Father to reveal Himself and to manifest all His attributes through you. It is of supreme importance that you understand that God has chosen you, as a vehicle for the expression of His Divine will, which is that Infinite Life, be expressed in and through you. God and you His Creation are one; rejoice that you have been created by God in His image and likeness and rejoice that He has made this known to you. God is first cause and when you accept Christ as the animating power within you, God becomes effect. Your oneness with God is a spiritual fact of your existence. This means that the Universal Consciousness of the Divine Mind resides in you, as the Christ of God in you. When you fully accept Christ, the Divine Mind will overshadow mortal mind and you will understand that your consciousness is the point through which God manifests Himself to you. The recognition and realisation of the Presence of Christ within you will produce a spiritual power that will bring forth, love, wisdom, peace, health, joy and happiness. Yes, it is possible to live a life of serene peace and contentment. Jesus gave the formula when he advised, "Seek ye first the kingdom of heaven and its right use and everything else shall be add unto you."

Life is from God and only through the acceptance of Christ resident within the soul can the secret of life be discovered. The purpose of life is revealed to all who live the Christ life, for the purpose of God is made manifest through the Presence of the Christ who resides in the immortal soul of every individual.

Christ is the universal creative principle of God and Christ resides in every atom and cell of every individual; recognise this truth and act accordingly and you are destined to gain entry into Paradise.

Chapter 7
Healing

Everything seen and unseen exists in the mind of God. Nothing can exist outside of Him. Before the healing process can begin, there are a number of things that must be clearly understood concerning disease or any other medical condition. Disease is not of God, and mastery over disease can only be obtained when we accept that God is not responsible for any form of illness or disease. Our God is the God of infinite love, compassion and understanding. It is totally wrong to believe that an all-merciful God could be responsible for all the dreadful diseases that cause so much pain, suffering and death. If you believe God causes disease your belief is based upon ignorance of God and yourself. This ignorance has of necessity to be overcome with knowledge, understanding, wisdom and truth.

Christ is the motivator of all spiritual activity including healing, when Christ's mission is fully understood which is to do the will of the Father. What God decrees, Christ is responsible for the manifestation. Crudely put Christ is the doer in all manifestations.

Let's at the beginning get a clear understanding concerning disease. Where it comes from, how it is caused and why it afflicts some individuals and not others. This chapter will not allow a comprehensive account of all aspects of disease and healing. However, you will be in receipt of the most important facts concerning all mental, emotional and physical abnormalities. Not only will you know what causes all the conditions you complain of, but also you will learn the healing methods to remedy all adverse conditions.

You must clearly understand that knowledge, of itself, will not cure disease. Knowledge must not only be learnt but must be given intelligent direction. You must first learn and then give wise direction to your new understanding. One fundamental lesson you must understand is this: your problem, whatever it may be is always within and never without.

Let's examine the cause or causes of disease and other forms of sickness. If God is not responsible for our ills who or what is? Where does disease come from? An examination of our world will be of tremendous benefit to us in our attempt to explain the origins of illnesses and all other ailments. God created the universe which includes planet Earth, with its mountains, seas, lakes and forests. Man has created cities, roads, ships, cars and all the other material goods we use many times every day. Everything you can see, feel or touch has been created either by God or man. Before anything can be created there has first to be a mental process of thought. Thought first, then the process of creating now. If everything is the result of the thought process then disease and all other negative conditions have their origins in our minds. Startling as it may seem we mentally create disease and all other forms of sickness by using the mind in its negative mode. If you have a diseased mind you will have a diseased body. Thoughts of hate, anger, fear and all other forms of negative thinking, are the cause of the medical conditions we complain of. The human body is a complex chemical factory, every thought, every spoken word, every deed, every movement causes a chemical reaction in the body. If your thoughts are of hate, anger, fear, resentment or any form of negative thinking, you set in motion negative chemical reactions and you suffer the inevitable consequences of poor health. It is of supreme importance that you clearly understand the relationship between mind and body. You go to sleep and have a terrible dream, a nightmare, and when your nightmare is about to reach an unbearable climax you wake up. You are drenched in perspiration trembling in a state of terror. You were never in any physical danger, it was all in the mind. Your mind created the non-existent terror, and the terrified mind caused the body to tremble and perspire, proof positive that the mind does cause adverse physical and mental problems. You need to understand that there are two phases to your mind called by different names, your ordinary mind and your subconscious mind, also known as your objective mind and subjective mind. Your outer or objective mind is the means whereby you are aware of the external world. Your objective mind has as its characteristics, prejudice, bias, emotion, anger, hate, fear and many other negative traits. Your inner subjective subconscious mind has different characteristics, reason, recollection, will and imagination.

The mind of man is dual in its control of the outer and inner actions. Your subconscious mind controls breathing, heartbeat, blood flow and is responsible for all your organs. This subconscious mind comes under the control of the outer mind and if given instructions from the outer mind will produce what the outer mind directs. Your mind will not always give you what you want or desire, but it will always produce what you believe.

You have seen the hypnotist at work and the weird and wonderful things he or she can make the hypnotised person do while in a trance. What happens is this, the hypnotist puts the person to sleep or trance and then gives instructions to the subconscious mind and the person in hypnotic trance will behave as told. If the person in trance is told that he or she is a monkey they will act the part of a monkey. The body and mind will act in accordance with the instructions of the subconscious mind and the subconscious mind will produce what the outer mind deeply believes.

Jesus clearly understood the law of mind, for he said repeatedly, "It's done unto you according to your belief." If you are totally convinced you will be a millionaire before you die, your subconscious mind will see to it and you will die a millionaire. Within you is the universal consciousness of the divine mind, which enters your body along with the life force with the first breath. The Universal Consciousness of the Divine Mind when clearly understood and called into action will allow you to control and give direction to energy. This control of energy when given proper direction can heal a diseased body. Throughout the whole of creation there exists a great vital energy and is directed and controlled by God Himself. This vital energy resides in the human body giving every individual the right to use this power. The mind of man when in harmony with the Divine plan becomes the regulators of this energy. Now if you are prepared to work in harmony with God's plan you can use this energy for healing in all sorts of ways.

Your mind, your consciousness and your intelligence are constantly in contact with the Universal Mind of God. The Universal Mind of God is all knowing and everywhere present, then the mind of God permeates our individual minds. And the startling truth is we can gain access to this Universal Mind to solve any human problem. Two laws apply to the use of the divine cosmic mind. The first law is to consciously allow our thoughts, desires or impressions to be released from our human mind into the Cosmic Mind of God. Second is to attune our minds with the Universal Mind of God, this enable us to receive any transmitted impressions. You should understand that it's well within the ability of God to convey impressions to us that are independent of the physical faculties. In mind silence and stillness God can and will silently communicate with you.

You must cleanse the mind of all negative thoughts and purify the heart by filling it with love, compassion and understanding. These conditions are absolutely necessary for union with God. Your oneness with God is a spiritual fact of your existence. It was God himself who created you—out of his perfect spiritual substance—in his image and likeness. God is perfect and if he has created you in his image and likeness then perfection is meant to be your natural condition. You were certainly meant to enjoy good health and all other benefits of a rich rewarding life of peace, contentment and happiness.

Every individual life was meant to be a blessed experience of joy in the truth that God and man are one. All that has gone wrong in your life has happened because of your ignorance of your relationship to God. You see it's only through spiritual understanding that we find release from all our troubles including sickness, ill health and disease. To recover your health and your life you must get close to God. Or more accurately you must become aware of your oneness with God. Paul tells us that we live, move and have our being in God. To be aware of his Presence is the road to healing and salvation. Your consciousness is the point through which God expresses himself in your life. And is the point through which you make conscious union with God. Later on, one of the healing methods to be explained will be Christ Healing, so it is important to get a clear understanding of who or what the Christ is. Christ is the Universal God individualised in each and every person. God personalised in you is the Christ in you. There is nothing more important in all of the universe or through eternity, than the knowledge and acceptance by you of the Christ within. Please do not confuse the universal Christ with the personality of Jesus. Jesus the man—the greatest prophet ever—showed us what is possible if we allow Christ to dominate our thoughts, words and deeds. The man Jesus became the Son of God because he allowed the Christ total control and authority. Jesus came on earth to be the great example; the Christian churches have made him the great exception.

"Of myself I can do nothing; it's the father who ever remains in me. He does the work," Jesus said. On another occasion Jesus tells us, "I only have to ask and legions will be sent to HELP me."

Yes, there were times when Jesus had to ask for help. He said repeatedly, "I am the Son of God, the son of man." Jesus' holy mission was to proclaim the truth of God and man united in Christ.

The Bible tells us that the Word was in the beginning and the Word was with God, that very Word that was God and that Word was made flesh. The Word

155

made flesh is the Christ of God in man. The universal God individualised in each and every one of us is the Christ. The personality of Jesus must fade out of your mind. Only then can you experience the reality of the living Christ within you— to realise yourself, one with the Christ, to be consciously aware of the Christ Presence within is, healing for soul mind and body. If you accept the Christ of God within you and allow the Christ to work in and through you, failure is impossible. When Christ is fully accepted and realised by you, when you are prepared to live the Christ life of love, wisdom and compassion and understanding, you will have found your real self and your future not only on earth is secure, but through all eternity. Think of the glorious prize waiting for you, an eternity of love, peace, joy and harmony. The mind of man cannot conceive the things that God has prepared for those who love him. This world is only a preparatory step in the unfolding of the Christ within. And should you fail to allow Christ Consciousness expression in you, you will have missed the whole objective of your earthly mission. And the consequence of your failure will mean that you must return again to earth in another body to give you, yet again, one more attempt to discover the truth. You will continue to return to earth until you learn the lesson that you and the Father are one, and to live the Divine Life of love. Don't hinder the Christ by clinging to your old limited beliefs and your negative thinking. If you want to be free from all your problems you must give up your present notions and outdated beliefs for these have blinded you to the truth of who and what you are. The greatest hindrance, to the expression of that which is divine in you, is ignorance of the Christ in you. Make Christ a conscious reality and you will know that Christ is the conscious expression of almighty God, who lives in you. The acceptance of this union between God and self is healing of soul, mind and body. To be constantly, consciously aware of the Presence of God as the Christ within is 'Truth Healing,' Jesus said, "You shall know the truth and the truth shall set you free." The freedom of Truth is to be free, for all time, from all human defects. Can this be true? You ask. Is it possible to leave behind all worry, care and woes? The answer is a definite yes, but only if and when you are prepared to live the Christ life. You may well ask, how do I live the Christ life? What must I do? You have the great example of Jesus. He lived the Christ life and he could do the wonderful things he did because Christ dominated his every thought, word and deed. The Christ life is a life of love and unselfish service to all of humanity. Every life should be a work of art, a very

156

beautiful experience. If you desire to live a beautiful life you must do beautiful things in and with your life.

"Your mission in life is to become and grow as beautiful as God meant you to be when he first thought of you." (McDonald)

It is the in-dwelling Christ who is responsible for all healing. When you accept the Christ Presence you gain a victory over all conditions. When you recognise and realise that it is the Christ of God who resides in you this truth will allow the healing power of the universe to manifest in you. The Christ Presence within, when fully recognised and realised will produce within you a power that will bring forth all that you require—health, wisdom, peace, love, joy and happiness. You must become constantly and consciously aware of the Christ living and breathing in you. With Christ awareness nothing can harm or hamper you from without. You can only know the Christ through the love of God and mankind, his children. God has decreed that Christ shall have dominion over all things; by accepting Christ into your life you are partaking in God's divine plan for humanity. The power of Christ is a mighty power indeed and is developed in you by recognition, then realisation. This acceptance must be followed by periods of mental quiet or meditation on the in-dwelling Presence.

If you accept Christ as the in-dwelling Presence and remain true to the Presence you will be glorified by Christ in the Presence of God. For when the Presence meets the Presence, glory, exaltation and bliss are yours. When Christ spoke and acted through the personality of Jesus it was part of a mission, which is ongoing and its purpose is to reveal the glory of God. Pray and entreat the Christ that his mission may succeed in you. Become aware of your oneness with the Christ and know that Christ is within you, always patiently waiting on your recognition of his Presence. If your recognition and realisation is strong the Christ power will arise within you and your body will be under your spiritual control. You have been placed on planet earth to overcome the world and all its follies and stupidity. Jesus said, "I have overcome the world." He had to struggle also, and was subject to many temptations. Jesus accepted he was the spiritual Son of God. He said, "I am the Son of God; ye are the sons of God." Christ was the personal expression of God in Jesus, and Christ being universal is the personal expression of God in each and every one of us. In your recognition of this truth you gain love, peace, power and healing of mind and body.

Know that it's the infinite spirit of Almighty God that dwells as the Christ in you and when fully realised nothing will be impossible to you. Jesus said, "Seek ye first the kingdom of heaven and its right use and everything else shall be added unto you." He also said, "The kingdom of heaven within you." When you discover deep within yourself the kingdom of heaven, you will have gained a permanent victory over disease and all other forms of physical and mental adversities. When Jesus healed, he advised the cured, "Go and sin no more least a worse thing come upon you." Good health you see is directly related to good living. A troubled mind will produce a troubled body. A diseased mind will produce a diseased body. When Jesus said, "Sin no more," he meant, don't think negative thoughts. Jesus was acutely aware of the link between negative thinking and disease.

You are now learning that the acceptance of the Christ Presence within you is the power that brings forth health, peace, harmony and lasting happiness. Thank the Father for making these things known to you. You may ask, how do I bring forth the Christ consciousness? The answer is through your own consciousness. Your consciousness is the only way of making contact with God within you. And it's through your consciousness you will know the Christ of God; you must become consciously aware of the Presence of God, personalised as the Christ, in you. Christ is the consciousness of God in man and this consciousness is aware of itself in man. I do hope you are beginning to understand the relationship between God, Christ and the whole of mankind. For this relationship to be realised by the individual, there has to be a cleansing of the outer mind of all negative thoughts, particularly thoughts of hate, anger, fear, contempt, malice, greed, jealousy and all other forms of mental sin. With the mind thus purified and the consciousness made aware of the Presence within, you have created the necessary mental conditions for the Christ to take charge of your life. Having purged the mind of all negative thoughts you are now required to charge the mind with positive ones—thoughts of love, peace, harmony and good will towards all of humanity. When you change your thoughts from negative to positive the healing process begins automatically.

Your body is a large chemical factory. Every thought, every spoken word, every emotion, every movement and everything eaten or drank causes a chemical reaction, either negative or positive. If your thoughts and emotions are negative you cause negative vibration in the body, which in turn causes negative chemical reactions. Thus, we are the creators of the pain, sickness and disease we complain of. By the power of the Christ of God that dwells within, you conquer all problems mental, emotional and physical. You should clearly understand that the reason for your life on earth is a preparatory step in the unfolding of the Christ within. This preparatory lesson can only be learnt during life on earth and if for any reason you don't learn this fundamental lesson, then it will be necessary for you to reincarnate on earth to be given another chance to learn. The Christ is incarnate and dwells within every living soul. The Christ did not leave us two thousand years ago. The Christ speaking through Jesus said, "I am with you always even unto the end of the world." The world is in the dreadful mess it's in because of the confusion concerning the Christ of God.

Christians—so called—find no difficulty in rushing into war with the expressed desire to murder and are quite content to murder fellow Christians. Know that the Christ of God is Universal and the Christ is the animating and creative power in the human mind; the mind that is dominated by the creative thoughts is the mind that will establish peace in the heart. If you want to be free from all bondage, all illusion and all folly, then you must become aware of the Christ of God within you. With Christ in your heart and mind you will come to know yourself as God knows you. Christ is the only means of overcoming all that troubles or concerns you. Know that with Christ all anxiety will pass away.

All will be revealed to you when you fully accept that it is the Christ who lives and breathes in you. Yes, it is the Christ who breathes and not the body. When breath leaves the body, what is called death takes place. In truth there is no death, there is transition. We leave the body but our conscious experiences continue and we go to a place that we have earned by the quality of our earthly humanity. For those who have diligently sought for an explanation for life and lived accordingly will, when they leave, find themselves in a very pleasant place and will enjoy their stay there. However, because they have not found the truth of their spiritual union to Christ, God, and their fellow man, then it will be necessary to reincarnate back on earth. Those who have lived the life of crime or wasted their time on earth chasing after material possessions, when they leave this earth, they will go to a very unpleasant place indeed. Jesus said, "There will be weeping, wailing and gnashing of teeth." Let me say clearly that God does not punish anyone. Our God is a God of Infinite Love, Compassion and Understanding. We will punish ourselves. When, all pretence, all illusion has been stripped from them, when they are faced with the reality of what they did and how they misbehaved, when they see, and they will be shown, where they could have gone to, and when they compare this place of beauty and joy to where they are, there will be such sadness that 'there will be weeping, wailing and gnashing of teeth,'

To return to the proposition that it is the Christ who breathes and not the human body, let's examine the story of the creation of man. The Bible tells us that,

'God created man out of the dust of the earth. Into his nostrils he breathed the breath of life and man became a living soul,'

Notice it was God who breathed, also note, and this is of tremendous importance for you, God breathed into the nostrils *'the breath of life,'* Life is breath. God is referred to in the Bible as 'The Holy Breath,' So breath is of great importance for us. It is only at the first breath that the soul enters the body. And when breath leaves the body so also does the soul.

Healing, said Plato is of the soul, meaning that healing was a spiritual experience. It is the Christ within you that heals and no one else and by your awareness of the Christ Presence are you healed. In deep silence, meaning silencing the mind, will unite with the heart and mind of Spirit, and this will produce the necessary condition for healing. Conditions in your body and mind will change and harmonise according to your realisation that it is Christ who is working in you and for you. Remember it is the Christ who breathes and Christ breathes through the outer body of flesh. If you co-operate with the Christ failure is impossible, because Christ cannot fail and neither will you if you give Christ dominion over your life.

If at this moment you are in distress and suffering pain, suffer in silence; don't complain even in your own mind, for silence has to be established for healing to take place. Allow Christ to reign in your life and clearly understand that God Himself, through the Christ, is working in you, for you. When you realise the Christ Presence your suffering will end. You, Almighty God Himself will you whole and complete; never again shall you know pain, sickness or disease. Healing can only take place when the mortal senses have been stilled and the consciousness is directed inward to the kingdom of heaven within you. Your physical body is composed of the dust of the earth and to dust it shall return. Your body is conditioned matter and has no power or authority of its own. Your existence in material form gives you individual awareness and when this awareness is realised establishes the Universal Christ Conscious in you. It is the Christ in you that has power and authority and this power permeates every cell in the body. The physical body of itself has neither power nor authority.

For healing to take place there has to be a clear understanding of the Christ principle and an awareness of the Presence of Christ within you. You must calm and still the mind. And you must accept that it is the Christ who is breathing through the outer body of flesh, from within. 'God in the midst of thee is mighty,' It is the holy and blessed Presence of God in you as the Christ that heals.

'In thy Presence is fullness of joy, at the right hand there are pleasures for evermore,' (Psalm 16: 11)

Please don't struggle with pain, sickness or disease; when you struggle with your problem you become possessed by the thoughts of it and you give it power and authority over you. Remember what Jesus said,

'For with God nothing is impossible,' (Luke 1: 37)

The principle of healing is to know that the Presence is present within you, and then you fulfil the law of silent healing. You should clearly understand that the Presence is love, wisdom, compassion, understanding and healing. Your thoughts should reflect the attributes of the Presence. Love should be the dominant thought in your mind, and if you require a reason for the acceptance of love, here it is. Love is the supreme spiritual law. It is the essence of all existence and the most dynamic force in the universe. The Bible tells us that God is love and love is God. The mind that is dominated by love is a mind dominated by God. The mind dominated by God is a healthy mind. The mind that is made healthy by God will produce a body bristling with vigour and health.

Now let's examine the best technique for putting into effect the 'Christ healing,' You have been told that periods of quiet contemplation and realisation are necessary to allow your consciousness to realise the Divine Presence of God as the Christ in you. Set aside two periods of 15 minutes duration per day, for the healing technique. Try, if possible to do, the healing process at the same times each day. Healing can only take place when the mortal senses have been silenced and the consciousness is turned towards the kingdom of heaven within. The Bible—Old Testament—gives this wonderful message, *'Be still and know that I am God,'* To be *'still'* means to still the mind. He who has control of his mind has control over everything else. The second important part is *'I am God,'* God appeared to Moses as a tongue or flame of fire and then God gave His holy name to Moses, *'I am who am; God is called "I am",'*

Now when your mortal senses indicate pain, disease or any negative condition, you must become aware that the Spirit of Almighty God as the Christ resides in you. Call into manifestation this power and authority of the Christ by the word of power and authority 'I am,' The name of God is the word of power and you now know that the name of God is 'I am,' You can say with total authority 'I am the life,' I live, because God's Life lives in me. Life is God and God is life. Paul has told us that we move, live and have our being in God.

As previously stated, awareness of the Presence fulfils the law of healing. But it must be a keen awareness. And the awareness can only really be true awareness when the mind is still. In the sanctuary of your heart, rest in the knowledge that the Christ of God is present. Know that the Presence is the healing power of the universe. In the sanctuary of your heart God is ever waiting on your recognition. And in your heart when full of love, comes healing, peace, joy and happiness such as the world can never give. The 'Presence', when fully realised, will permeate every cell in your body, correcting, harmonising and perfecting.

Go somewhere, where you will not be disturbed, a quiet place. Sit erect, hold your spine and neck straight, and plant your feet on the floor, rest your hands on your thighs. Next, offer the following prayer to the Christ within. *"It is you, my beloved Father, who ever remains within me; you are doing the work, for which I lovingly thank you."* Now this prayer must be said with love and devotion, make every word live. Now say, *"Father, thy kingdom come,"* and you should immediately adopt the attitude of expecting a spiritual revelation while engaged in meditation.

Now watch the breath of life entering and leaving the body. Remember it's not the body that breathes, but the Christ. As you breathe in mentally offer love to the Presence within and on breathing out offer love to every being in the Universe. Repeat this breathing exercise six or more times. You should, when exhaling not alone, offer love; you could, when breathing out, offer healing and peace. So, on every inhaling of breath you mentally say love to the Presence. When exhaling for the first time offer love to all of God's children; on the second exhalation offer to all healing; on the third exhalation offer peace. Now you know that it is the Christ who is breathing in you. Imagine Christ situated behind your physical heart in the middle of your chest. And as the Christ breathes, he breathes in through the outer flesh. Imagine the breath entering the flesh through every pore into the Christ Presence. As you exhale imagine the breath entering and remaining in every cell of the body. When you breathe through the nostrils unaware of who is doing the breathing you take into the lungs a mixture, oxygen, hydrogen, nitrogen and other gases that compose air, which is vitally important, for without it life could not be sustained in the body. However, there is something else in the atmosphere; in fact, it exists throughout the Universe. It is the Spiritual Substance out of which everything has been created. The Spiritual Substance is everywhere. It is intelligence and the highest form of energy that sustains the Universe and everything existing. Without this intelligence and this energy, the planets would be without guidance and the Universe would collapse in chaos. When you are aware that it is the Christ who breathes through the outer flesh in the manner already explained, this intelligent energy is breathed into the body and distributed to every cell, which in turn is revitalised.

When you have finished the first breathing exercise and your breaths should be of normal duration, no forced effort of any type should be attempted. Continue with the breathing exercise. As you breathe in mentally, say, *"I am,"* and as you breathe out mentally say *"the life."* Continue with meditation exercise for ten minutes.

It would be of tremendous help if you could be constantly aware of the Presence at all times. Were you to do this, then you would reach a point where you could do the things Jesus did. He gave us the explanation for his great deeds when he said, "It is not I but the Father who ever remains in me (the Presence) He does the work."

During the course of every day, repeat this statement of truth, *"I am the life; I know myself to be the life, and in my knowing I become the life."* Repeat this as many times as opportunity permits during the day, every day. You can if you wish abbreviate it to *"I am the life."* You could include the following statement of truth, *"Almighty God you and I are one."* Dramatically short and dramatically true. God himself created you out of his perfect spiritual substance in his image and likeness. Perfection was meant to be your natural condition. Jesus has advised us, "Be ye perfect as your Father which is in heaven is perfect." The way to perfection is to constantly be aware of the Presence of the God within you as the Christ. There is no other way; there never was, nor will there ever be. If you want to be free from all pain, mental, emotional and physical; if you want to be free from fear, anger, resentment and all other forms of negativity, you must accept the truth of your oneness with God. There can be no other source of your being. You live because God's Life lives in you. God is the Life in you, Life is God in you; it's of critical importance that you accept the proposition that you and God are one and act accordingly.

You and the Father are one. Take hold of this truth and you shall be free from all that pains and more importantly you will be freed from the need to return to earth. Realise that you are first and foremost Spirit. Call this Spirit into manifestation by recognition and realisation. The method you now know. It is only by the power of your consciousness that you can bring forth the Christ consciousness within you. Awareness of the Christ Consciousness is healing of mind and body.

Welcome to the experience. Everyone has the power to heal; you only have to accept you have the ability to heal and know how to make contact with the healing power. This healing power is within each and every one of us and freely available for all to use at any time. The technique is very simple. There is little to learn but much to understand. Mastery over disease can only be achieved when you accept that disease is not of God. If you are in ill health and you wish, hope and pray for a cure, nothing happens except your health gets worse. What is happening is this: your belief in disease is stronger than your belief in a cure. So, you continue to suffer. When your conviction of healing becomes stronger than your belief in disease, you will be healed. It's as simple as that. In the Bible we read in Job, *'What I feared has come upon me,'* Fear is the strongest emotion in man. If you fear you won't be healed then you condemn yourself, but don't despair, you only have to reorient your thinking. In Romans chapter 12 verse 2 we read,

'Be ye transformed by the reviewing of your mind,'

Jesus has told us, "The kingdom of heaven is within you." You will notice the last word in the quotation is 'you,' Jesus also said, "Seek ye first the kingdom of heaven, and its right use and everything else shall be added unto you." Notice again the last word in this remarkable piece of advice and promise. So we clearly see that, we must seek within ourselves for the solutions to all our problems. All that happens to us in the outer world influences the subjective mind. Our emotional reactions are invariably negative; consequently, the objective or subconscious mind is fed a diet of anxiety, fear, hate and all other forms of mental poisoning. Is it any wonder then that our bodies become diseased? There cannot be an effect without a cause; a diseased mind is the cause of a diseased body. What you require of yourself is the acceptance that you have been the cause of the condition you now find yourself in. Also, that you can with the help of Almighty God put things right again. You need to reorient your mind from being the tyrant that rules over you with dictatorial authority.

Your mind is meant to be your servant, and it will be if given intelligent direction; unfortunately, all too many allow their mind to be their ruler. We should seek for the highest form of inspiration, encouragement and hope. Where can be found that which is required to regain health, peace, joy and happiness? Let's turn our attention to God within. Scripture tells in Isaiah 14: 31, *'For I the Eternal your God holds you by the right hand whispering Fear not, I shall help you,'* The meaning of this text is crystal clear, however certain aspects have to be emphasised. For God to take hold of your right hand you must get very close to Him. And God will whisper, *"Fear not."* You must listen very carefully for this whisper. Yes, if you prepare yourself, an inner voice will be heard and its message you already know. *"Fear not I will help you."* Note again the last word in Gods promise; yes, God makes this remarkable promise to you.

In Jeremiah 30:17 we are told, *'I will restore health unto you and I will heal thee of thy wounds says, the Lord,'*

The truth is that God, as the Christ in you will heal any condition if you are prepared to embrace the loving presence of God within you. There are many wonderful promises contained in sacred literature particularly in Psalms. The book of Psalms is the hymnbook of the Bible and we can profitably examine at least one of them for encouragement and inspiration.

There are 150 Psalms in the Christian Bible ranging from songs of praise to tales of woe and lamentation. For those in any type of difficulty be it of health, domestic, financial, or anything else, the promise of the 91st Psalm is a divine guarantee of help and protection. Its meaning is crystal clear and requires no explanation. Its importance is, however, overlooked, not properly understood. It's full of spiritual advice and more importantly it gives cast iron guarantees of protection. You will come under the protection of God himself. If you are in crisis take encouragement from its promise, *'I will rescue him,'* This is God's promise to you. It matters not what your problems are, be it health, emotional or physical. No matter what ails you there is no problem that God can't solve. There are of course certain conditions and obligations on your part. There is one fundamental requirement, you must dwell in the shelter of the most high. You must get close to God; you must be prepared to conscientiously and consciously be at one with God. The best method, indeed the only one, is to become aware of God resident within you. Paul says, "We live, move and have our being in Him." You and God are one. It was He who created you in his image and likeness. Jesus understood this truth when he said, "I and the father are one." The truth is the truth for each and every one of us. The truth belongs to everyone who has ever lived. It belongs to you and me. When we limit the truth we limit ourselves and cause the problems we complain of. It can be truly said that those who don't aspire to the truth have missed the whole objective and inner meaning of Life. We come to the truth through the diligent recognition and continual realisation of the Presence of God working in and through each one of us.

Let's return to the 91st Psalm and try to understand what message it has for us and what, if any benefits are gained from acceptance of its tidings. The first sentence contains a remarkable promise, *'He who dwells in the shelter of the most high will rest in the shadow of the almighty,'*

Let's examine this extraordinary statement in more detail, *'He who dwells,'* Dwells means a place of residence, a place or accommodation where you choose to live. Somewhere you have decided to settle, a place where you wish to remain. *'In the shelter of the most high,'* Shelter means a covering, something to protect you. It can mean a harbour, a place of safety from the troubled waters of a turbulent life. The most high is God himself. God is all there is. Everything exists in the Universal Mind of God and nothing can exist outside of God. God is the life in you and me; there is no life outside of God. If you dwell (conscious awareness) in the shelter of the *'most high'* (God). You will find meaning, tranquillity, peace of mind and perfect repose, if you rest in the shadow of the Almighty. To be in the shadow means to get close and there you will find rest from all your cares. All your burdens will be lifted from you and all grief will end. What a fantastic promise. You need only dwell in the shelter of the most high.

'I will say of the Lord; He is my refuge and my fortress, my God in whom I trust,' This is a statement of faith on your part. You must believe it with all your heart, and mind, and with all your strength that God is your refuge, your fortress, and that you have complete trust in him. The law is 'unless you believe,' If there is not total belief, absolute certainty, then you will find no refuge in God. A refuge is a place where you find protection, help or relief. Make God your fortress and you will find yourself in a fortified and sanctified place, a blessed abode. To gain entry to this paradise you must have a strong faith. 'Faith is a continuous constructive thought,'

'Surely He will save you from the fowler's snare and from the deadly pestilence.' Here is a cast iron guarantee of direct divine intervention, an assurance of help by God who will save you from the fowler's snare. A fowler is a person who hunts and kills birds. A snare is a device such as a noose used as a trap to ensnare and kill. You will be saved from all types of enemies, even those whose intention would be to kill you. You will also be saved from the *'deadly pestilence,'* Deadly means the highest form of danger, destructive and lethal, all that is venomous and fatal. God will save you. Pestilence means disease, an epidemic, a plague and a deadly visitation. You need have no fear for God has promised to save you.

'He will cover you with his feathers and under his wing you will find refuge. His faithfulness be your shield and rampart.'

'He will cover you,' Cover in this context means to protect, to shield you, to allow no harm near you. If God be your protector you will enjoy complete safety; no one and nothing can harm you. While God is above the greatest conception of mind intelligence, if you are prepared to shelter under his wing you are assured of his personal involvement in your life.

'His faithfulness will be your shield and rampart,'

You can be certain that the Divine shield of God will protect you from all blows and missiles. God's shield means his love. His love is the only energy that sustains all things and perfection is the aim and objective of love. When genuine love exists nothing will go wrong, no pain mental, emotional or physical, because unconditional love is complete in itself. And God's rampart is his commitment to you and he will fulfil His obligation to you in every way. Man-made ramparts have been breached many times by determined attackers and many lives have persisted in the false belief and hope that man-made defences could offer security. How foolish.

'You will not fear the terrors of the night, nor the arrow that flies by day nor the pestilence that stalks in the darkness, nor the plague that destroys at midday.'

If you decide to reside in the presence of God, he will banish all your fears and all that would cause any type of apprehension. If you fear nothing, this makes you as powerful as the person who is feared by everyone. Fear is always propelling us towards a painful and an uncertain future and our future must of necessity be as uncertain and fear ridden as our past. The only way, not one of the better ways, to escape fear and uncertainty is to move closer to Him, the only One capable of banishing all fear and uncertainty. Imagine life in which fear and uncertainty have been completely eradicated. It sounds too good to be true, almost too much to be hoped for. Yet we have the Divine promise if God is at the centre of every consideration. Divine help is always available. God can't possibly be at the centre of our life if hate, fear and malice dominates the mind. It must be stressed that we must not fear God. God should be the object of our love and veneration. You have within your power to do what pleases him and by so doing peace, harmony and contentment will be yours. You need not fear the pestilence that stalks in the darkness, or the plague that destroys at midday. You will be protected night and day from pestilence and the plague. Pestilence means disease, epidemic, deadly visitation. Plague means an affliction, an epidemic of disease and does include infection. Yet you need not fear for your health because God himself will protect you. You need have no anxiety, no dread. The promise is you will not fear the terror of the night. Terror means to be obsessed by fear and fear is the parent of folly and stupidity. No person can be free or happy if fear is not totally banished and finished with. If fear and all the other problems in our lives are to be overcome, we must become united with God. Love is the union between God and man and is the way of God and His way is the only way. But love must be the finished product; it must be total, complete and unconditional.

'A thousand may fall at your side, ten thousand at your right hand, but it will not come near you. You will only observe with your eyes and see the punishment of the wicked.'

This has to be the most remarkable of all. You are guaranteed safety from fear, the terror of the night, this means spiritual darkness. Spiritual blindness is a condition worse than physical blindness. All of the crimes perpetrated throughout history, all that is evil, vile and reprehensible has happened because of spiritual blindness or active ignorance. If we had a clear spiritual understanding of who and what we are and our spiritual relationship to each other then we would not rush into acts of violence, murder, child abuse or any act of folly or stupidity. God has created everyone in His image and likeness and when we say the first two words of the Lord's Prayer, *"Our Father,"* we proclaim one God and one family of God. We are all spiritual brothers and sisters. If this spiritual reality was clearly understood and accepted the world would change from what it now is—a place of hate, fear, violence and madness—to a world of peace, harmony, love and consideration for all irrespective of gender, colour, creed or class.

Most intelligent individuals would choose to live in a world dominated by love, peace and harmony. You may believe it's impossible to change the world to make it a place of joy and tranquillity—maybe so—but by changing yourself, by becoming a loving, caring and considerate person, really loving, really caring, really being considerate of others, you help in the most practical manner to make this blood-stained planet better, not only for yourself but everyone as well. Yes, *'A thousand may fall at your side, ten thousand at your right hand,'* Yet God will be your proctor. Your awareness of God's Presence within you is your guarantee that no harm will come to you. It may come near but never touch you. You will see with your eyes the punishment of the wicked; you are safe in this life and in the next life also.

'If you make the most high your dwelling—even the Lord who is my refuge—then no harm will befall you no disaster will come near your tent,'

In almost every sentence you are reminded of God's divine promise of protection against all foes, all perverse conditions and all unfavourable circumstances. But you must make God your dwelling place. Jesus was able to do the wonderful things he did because he dwelt in God. "I and the Father are one. It is the father who ever remains in me. He does the work." Jesus was constantly, continuously aware. You must become aware of God's Presence, not in churches made by human hand, but in every cell of your body. God lives in you and you live in Him. If you accept this truth in your heart and mind your life will change dramatically. No harm will befall you, no disaster will come near your tent. Tent in this context means your life.

'For he will command his angels concerning you, to guard you in all your ways; they will lift you up hands so that you will not strike your foot against a stone.'

Jesus once said, "I have only to ask and legions will be sent to help me." Jesus was extremely close to the Father. Jesus also said, "I and the Father are one." He dwelt in God and knew because of this awareness of unity with the Father that God would send his angels to help. Turn completely to God and give yourself totally to Him and from the Divine Life of God and you will be healed. God has promised to send his angels to protect you in all your ways. What a wonderful promise made by God himself to you personally. You only have to believe and it will be done.

Jesus said, "It's done unto you according to your faith."

God's angels will lift you upon their hands. The promise is that God himself will command His angels to care and protect you. Your foot—meaning you— will not strike against a stone. Stone means adverse circumstances. If and when you get close to God, His angels will be at your side night and day to guard and protect you in all your ways, a truly wonderful promise.

'You will tread upon the lion and cobra; you will trample the great lion and the serpent.'

This passage simply means you will be triumphant over all adversity. Not only will you tread—be triumphant—upon the lion, but you will trample. *The great lion,* meaning you will triumph over your greatest adversity. 'I will rescue him; I will protect him, for he acknowledges my name. He will call upon me and I will answer him. I will be with him in trouble; I will deliver him and honour him. With long life will I satisfy him and show him my salvation.' Here you have in stark and unmistakable language the promise of God to rescue you, to protect you, to answer you, to deliver you, to honour you, to satisfy you and most important of all to grant you salvation. However, you must get close to God. In truth you are very close already but you must become aware of this togetherness.

Love is the golden link between God and man, the crowning glory of spiritual wisdom and intelligence. You need to make unconditional love the dominant factor in your life. When you allow love to become dominant in your life, you will be divinely guided by God himself to peace, wisdom and healing. Every disease is curable, but not every patient. You must have faith and believe with all your heart, mind and soul that God will heal you and He will. Jesus has told us, "As thou hast believed, so be it done unto you." And, *'For with God nothing is impossible.'* (Luke 1: 37)

'Then shall the light break forth as the morning and thy health shall spring forth speedily.' (Isaiah 58: 8)

'I will restore health unto thee, and I will heal thee of thy wounds saith the Lord.' (Jeremiah 30: 17)

I have quoted these promises from the scripture to encourage your faith in God's ability to heal you. For many patients the first healing has to be of doubt, despair or disbelief. You must cleanse your mind of all negative thoughts. Keep the consciousness of the Father before you at all times. With Him in your heart you cannot fail. Know that He is ever seeking to make you a channel of his love and wisdom. God's wish for you is that you may become a perfect instrument of love, wisdom and intelligence.

Jesus asks you, "Be ye perfect as your Father in heaven which is perfect."

If your life is not dominated by love, then your life is not the blessed experience it could be, should be and was meant to be. You now know the secret of Eternal Life. Love totally, love completely and love unconditionally. It is love that seeks, that asks, that knocks, that finds and is true to what it discovers, which is the truth that God and man are one. God is Love, Love is God; to live in love is to live in God. To live in God is the end of all troubles and tribulations. If God is Love then love has to be the greatest healing power in the universe and is freely at your disposal. Should you decide to live in love, not only will you help yourself, but you will be of spiritual benefit to all of humanity.

All great thinkers, saints and mystics including Jesus believed love to be the core of individual and world reconstruction. It certainly is the link or bond between God and mankind. Love is the only way to keep the heart pure and the body strong and healthy. According to all of the sacred books including the Christian Bible God is proclaimed as the God of Love.

The New Testament informs us and I quote: *'The fruits of the spirit are love, joy, and peace,'* We all want to be loved; to experience the bliss of joy; to know that peace which surpasses all understanding. Love has the power and authority to overcome all conditions, all circumstances. God is love. Love is God; then love has to be the greatest power in the universe. And love can and will heal any person who is prepared to love all irrespective of class, colour, gender or creed. For love to become effective as a healing agency it has to be unconditional.

It has been wisely said that human thing must first be known to be loved, but spiritual things have to be loved to be known. You should know that God created you to be a vehicle for the expression of His love. And if you are expressing love for God and all his children then you are fulfilling your spiritual mission in life. For the expression of love is the true science of life. Love is the golden key to God's inexhaustible treasure house. Any and everything you desire can be yours but you must live in love, not in part. Your love must be a finished product. It has to be total, unconditional and complete without reservation. In love all mysteries and all of life's secrets will be revealed to you. All your faults all errors are the want of love. Love being infallible bestows infallibility unto those who know how to love.

The Bible has this wonderful promise concerning love, *'The eye has not seen, the ear has not heard, the heart of man has not conceived the things that God has prepared for them that love Him,'* If you want to elevate your life, to affect the quality of your existence you have to live the life of love. Healing, you see, is of soul. To understand the part that love can play in our lives is to see clearly and is poetry, prophecy and spirituality all in one. We can't conceive the things that God has prepared for us if we love. Yes, the table is already set; everything is in place and the good news is, you are invited. Some find it hard to love, difficult it may be, impossible it is not.

Before you can love properly you must first forgive all those who have wronged you. Your mind has to be free of hate, fear, anger and all resentment. In fact, you must rid the mind of all negative thinking. You should know that a diseased mind produces a diseased body. One is directly related to the other. When the mind is allowed to operate in its negative mode it produces the physical conditions we suffer from. The Bible tells us: 'As a man thinkest in his heart that he is,' Learn this truth, that mind and body affect each other.

Were you to live in love of God and all his children you would soon acquire the wisdom and power to accomplish all things. With your heart full of love your soul would rejoice, your mind would be at peace and your body perfectly healthy. Love has power and authority to draw a veil over all folly, over all wrongdoing. Love will confer this mighty power and authority on you when you live the life of love. In love you will be the conqueror. Nothing can harm you. Your life will be full and free. Your body completely whole without a defect. God's love is constantly flowing into the soul, heart, mind and body of every individual. All you have to do is receive and give expression to this marvellous gift of Divine Love, and all you could hope, or wish for will be yours. Do everything for the love of God and you have learnt the secret of all power in heaven and on earth. And if you have the wisdom and intelligence to act on this advice you will, most assuredly, experience the beneficial effects in all aspects of your life. Love, you see, is the power. All may use the wise and the intelligent, so also the foolish and the weak.

Love, when combined with faith is the means for ending all problems, be they medical, mental or spiritual. God has made promise after promise to you of His continuing concern and His willingness to help you. In Isaiah chapter 41 verse 10, God says, *'For I the Lord thy God will hold thy right hand saying unto thee fear not I will help you'*, a remarkable promise made by God to you personally; yes, God had you in mind when this promise was made.

The Bible tells us, *'For with God all things are possible'*, and in Jeremiah chapter 30 verse 17, God again repeats his promise of help, *'I will restore health unto thee, and I will heal thee of thy wounds, saith the Lord,'* And yet again another wonderful promise contained in Isaiah chapter 58 verse 8, *'Then shall thy light break forth as the morning and thy health shall spring forth speedily,'*

Could you ask for anything more definite, more encouraging than this? Notice that before healing your light must break forth; light in this context means spiritual understanding. Spiritual understanding could take years of study. However, the Bible tells us, 'Love surpasses all understanding', Love, then, is the fast track to success. Love is the means of ensuring that your health shall spring forth speedily. But your love must be pure, positive and unconditional.

Seek to express the Divine love that dwells in the silence of your soul. In silent communion with God become consciously aware of God's presence within you. His presence is a loving presence and as you become aware of this loving presence, send thoughts of love to all on earth and in the universe. Love all, even those who hate and despise you. Don't let hate blind you to all that you may achieve, to all that you may become. The power that is of God and is God dwells in the heart of those who love Him. Make love the dominant factor in your life and God Himself will be your constant companion. God will express Himself in you and through you. You will become a channel for all types of healing; you will be of benefit to all who come into contact with you. With the love of God in your heart and consciousness you will become a means of influencing others to an understanding of God and His infinite love for all humanity.

Gaze upon the golden fountain of love and you will be complete in soul, mind and body. Give loving thanks to the Father that He has made these things known unto you. Only through love can you partake of the feast that God has prepared for you. Love is beauty, the infinite law of perfection. Nothing in this world or in the whole of creation is of more importance than that you should live in love. Not only will it affect the quality of your life here on earth, but will determine where and how you spend the rest of eternity.

It is of supreme importance that you fully understand and by understanding accept that you have been created by the God of love and love is the real you. And when you become what God intended you to be—the complete human being—you will know yourself to be a radiant loving expression of God himself.

Listen to what Paul has to say about love in his letter to the Corinthians, 1, chapter 1, verse 13,

'And now I will show you the most excellent way. If I speak in the tongues of men and of angels, but have not love, I am only a resounding gong or a clanging cymbal. If I have the gift of prophecy and can fathom all mysteries and all knowledge and if I have a faith that can move mountains, but have not love, I am

nothing. If I give all that I possess to the poor and surrender my body to the flames, but have not love. I gain nothing. Love is patient love is kind; it does not envy, it does not boast, it is not proud. It is not rude, it is not self- seeking, it is not easily angered, and it keeps no record of wrongs. Love does not delight in evil, but rejoices with the truth. It always protects, always trusts, always hopes, and always perseveres. Love never fails. But where there are prophecies they will cease; where there are tongues they will be stilled; where there is knowledge it will pass away. For we know in parts and we prophecy in part, but when perfection comes, the imperfect disappears. When I was a child, I talked like a child; I thought like a child, I reasoned like a child. When I became a man I put childish ways behind me. Now we see but a poor reflection; then we shall see face to face. Now I know in part; then I shall know fully, even as I am fully known. And now these three remain; faith, hope and love. But the greatest of these is love,'

Become consciously aware of the loving presence of God within you. Give two periods of silent reflection in God's presence within. Don't think about God. God is greater than human thought. Still your mind and use your awareness freed from thought. The Old Testament has this tremendous advice, *'Be still and know that I am God,'* This short piece of advice should be clearly understood. To be still means to still the mind or more directly to put a stop to thought. Only with the mind at peace have you created the necessary conditions for God to manifest within you.

The New Testament has this wonderful advice, *'Study to be quiet,'* The universe will reveal all her secrets to the mind that is still. Still the mind and be consciously aware of the presence of God. That is complete healing for mind, spirit, heart and body. You now know that God's Presence is a loving Presence. This healing technique is infallible and can be practised by anyone. Practice love, that your love may be perfect. When this happens, you will be without a defect. You will enter heaven while in your present body. You will know heaven is not a place to be entered, but a spiritual reality to be experienced.

God tells us in the Bible, *'Before they call I will answer and while they are speaking I will hear,'* If you listen carefully you will understand what is being said. The message is crystal clear. God is saying, if you ask, He will answer. Prayer and the solution are one. Don't pray in the hope of a solution; know that your prayer is answered and it will be.

Chapter 8

Reincarnation

The Christian Churches—for reasons that are not entirely clear—no longer teach the doctrine of reincarnation. It is, therefore, hardly surprising that the average Christian has problems accepting a philosophy long abandoned by institutionalised Christianity. You can be sure that it's God's wish that mankind should have a clear knowledge and understanding of his Divine plan for all of creation. God would have us understand his Laws by which creation is governed, that we, his children, may work in harmony with them to overcome all of our human faults and failings.

Life cannot be properly understood until and unless we accept not only the doctrine of reincarnation but karma also. Reincarnation is a spiritual devise that provides humanity with the wonderful repeat opportunities to redress any and all karmic debt incurred during any lifetimes spent on earth. The majority of Christians believe that karma and reincarnation are exclusively eastern philosophies and make a great mistake in believing that somehow, it's alien to western culture and Christianity. If the Christian Bible is read with some diligence there can be found many references to reincarnation and if we are ever to gain a complete understanding of life and its spiritual implications the twin doctrines of karma and reincarnation must be studied, and the lessons learned must be applied to life. The inequalities of life that are endured by the poor and dispossessed and the advantages enjoyed by the rich and powerful can only be explained by Karma.

Jesus explaining karma said, "As you sow so shall you reap." All that happens in our lives, good or bad is the result of karma. Many westerners are unfamiliar with the law of karma. The Oxford Dictionary defines Karma as being, *'The sum of a person's actions in previous states of existence, viewed as deciding his or her fate in future existences,'*

175

Karma is the law of cause and effect. Jesus said, "Even a cup of water given in my name shall not go unrewarded." Jesus was explaining the universal law of Karma. Reincarnation and Karma is, if accepted, the means of explaining many of the difficulties and tribulations experienced in earthly life. The doctrine of what you sow you reap as explained by Jesus is a very beautiful just and natural law. Karma is a two-edged sword, it demands compensation for all wrongdoing, conversely it will reward all good that is done by any individual. Since the immutable law of Karma is universally just, then justice is assured for each and every one.

Absolutely no one can hope to escape the consequences of their thoughts, words or deeds. Pain and frustration are the inevitable consequence to be endured if life is lived in ignorance. To be free from all pains we must end all doubt and ignorance concerning the reasons for our existence in and out of the human body. When physical death occurs, we leave our bodies and we pass into another dimension. You will still be alive; you will be the same person, the difference being that you leave your human body of matter at physical death, but you still exist as spiritual entity in a spiritual body. Ignorance and wisdom still exist until you can finally understand the truth of your spiritual existence.

You are a spiritual soul presently housed in a physical garment of gross matter called a human body; your earthly existence is only part of God's plan for you and your duty is to become fully aware of God's complete plan. Its only by understanding the Creator's Master Plan that we can hope or expect to successfully fulfil our spiritual obligations. God in his goodness has bequeathed all his children, all of his attributes, which include intelligence and wisdom that all may use these God-given gifts in seeking to comprehend our part in creation. Understand clearly that absolutely nothing in the whole of creation is left to chance or blind fate. Jesus advised us, "Seek and you shall find." Take encouragement from the wonderful promise. It is much more than a promise; it is a guarantee of success for any sincere seeker after truth. How reassuring to know that all genuine seekers will in time be led to all spiritual knowledge and the resulting freedom. God governs his creation by means of his spiritual laws and we his children are subject to these laws. Reason demands from us that we comprehend the law and what precisely are the consequences to us of our ignorant or wilful violation of the law. And what are the advantages to us if we live in harmony with the law. If we are to live as God intended then we had better discover the reasons for our existence and the laws governing all of us. Yes, we can continue to live in ignorance; life in human form can continue without a clear understanding of the spiritual science of life and how the law affects our daily lives. However, the life of ignorance and neglect must of necessity be a totally unsatisfactory existence lacking any real or lasting satisfaction.

If we are ever to possess life to the full, we must establish the truth for our existence. What we do not clearly understand we can never possess.

The story of creation and humanities' part in it has already been stated. Each of us is in truth is a spiritual being—a living soul housed in a physical body. Bodies are composed of matter and subject to the laws governing matter. The soul is spiritual, meaning immortal, timeless and ageless. The human body, composed out of the dust of the earth, is constantly changing and with time grows old and weak and when the time comes for the soul to leave the body, what is called death takes place. Soul with its spiritual consciousness continues in existence throughout eternity. The soul personality is the real personality and this is the truth that must be grasped if we as individuals are to know and understand our place in the cosmic scheme. Mary, the mother of Jesus, clearly understood the supreme importance of the soul for she made this wonderful statement: "My soul does magnify the Lord." Awareness of the soul's presence and the willingness to be guided by it is the chief means of understanding God.

The infinite consciousness of God resides in the soul and the soul's understanding of all things spiritual must therefore, be complete. The soul, prior to being united with the human personality would have no experience of earthy existence or human behaviour. Human desires and emotions, be they of joy or woe, would be unknown to the soul before union with the human personality. The reason for the soul's earthly experiences is to gain knowledge of, and triumph over all negative emotions and deeds. Soul brings to human existence spiritual consciousness, divine wisdom and cosmic intelligence. Your soul is the means of attaining spiritual power and authority because the soul being of the spiritual world is in constant communication with all spiritual forces. The power of the soul is the power of God existing in the consciousness of man and this power can be communicated to the outer man, but only when the outer becomes as the inner.

Karma and reincarnation are inextricably linked; reincarnation is made necessary because of Karma. The Christian Bible in a statement in the Old Testament reads: *'He who spills the blood of man, shall have his blood by man spilled,'* Now we all know that there are thousands of murders every year that are never solved. Many killers are never detected and seemingly escape any form of punishment. While it's true some murders never face any type of human censure, they cannot hope to escape cosmic retribution. The Bible statement of the Old Testament concerning murder will be fulfilled. Murderers will reincarnate on earth to be murdered, cosmic justice will triumph, and of that there can be no doubt. There is no real escape from the consequences of our deeds; karma will demand that our sins be paid for. Karma, when wisely understood can become a powerful motivator directing our energies towards wise and intelligent decisions. Mankind would do well to learn that each of us carries our individual fate with us every step through life. The most horrendous physical Karma is created by mass murder and those responsible will at some time be the victim of murder, most likely in a future incarnation.

Not only is there physical Karma but mental Karma also, and the worst type of mental Karma is generated by hate. Many of the worst diseases are the result of intense hatred over many incarnations. Our mental tendencies are the result of past life's negative thought patterns. The person you now are, is the result from the quality of past lives and how you behaved towards other persons. You are now the result of your past and present thoughts and deeds. Previous thoughts and deeds have brought you the quality of life you are now experiencing; your present experiences, good or bad, are due exclusively to the quality of your previous lives spent on earth. The acceptance of the doctrine of karma can be a potent instrument in shaping our future destiny. The past has gone, but we continue either to pay the cost for the transgression of the past. Or if our past lives were lived in love, wisdom and intelligence, we are reaping a rich harvest of peace and contentment.

In God alone and only in him can be found liberation from all our troubles and tribulations. A constant awareness of His presence within you is the only means of ending the cycle of reincarnation. Awareness of your oneness with Him, your creator, will lead you to spiritual love. And love is the golden key that will open Heaven's gates. Let's return to the Bible for further evidence of the doctrines of Karma and reincarnation.

In John Gen, verse 2, we read, *'And he went along, he saw a man blind from birth. His disciples ask him. Rabbi, who has sinned that this man or his parents that he was born blind? Had the man, in question "sinned" to be born blind then the sins would have had to be committed in a previous life,'*

178

In this story of the blind man we have confirmation of Karma, for the man's blindness could only have been the consequences of having *'sinned',* The purpose of asking Jesus the possible reasons for the man's blindness was for the sake of clarification. It is logical to assume that Jesus and his disciples had had a discussion on karma and reincarnation.

Again, in the New Testament we find more evidence in the belief of reincarnation. In Mark, 9th chapter, verses 10 – 13, *'And they (disciples) asked, why do the teachers of the law say that Elijah must come first?'* Jesus replied, *'To be sure Elijah does come first, and restore all things. Why then is it written that the Son of Man must suffer much and be rejected? But I tell you Elijah has come and they have done to him everything they wished, just as it is written about him,'* Here you have it from the mouth of Jesus that Elijah had, in fact returned to earth. Elijah had reincarnated as John the Baptist. You might argue that as Elijah was a prophet of God, he was granted a special dispensation to return to earth. The law of reincarnation is a universal law and does not change in any circumstances. Love, wisdom, intelligence and loving deeds will change karmic debt to compensation. The only effective means of understanding fully the joys of love, wisdom and intelligence is to live as many lives as are necessary. For only when we finally arrive at human perfection will spiritual deliverance eventually happen? Frustration, emotional and mental pain, misfortune and the hell of greed, fear, anger, is all the result of karmic debts incurred by past deeds.

Knowledge and the wisdom to use new knowledge wisely are the means of overcoming ignorance. The soul with its spiritual understanding is fully aware of its divine origin and longs for a permanent return to its spiritual home; however, this cannot happen until the soul personality triumphs. The ever-present 'longing' of the soul can be the means of spiritual inspiration and deliverance from all human weakness. Emerson, that wise and thoughtful American, was right when he suggested that every wrong has a remedy and that satisfaction exists for every soul. Only in the sanctuary of your soul can you hope to experience the truth and the spiritual reality that you are the divine child of God. As you understand the soul's attributes better, your true spiritual identity will manifest more and more, until that blessed day when you recognise your true spiritual identity. The soul is always aware of its origins and while it is housed in the human body it longs for a reunion with God. This longing of the soul for a return to God can be of great benefit to those seeking inspiration. The soul in each and every one of us is the divine channel that leads directly to God.

Your soul is the repository of all understanding, wisdom and knowledge. All that you seek, all that you could wish for is contained within your immortal soul. When you accept your soul's presence within you and when you clearly identify the soul's spiritual attributes you have taken a giant step towards spiritual redemption. Only by the means of the soul can we come close to God. And only in God can be found the love, peace and happiness all are seeking. Don't seek in the outer world for spiritual guidance. Hold communion with your divine immortal soul; this is the highest form of wisdom and intelligence. The soul cannot lie or deceive; its purpose is to allow the outer person access to all-spiritual wisdom, knowledge and spiritual intelligence. When the soul triumphs over the inconsistencies of the outer personality the Holy Ghost will descend into the elevated consciousness and spiritual liberation will manifest.

Mankind has become possessed by the acquisition of material possessions, which cannot provide the spiritual security that the intelligent are seeking after. The only prosperity that can bring lasting peace is mental and spiritual prosperity and the soul alone is the provider of what mankind desperately needs. Because soul is resident in everyone, spiritual inspiration is freely available to all that have the wisdom to seek it from within the soul. The greatest obstacle to spiritual growth is ignorance of the soul's attributes and abilities. It is the mortal senses that blind us to our divine potential and keep us spiritual pigmies. Clearly understand that you are first and foremost a spiritual soul; you are not your physical body. Your body is temporary dwelling place for the real you. It is imperative that we as a species find the solution to human folly, limitation and all forms of irrationality, so that we may clearly understand the divine attributes of the soul. There has to be a reason why we experience all of the tribulations of human existence and until we arrive at a satisfactory explanation for our troubles they must continue and we must continue to suffer. Ignorance of who and what we are and of who and what God is, is the cause of all our troubles. If we continue to be unresponsive to the presence of the soul within then we are certain to continue to suffer sorrow, pain and daily frustration. Suffering is of course nature's means of informing us that we are treading the wrong road. Accept the fact that you are dual in nature, that you have a temporary physical dwelling in which is housed the real you, which, is soul.

You are not the human form you see when you look at a mirror. When you allow your intelligence to mirror your soul you will recognise yourself as being spiritual and divinely conceived by God Himself. Your immortal soul is God's consciousness within you, and your soul is the means always available to you—to overcome any problem or difficulty. Because of the presence of your soul you are a spiritual being with divine qualities and abilities. It is the soul that reincarnates and will keep reincarnating until the soul is triumphant over all negativity and ignorance.

There are many conflicting opinions concerning life and the confusion is the result of ignorance and ignorance is the cause of mental and emotional pain. Individuals, at times of distress ask serious questions concerning life and at that moment they genuinely want meaningful answers, but don't have a notion that they are spiritually unprepared to receive that which they seek. To receive that which must be known don't judge anything new by what you already believe. Your consciousness must be used intelligently and with sensitivity. Consciousness means to be aware, so that you may gain in knowledge and understanding of your relationship to God and mankind. You should use your consciousness to gain a clear and comprehensive understanding of the soul which, as you now know, is the real, you. The soul contains all knowledge, wisdom, understanding and truth; all of soul's spiritual attributes are available to us that we may use these wonderful spiritual attributes to arrive at a clear understanding of our divine origins. It takes courage and wisdom to accept the doctrine of reincarnation and karma. Rejection of the laws of karma and reincarnation invalidates neither, and by rejecting them we only retard our spiritual understanding and growth. And by clinging to limited and false beliefs we hinder our spiritual growth. The principles of spiritual laws must be accepted before the law can be made effective in our daily lives.

Our experiences and circumstances can best be explained by the acceptance of Jesus' statement on Karma, "As you sow, ye shall reap." The present experiences you are reaping are the results of what you sowed in previous lives lived on earth. When Jesus healed the sick, he often said, "Go and sin no least a worse thing befall you." If you sin, then you will be subject to the law of karma. Good deeds, loving thoughts, repentance and prayer will eradicate all negative karma. While we have choice over what deeds we engage in, we can never be free of the consequences of our thoughts and actions.

Karma and reincarnation are the most effective means of acquiring wisdom and helping the soul in its quest to establish the kingdom of Heaven in the mind of humanity. The soul is the divine spiritual essence of Almighty God and is responsible for sustaining life in the human body. When fully recognised and realised the soul is the divine channel of God's presence. And when this awareness takes hold of the individual, it leads to true love, perfect harmony and peace profound. When Jesus spoke of The Kingdom of Heaven being within, he was speaking of the presence of God in the soul of every person. Your immortal soul is the only source of mortal happiness. As human life is totally dependent on the presence of the soul, a spiritual life cannot be lived until you charge the soul with the responsibility of taking control while in the human body. Give full recognition to the presence of the soul within you and when the soul responds, as it most assuredly will, all struggle and effort will be at an end. Your immortal soul is the repository of all wisdom, knowledge and intelligence. It knows all that is to be known because of the soul's supreme importance. It is imperative that a clear and comprehensive understanding is mastered of the soul's attributes that we may give to soul it's spiritual due. Souls, as all living entities are subject to the laws of evolution and its experiences in different bodies, are for evolutionary purposes. Each and every soul has divine consciousness and because the soul is incarnated in different bodies it must have individual consciousness, and this individual consciousness produces distinct personalities.

The soul being of God is the eternality spiritual reality; the divine channel of love and peace, and all spiritual knowledge is gained by means of the soul. Soul is closer than hands and feet and is the source of all spiritual understanding and wisdom. To our great cost we have forgotten soul and its spiritual potential; there is no need for any other form of spiritual guidance. The in-dwelling and purified wisdom of your immortal soul will lead you to spiritual freedom. The soul is the repository of all knowledge, and contains all the sought-after solutions to every human problem. The acceptance of the presence of your immortal soul within you is a necessary first step that must be taken on the road to spiritual freedom. When you decide to leave behind your mundane life of pain and misery your soul will inspire you to find the new life. But, you must first get to know your soul and understand its role in the universal scheme of things. When you accept your soul's presence and clearly understand its divine mission and hold communion with it you will be engaged in the highest form of spiritual wisdom. In the sanctuary of your soul, and there alone, will you experience the spiritual dawn of reality. To discover the truth of your immortal existence you must first intimately know your soul. Your soul in its wisdom is ever seeking union with its creator and when you decide to seek union also, nothing can stand in your way. Soul is the key to all understanding in heaven and on earth. The mind and body of man have consciousness and awareness, so also has your soul mind and consciousness. The difference between your outer body mind and consciousness and your soul's consciousness is, that your body consciousness is concerned with the mundane world of matter and form; your soul's consciousness is concerned with matters that are spiritual and divine.

Your soul is continually receiving influences from all spiritual domains and has the ability to understand all that is happening throughout creation. The soul being divine, sees all, hears all, knows all and is the unlimited source of all spiritual knowledge and wisdom. Jesus clearly understood that the divine spiritual essence of God resides in every person and that the soul's personality is immortal and eternal. When Jesus spoke of "the kingdom of heaven within," he was referring to the presence of God in the soul of every person. The acceptance of your soul's presence provides the opportunity, to seek soul guidance and the soul with its divine consciousness, knowledge and understanding is continually available to you. You are the heir to all of God's attributes; all that God has is yours when you place your inner spiritual world first in your order of priorities. When your inner spiritual world is right so shall your outer world be also. Become aware of the presence of God who dwells in your immortal soul. Know that God is alive in you because there is no life outside of the Almighty. Accept the spiritual reality that God and you are one, that the real you is spiritual and divine if you can fully accept the truth of your union with God, then you must become the living reality of truth itself. This can only be experienced by the acceptance that your soul is present, eternal, immortal and divine. You are the soul that has temporary abode in your present body. The material body has been created out of "the dust of the earth" and will after so-called death, return to dust. You are not your body, you are a spiritual soul and will live forever.

Just as there is one God, there is one Soul throughout all of creation. All souls are portions or fragments of the one Universal Soul that is God. There cannot be separate or individual souls. The soul in every person is a constituent unit of the universal soul of God. To explain this further let's examine the concept of space. Space exists everywhere. There is nowhere where space does not exist. You occupy a segment of space and so does every other person on this planet. You have your individual space and so does every other person, yet space remains an area that extends to infinity. Every soul unit is in constant communion with every other soul segment and maintains awareness of the universal soul. The soul in every person has full spiritual power and abilities and will in certain circumstances communicate these to the outer physical being. Embracing love, compassion, tolerance, generosity and understanding is the means required to allow the souls spiritual powers and abilities to manifest in the outer world of form. In genuine love the sincere seeker will, in time, discover nothing is hidden, that all will be revealed. Soul knowledge is freely available to all and is constantly on tap for those who choose to live the life of love. In your spiritual state you are the image and likeness of God; this image and likeness is contained in your soul. Birth and death are but episodes in the eternal life that lives in you. The real you, which is soul, has always existed and will continue in existence throughout eternity. You are spirit and spirit is indestructible, and your soul is the universal spirit of God in you. To become fully alive, to live the life of love, peace and contentment there must first be the recognition and realisation that you are much more than a mere physical being. Your physical existence is finite; in truth, you probably have experienced other physical existences and will go on to future physical experiences in different physical bodies. You are, in truth, a spiritual soul with eternal life.

The problem confronting you is this. You know for certain that you live; consciousness makes you aware of your physical existence. You have an identity composed of different facts. You have a name, a physical body, a mind brimming full of opinions, you have an occupation and you have family. You are continually conscious of your existence in your present physical body; you are subject to the physical reality of human existence. Human reality however, is only a shadow; the only genuine reality belongs to the spiritual realms. In reality God has created you and you are a soul entity resident in your present physical body. However, spiritual reality can only be realised when we love God and all of His children. Divine things must first be loved before they can be truly known. The physical fact that you live is probably painfully obvious. Most lives are destroyed on the emotional rocks of pain, grief, anger, resentment, envy, and general indifference to spiritual matters. Yet with proper awareness it can become so wonderfully different, life can become an experience of joy and bliss. But, you must first observe spiritual reality; you did not come into existence because of a physical act of copulation. You have always existed and will forever remain a living soul. The soul has consciousness and your soul has its own distinct personality. Soul personality is the result of succeeding earthly experiences while in the physical body. Your physical body may be imperfect. It may be deformed, your limbs may be twisted, your mind may be mentally deformed, but your soul is perfect. The soul, which is of God, cannot in any manner be harmed by a human activity. It is not in the power of the flesh to be able to harm or do any type of damage to spirit. The soul progress or mission can and often is retarded or impeded by the unwillingness to accept its presence. The soul is the means that is constantly available to all of us to gain in spiritual stature by means of its inspiration.

Your immortal soul, because of its consciousness of itself, has to have a personality of its own. And the soul like everything else in creation is subject to the law of evolution. It is the soul quest for universal experiences and wisdom is the chief reason for the necessity of reincarnation. The soul has a critical role or function in the creative scheme of God's plan for all of creation. The evolutionary process demands that the soul is continually seeking, to gain, by earthly experience wisdom and understanding. Soul is an inner spiritual essence a divine consciousness and the function of the soul is to gain total influence over all human behaviour and inclinations. To bring mortal mind, with all of its dreadful inclinations under spiritual control, there has to be an awareness of the in-dwelling presence of the soul.

Each soul segment is continually seeking reunion with the universal soul and if allowed, this longing of your soul will guide you towards the ultimate destination of spiritual love and freedom. Direct your mortal consciousness with intelligence towards soul consciousness. This can only be done by the combination of recognition, awareness and realisation. You begin with the acceptance that the soul lives in your mortal body; this acceptance is in fact recognition. Next you must become aware of the soul's presence. Realising that every good or noble thought or deed performed is the prompting of your soul, your soul consciousness will, with your co-operation, influence you to think refined thoughts of understanding and compassion and will encourage you to perform good words and noble deeds. If you work in harmony with your soul at this level of human activity, it's only a matter of time before your soul will reveal spiritual realities. The soul will provide the necessary inspiration and support at all times, but you must make your mind receptive. Cleansing the mind of all negativity can do this. Should you think thoughts of anger or resentment, become aware of the damage you are doing to yourself. When you gain composure over your mind, immediately counter the negativity of your mind by sending thoughts of love, healing and peace to the person or persons whom you thought had angered you. If you allow your mortal consciousness to be guided by soul consciousness the result will be that both consciousnesses will benefit. There will be a perfecting of both. Your understanding of life on earth becomes deeper the more you understand the spiritual attributes of your soul. Our painful tribulations are bitter testimony to the folly of trying to live life without a deep spiritual understanding of our relationship to God. When will mankind learn that all our problems are the direct result of trying to live apart from God? Only when we realise that we possess eternal life and that our earthly task is to become more and more intensely spiritual can our lives become the happy experience of profound love and peace. It's only when the solution is found to the problem of earthly existence can contentment, peace and harmony be experienced. Your soul is the divine essence or energy of God Almighty and this divine energy is the vital life force that sustains all of creation including life in the human body. Life should mean spiritual growth culminating in spiritual reality. Spiritual reality cannot be properly explained. There are no words in any language that can convey the experience. Man has written on this matter, but reality must of necessity be a very personal and private experience.

To know yourself as God knows you, you have to be the greatest human experience possible and this knowing of your true spiritual identity is the reason for your earthly life. When finally this 'knowing' or realising of your true spiritual identity is experienced, your earthly mission has been successfully completed. Now that you have discovered the reason for your existence in human form here on earth do two things, give thanks to God for making this known to you and place your trust in the presence of God who resides in you as the in-dwelling soul. You now have the knowledge to choose wisely between remaining on the path of folly and being prepared to remain the prisoner of chance, or to become the creator of a beautiful life of truth and tranquillity.

It is only when a deep understanding of reincarnation and karma is reached can a satisfactory explanation for life's experiences be found. Our greatest need is to clearly understand the mysteries of life, that we may bring to an end the miseries of life. Reincarnation and karma, when properly understood, will radically change existing attitudes towards death and hell. Death loses its sting when we realise that life is immortal and reincarnation provides further opportunities to gain in knowledge and wisdom, and to repent of our follies, mistakes and sins. God in His wisdom and love has decreed that we, his children, should have every opportunity required in our quest for the glory of perfection.

Christian churches preach a vengeful God and eternal damnation in 'hell-fire' for our sins. And in complete contradiction the same churches preach that our creator is a God of love. Either God is the God of infinite love which means that His love is inexhaustible, total, complete and unconditional; or God is a revengeful deity seeking retributions and reprisals for our wrongdoing. There can be no reconciliation between the notion of the God of infinite love and the God of retribution and vengeance.

The notion of a vengeful God who is prepared to condemn his children—whom He created in His image and likeness—to everlasting torment in 'hell-fire' is too terrible to contemplate. The doctrine of reincarnation provides a more humane explanation of God's will for we, his children. If we get it wrong in this life, God in His goodness, through the doctrine of reincarnation, provides us with a further opportunity for atonement. Reincarnation is the means chosen by God to allow the soul to gain an understanding and awareness of spiritual realities, even if this understanding takes many life times. The soul's personality has to confront every conceivable human condition and situation and come through the experience with the soul's personality enriched by overcoming all adversity. The soul's personality must overcome the world and when the soul personality has reached the state of perfection the need to reincarnate is ended. For the soul to gain the multiple experiences required for the perfection of its personality, it simply cannot be accomplished in the brief period of one earthly lifetime. Every experience, good or bad, moulds the soul's personality and this personality because of its many experiences is evolving and seeking perfection. The purpose of life seems to be that we must come to the spiritual realisation that humanity is the divine expression of almighty God. And this realisation has to be experienced in our human form. This then explains the need for the law of reincarnation. When will the requirements to reincarnate on earth end? The answer is simple to give: when every thought, word and deed is dominated by love, your earthly task will be complete. Love, you have been told, is healing and harmony for the soul and body. An enlightened consciousness will end the necessity for reincarnation and the total acceptance of unconditional love is the only means of acquiring an enlightened consciousness. Jesus has told us that the 'truth' would set us free, and when he made this wonderful statement he was referring to freedom from the need for reincarnation. The Christian churches do not propagate the doctrine of reincarnation, choosing instead to suggest that spiritual souls are provided for physical transient human bodies. This suggestion is classical cart before the horse syndrome. This nonsense is further compounded by the suggestion that the soul has one, and only one, earthly life in which to complete its spiritual quest. At the completion of one earthly life, the soul, we are told, will be dispatched to some part of the universe to wait for a judgement day and if found waiting it is to be punished in hell-fire for all eternity. It is stretching credibility beyond comprehension to suggest that God would take revenge against any soul remembering the divine essence of God. In human terms it would be the equivalent of cutting off the nose to spite the face. This doctrine of divine retribution against the soul is at best deeply flawed and at worst morally primitive.

God calls every person to live the life of love, compassion, wisdom, peace and understanding; the notion of a vengeful God is in total contradiction to all that God represents. God can't demand from humanity love, charity, goodness and other moral values that He does not possess. Our creator possesses all moral values to an infinite degree, and is incapable of the type of punishment suggested by the Christian churches.

Life can be explained in many different ways, theories and theorists abound everywhere. There are too many cooks and the broth gets spoilt. Is it any wonder that confusion reigns supreme and the purpose of life is surrounded at best by mystification, and at worst dreadful ignorance? Clearly understand that life is of God and as God is eternal and universal so the life in each person is also universal and eternal. There are, of course universal principles or laws that govern our existence in and out of human form. These laws of universal principles apply to every individual, yet the laws are impersonal. If you violate the law you will be punished; ignorance of the law does not in any way effect the operation of the law. When you know and understand the law you can work in harmony with the law to make your life the pleasant experience it was meant to be. What trial and tribulation you experience in life is the direct result of violating the law of life. You already know the law of life, "As you sow, so shall you reap." If you want to avoid all the emotional pain associated with human existence you must sow good seeds. Good seeds are good deeds; to become the happy and contented person you would like to be, you must understand the purpose of life. Only when the eternal truth of life is discovered, can life be lived as God intended. When the truth of our existence is realised we graduate, beyond mortal existence, in human form and beyond the law of karma and reincarnation. Every day indeed, every minute of every day, should be spent in a conscious effort at improving our humanity. It is only when we reach human perfection that the soul can reveal its presence in all of its glory. We can only experience life, as it truly should be lived when we become fully aware of the consequences of the choices we make and the impact they have on our spiritual evolution. We all share the one life that is God created, and if God is not at the centre of every thought and deed then our experiences will be mundane. And life will be a continual struggle against conditions that we create. For there can be no lasting satisfaction unless and until we acknowledge the presence of the soul.

Begin, this day, to correct all faults that you have allowed to develop over your life time in this incarnation. The task facing everyone is to become the repository of all that is good and decent in human nature. This can only be achieved by the total embracing of unconditional love. For the soul to make its presence known, love has to the motivating factor behind every thought, word and deed. The soul being of God must have had an awareness of itself and every experience encountered in and out of the human body. Your divine soul is in reality, the real spiritual you. The soul takes up residency in different human bodies that it may experience every facet of human behaviour and the consequences of behaviour. Human bodies are formal out of physical matter, while bodies are formed out of physical elements. It has to be remembered that everything seen is the result of the unseen. God being the only creator is the creator of human bodies and God intended the body to be the physical temple for the soul. All matter is in fact a form of spiritual essence; however, the soul is of the Consciousness of Almighty God. The human body requires the direct involvement of God. By breathing into the nostril of every individual shortly after birth, the soul enters the body and only then does life begin. Human bodies come into and go out of existence; the form of human physical existence is subject to involuntary change, but not the soul. Were we to sing from the hymn sheet of the soul, our bodies would undoubtedly benefit; disease and all forms of bodily ailments would be things of the past. God in His wisdom has decreed that all souls should be subject to human earthly experiences and each soul is meant to overcome all earthly problems. It is the task of the soul to overcome all difficulties and if the soul's personality fails in its mission then it must reincarnate in any other body to be confronted with the same type of trials and tribulations. Should the soul's personality fail in its earthly mission, which is to overcome all problems encountered, then its earthly mission must continue. The soul that resides in the human personality and whose characteristics are exclusively concerned with earthly matters, should the soul be unable to correct these tendencies, then the soul must meet the same challenge in any other incarnation. The number of reincarnations for the soul depends on its ability to influence, for good, the human personalities into which the soul is incarnated. This book is all about how to end the cycle of reincarnation and the chapter on love is of supreme importance in regard to this subject.

Reincarnation can be brought to an end by the intelligent use of the law of karma. It is, therefore, important that a clear and comprehensive understanding of the law of karma is mastered. Karma means compensation, if you behave wrongly you must pay compensation; conversely, if you engage in good deeds, if you act at all times with love and compassion your good deeds must also be compensated. Karma is constantly at work in every life; happy thoughts make for a happy person. Thoughts of anger rob you of reason and intelligence and you are disappointed with yourself. These reactions are karma at work. When behaviour is constructed on wisdom and intelligence, karma confers blessings. Conversely, thoughts and deeds of a negative nature demand that we pay an unpleasant price. The minimum penalty is loss of peace of mind; the maximum, another round of trials and tribulations back on earth in another human body. Jesus in his wisdom advised those be healed saying to them, "Go and sin no least a worse thing befalls you," an unmistakable reference concerning the law of karma. Jesus also made a number of suggestions regarding the constructive use of law of karma. In St. Matthew, chapter 5, it is said (I will list but a few of the more important suggestions), *'Blessed are the poor in spirit for theirs is the kingdom of Heaven,'* Poor in spirit have nothing to do with economic deprivation, but everything to do with modesty and humility. *'Blessed are they that hunger and thirst after righteousness for they shall be filled'*, *'Blessed are the merciful, for they shall obtain mercy,'* In the same chapter at verse 18, Jesus makes this comment concerning the law, "For verify I to say unto you; Till heaven and earth pass away, one jot or one title shall in no wise pass away from the law till all things be accomplished." Jesus is adamant the 'Law' exists and must be obeyed. Your spiritual prosperity throughout eternity is dependent on the wise use of the law of karma. This law can be used by anyone to great effect. So, store up for yourself treasures in heaven by good deeds. Give to the poor, visit the sick and those in prison feed and care for the hungry of the 'Third World,' Care for elderly, guide the young, and be a good neighbour, a loyal friend. Work conscientiously, minute by minute, at becoming a loving, kind, and considerate and compassionate human being. Set for yourself exacting standards of behaviour; make decency, courtesy, propriety and modesty, your main ambition.

In Matthew chapter 25 verses 34-46, we are informed of the divine reward for good deed performed,

'Then shall the king say unto them at his right hand. Come ye blessed of my Father, inherit the kingdom prepared for you from the foundation of the world. For I was hungry and ye gave me meat. I was thirsty and you gave me drink; I was a stranger and you took me in. Naked and you clothed me: I was sick and ye visited me: I was in prison and ye came into me. Then shall the righteous answer him saying Lord, when saw we thee as hungered, and fed thee or a thirst, and gave thee drink. And when did see thee a stranger and took you in or naked, and clothed thee? And when I saw we thee sick or in prison and came into you? And the king shall answer and say unto them. Verify I say unto you; in as much as ye did it unto one of these my brethren, even these least, ye did it unto me. "Then shall he say unto them on the left hand: Depart from me; ye cursed unto the eternal, which is prepared for the devil and his angels". "For I was hungered, and you gave me no meat." "I was thirsty and ye gave me no drink." "I was a stranger, and ye took me not in, sick and imprisoned and ye visited me not. Then shall they also answer saying lord when say we thee hungered, or athirst or a stranger, or naked, or sick, or in prison and is not Minster unto me." Then shall he answer them saying: verify, I say unto you in as much as ye did it unto one of these least, ye did it unto me. And these shall go away into eternal punishment, but the righteous into eternal life.'

Everything that happens in our lives is the result of the law of karma. Nothing happens to us because of chance. The notion that the perversities of fate or benign circumstances are randomly responsible for the good or bad that we experience is totally wrong. Karma is an inviolate cosmic law, that is impersonal and impartial and all are subject to the law. If the Law is violated, there will be punishment; conversely, working in conscious harmony with the law means rewarding compensation. The beautiful law of karma guarantees universal justice for all.

Your spiritual duty to yourself is to make restitution for past infringements against the law of karma. And if you now accept that your present difficulties are the direct result of infringements by you of the law of karma, you have learnt one of nature's greatest lessons. We are exclusively responsible for all that happens in our lives be it good or bad. If we are in difficult circumstances, we should now be prepared to accept our fate with understanding and forbearance. We should take encouragement from the fact that our new knowledge means we can end the cycles of pain and frustration. When we banish ignorance, we can use the law in our own behalf. And the road to freedom lies under our feet and we now know for certain that the journey must end in total liberation. Why is it you suppose that some individuals live in poverty and deprivation while others live in privilege and wealth? And why is it that some individuals become drug addicts, thieves, murderers, and child molesters, while others are loving, kind, compassionate and considerate? Why do some, seemingly lucky individuals enjoy all of the best advantages in life, i.e. good health a devoted wife and loving children, while others are living in diseased bodies and in impoverished financial circumstances? The circumstances, experience, be it good or bad, is the direct result of the deeds performed in past earthly lives. We are currently reaping the rewards of the seeds sown previously. Luck or chance is not on the divine agenda of God's master plan regarding we, His chosen children. The doctrine of what "you sow you reap" is the cause of your present situation, good or bad. As you sow you reap, is a wonderfully just and natural law and its justness is compounded by the wonderful opportunity it constantly provides us with to sow good seeds. Should you decide to use the law of karma, dedicate your good deeds to God as an act of love and devotion. You now know that you alone are responsible for whatever tribulation you endure. By the acceptance of this fact you become more emotionally equipped to handle all unpleasantness. An understanding of the law of karma will help us better understand our human experiences and why these experiences are directed towards us. When we rid ourselves of ignorance, at the same time, we rid ourselves of confusion, frustration and resentment. These are some of the wonderful benefits of knowledge, but the knowledge has to be acted upon. Decide to end all transgressions against the law of karma, then take the next logical step and work in harmony with karma. Theoretically it's all so simple—to change the effects, you must go to the cause. There really isn't any point in struggling against perverse circumstances; only by understanding the cause can tribulations be ended forever. Rebellion is no solution; it won't bring an end to your pain, but understanding the cause will. All of us have the choice between right and wrong, good or evil of ignorance or knowledge. The choice is between knowledge and understanding of God's universally just laws, or continuing with human folly that breeds an ignorance and delusion. You are the only one who can save yourself from the pain and tribulations you endure by admitting you are the cause. What is required is a new deeper and more profound appreciation of the laws by which we are governed. Life does not begin at human birth and won't end at physical death. And life does not consist of one earthly existence. Life is from God and because God is eternal so also are you. The real you, which is spiritual and eternal means that you have always existed and must continue to live throughout eternity. You are soul that is divine, spiritual and eternal and that you are at present temporarily housed in a human body, does not in any way distract from your spiritual and divine origin. Take firm and convinced hold of the truth of your being. It was God who created you and you are the divine expression of His love, compassion, peace and understanding. When you accept yourself as being God's creation and give human expression to your divine attributes you will be living in harmony with God's Laws. The alternative is to continue living the mundane life, a continuous struggle against conditions that you now know are self-created. The acceptance of the doctrine of karma and reincarnation will be of immense benefit; it teaches that there is no escape for wrongdoing, from wicked or sinful thoughts.

Karma teaches that all wrong thoughts, words and deeds must be compensated for. If you deliberately injure anyone by word or deed karma will insist that you suffer exactly the same fate. The converse is also true, karma will insist that every good thought, and word or deed is reward—to know that we are born of God created by Him in His spiritual image and likeness, to know that we eternally should provoke within us an unquenchable desire to arrive at a comprehensive understanding of God and mankind. When the doctrine of reincarnation and karma is accepted and understood much of the mystery of life will disappear. Events and circumstances that confused and frustrated, will be clearly understood. Knowledge conveys power, the ability to know why being hurt, angered and frustrated by all the obstacles, manage to get in our way and rob us of peace and contentment. How much pain we heap upon ourselves because of our ignorance or worse still, the wilful refusal to obey the law—of what we sow, we must reap. Anyone, who escapes paying for their evil deeds in this life cannot hope to escape retribution in the following earthly existence; the law is, karma will have the last definitive word. Blind emotional and negative reaction to events causes all the problems we complain of. Spiritual blindness can be eradicated by knowledge, emotion can be conquered by wisdom, and negativity can be overcome by the wise use of knowledge. Spiritual laws are impersonal, natural and based on infallible justice, for the law to become active in a positive manner in our life we must personally work in a constructive manner with the law. Your soul's personality, like everything else in creation is subject to God's laws, meaning that every soul is subject to reincarnation, karma and evolution. Love is the only means available that will allow us to work in harmony with all laws. Love is not only the means, but also the object to be achieved. The road to perfection begins and ends with love and human perfection comes before spiritual revelation, when you realise in reality that you and God are one; however, this spiritual revelation can only be experienced when we love unconditionally. The soul's liberation from the need to reincarnate is one of the beautiful rewards that love confers on all who live in love. The paradox is that while reincarnation and karma are blessings, our greatest good is only experienced when we win liberation from both.

Many individuals believe that physical death is the gateway to eternal oblivion; not so, at transition the soul complete with its consciousness returns to the spiritual realm to wait for another human body in which it can continue gaining earthly experiences. And until the soul is master over every human emotion, situation and circumstance, the requirement for reincarnation will continue. For if the soul's personality fails to resolve all human problems encountered, it has failed in its earthly mission. The soul alone is the repository of all knowledge, wisdom and virtue, and if we have the intelligence to seek soul's help, we will, in time, be led to the gates of heaven.

In finishing this chapter on reincarnation, we should briefly examine the widely held but mistaken belief that the individual may reincarnate into the body of an animal. Most individuals would be repulsed at this notion. No one in his or her right mind would want to live life as a spider, a crab, a snake or any other animal. This idea is inconsistent with the known laws of evolution. Evolution means the development of species from earlier forms. Soul's personality is, as is everything in the universe, subject to the law of evolution. While it is true that each species of animal is subject to evolution there is no creditable evidence that it spawns different species. If human souls were to return to earth in animal bodies that would represent devolution and not evolution. The soul is placed in the human body, which has the highest form of evolution of any species that we have knowledge of. There could never be beneficial consequences for any soul to be incarnated in animal from.

Not only is there scriptural evidence to support the doctrine of reincarnation, books and television documentaries have revealed startling and dramatic evidence of past lives lived on earth. One case revealed in a television documentary involved a young English woman, who, while under hypnotic state gave a remarkable account of a previous life. As a Jewess she lived in the English town of York in the middles ages and in those dark days Jews were the victims of pogroms and other forms of persecution. During one such episode a priest gave sanctuary to a group of Jews that included the young woman in question. The young woman identified the church and gave details of a crypt, situated below the church alter; she gave details of its shape and size. It was decided to search the church, which still stood as ruins, for evidence of the crypt. In spite of thorough searching no trace of the crypt could be found. The team involved recommended to the local museum that the altar should be saved and placed on display. Some months later a salvage crew was sent to remove the altar and during the attempt to do so it suddenly fell into a crypt below. The crypt was as described by the hypnotised young woman. The only explanation for this woman's knowledge of the existence size and shape of the crypt, is that she had in fact, been in the crypt at some time.

In another case of hypnotic regression involving the same female she is taken back to a period in the 17th Century and startles those involved by speaking in fluent French. This was quite remarkable considering she never had a French language lesson in her life, nor had she ever visited France. This session of regression was aborted for several days to have a fluent French speaker present. When the new session was held the young hypnotised woman was taken back to the 17 Century and again was questioned about her name and family. She gave both, where when asked her occupation she admitted to being a maid in a large chateau. She was able to give the name of the chateau, its location and the names of each member of the family and the names of all employed at the chateau. All these details were checked and found to be accurate. During one of the regressions she was taken back to a particular day and time and was asked what she was doing at that moment in time. She replied she was dusting in the hallway. When further asked if any member of the family or staff were present, she said the master was. When asked what he was doing, she replied that her master was placing papers in a secret chamber behind the clock on the mantel piece. It was decided by the regression team to visit the chateau and check the validity of the secret hiding place. Upon arrival at the chateau in question, it was found to be exactly as described by the young English woman who had, up to then, never been to France. When the owner of the chateau was asked about the secret hiding chambers neither he nor anyone else knew anything about it. He did however, agree to a search being made and to every one's surprise a wooden panel behind the clock was found to move revealing a secret chamber. Again, the only plausible explanation for this young woman's ability to speak flawless French, without ever having a single French language lesson—her details concerning the house and its inhabitants and her knowledge of the hiding place—is that she had, in fact, been employed as a maid during the 17th Century.

With these two contemporary pieces of dramatic evidence this chapter on reincarnation and karma closes.

Chapter 9

Love

"Lead life of love: that others who
Behold your life may kindle too
With love, and cast their lot with you."

(C G Rossetti)

Jesus was challenged by a lawyer who asked this most important of all questions question, "What shall I do to inherent eternal life?" The response from Jesus was, "Thou shall love the Lord thy God with all thy heart, and with all thy soul, and with all thy strength, and with thy entire mind; and love thy neighbour as thyself. Nothing in all of the Cosmos is more spiritually important than unconditional love. If you can accept this self-evident truth you will in the process take a quantum leap of understanding the reasons for life in a human body here on planet Earth."

Love, and it alone, will create the spiritual circumstances that will purify heart, soul, mind and supply the strength required to live a life of profound peace and everlasting harmony. Theoretically it's very simple, love unreservedly and your earthly experiences will be of harmony, peace, and everlasting serenity. All human problems have their origins in ignorance of the power and authority of purified spiritual love; elevated wisdom is love in action. The Christian Bible gives us a concise yet beautiful definition of God. It tells us that *'God is Love'*, meaning love is the main or most important attribute of God. If love is God, then Love has to be the most potent power in the Universe. A panacea for the problems of mankind, no matter what the problem or problems may be, Love is the perfect antidote.

The New Testament tells us that: *'The fruits of the spirit are love, joy and peace,'*

This message is both clear and of immense importance for all of us. If you want to live a life of joy and peace then you must embrace the divine essence of love. In love your life will be complete, your body strong, your mind freed of all negative thoughts and you will be at peace with yourself and all of mankind. The New Testament also informs us that: *'Love is the fulfilling of the law,'* God's law is the principle upon which God's plan, for all of His creation, is manifested and governed. It will be of considerable benefit to us at this point to examine what some of the greatest thinkers have to say about love.

"Love is ever the beginning of knowledge as fire is of light." (Carlyle)

According to Carlyle, love is the means of attaining knowledge; knowledge of God; knowledge of self and knowledge of mankind. Love, being God, has the divine power and spiritual authority to overcome every obstacle and to achieve all things. Should you embrace the divine essence of love it will correct all human errors and revitalise every cell in your body making it strong and healthy. The motive for all creation is love; it is first cause and is harmony and healing for soul and body. Love has no limits and because it is infallible, has no errors. It is pure in its intentions, precise in its actions. Love will not deceive or cheat you; it will not betray your trust nor disappoint your hopes. Not only will love heal mind and body, but will also reveal the hidden mysteries of the Universe. Love will not be fooled; it insists on total commitment. It will accept no percentages or partial obligation; to gain the benefits of love there has to be complete engagement in it. To receive all, you must first be willing to give all. In love giving is receiving. Should you choose to live in love, you will be missing many things. You will be without enemies or foes, you will be missing fear, you will forgo all emotional and physical pain, and all problems will come to a permanent end. Love is the spiritual antidote that corrects all human errors and eradicates all ignorance.

Another of our great thinkers has said, "Love sees what no eye sees; love hears what no ear hears." (Levanter)

Love goes beyond human thoughts, beyond our collective comprehension. The human intellect cannot comprehend the divine power and spiritual authority that love is capable of. All knowledge, all wisdom, all understanding is to be found only in love.

Love, being God means, that love cannot be intellectualised; it goes beyond all human understanding. The human finite mind is incapable of comprehending the Infinite Mind of God. Nor can the finite mind understand the infinite potential of love. But, understand clearly that love is the golden chain that binds mankind eternally to God. The real you, who has been created by God in his image and likeness, you are the spiritual expression of infinite love. Let this truth take hold of your mind and flood your soul that you may become a conscious living expression of divine love. Keep your heart full of love for God and mankind and much will be revealed to you and through you to others. All may use love for it is the healing balm that will bring peace and contentment in every situation. Love is beauty, splendour, grandeur and with its limitless potential and unending possibilities is the only means of achieving liberation from all human problems. Love provides deliverance from all that pains you, it will make you master of fate and raise you to sublime heights of understanding and spiritual revelations that you cannot at this time begin to comprehend.

Love will reveal the *'new heaven and the new earth,'* spoken of in the Bible.

However, you must clearly understand that you must love totally, completely and unconditionally. This will not be easy; we all know some very objectionable individuals; persons whose chief characteristics are dominated by utter selfishness; who care for no one and who will trample over all in pursuit of their personal ambitions. To love such individuals is impossible you say. The truth is, the less love a person has in their life the more they require it from others. Yes, we are obliged to love all, those we like and are fond of, and those objectionable individuals for whom we have neither love nor esteem. Love is not about your personal feeling, thoughts or emotions. Love, when fully embraced, will raise you above all mundane thoughts and feeling. And love will make it easy for you to forgive all who have wronged you. It is important to remember that God has created all, including those who have pained you, in His image and likeness.

Tragically all of us have smothered our spiritual identity with thoughts of hate, envy, greed, stupidity and ignorance and, of course, such thoughts are the parents of vile deeds. Understand clearly that practising love can never harm you. For love is the union of self with God. The answer to all human folly, folly that allows us to spend our wakened hours dominated by our negative thoughts, with all of the resulting consequences, is to clearly identify us with the Infinite Universal Life of Love. When we look at another individual, we don't see the real person, we see a human personality that has been constructed upon totally human experience, mostly of folly and compounded by ignorance. And can you, at this moment in time, declare yourself free of these terrible human burdens. Someone pains you by word deed or omission. You are angered and hurt when someone tells lies about you. You are outraged when someone deliberately causes you physical harm or for stealing from you. How could I love anyone guilty of such behaviour? Love insists that you forgive wrongdoing not only against you, but all wrongdoing. The intelligent reaction to human folly is not to condemn it, but rather to understand it.

How are we to react to those who murder or sexually abuse children? Outrage is the understandable reaction to such terrible events. Such behaviour must be condemned and those involved must be punished. You don't have to love the outer person, those individuals who wallow in evil deeds who prey on the innocent. But, while the purveyors of such vile and reprehensible deeds prey on their victims, we must respond by praying for those pathetic creatures. If you fully realised the dreadful future experiences awaiting those individuals when, as they must, leave their bodies at death, you would be full of compassion for them. You don't have to love the outer person and the dreadful deeds sometimes perpetrated by them. But, you are spiritually obliged to love in inner person who is in essence a creation of God himself.

At this junction we should remind ourselves of what Jesus had to say about love. When asked what was the chief commandment he responded, "The chief one is: Hear. O Israel, the Lord our God is one Lord, and you must love the Lord your God with your whole heart, with your soul, with your whole mind, and with your whole strength. The second is this; you must love your neighbour as yourself. There is no other command greater than these." Jesus is clearly saying that you must love God and all his children totally, completely and unconditionally.

Love, you see, is a sacred spiritual obligation decreed by God and no one can opt out of it. If life is to have any genuine meaning, any worthwhile relevance and if you want to be elevated above the current confusion and insensitivity of today's world, this 'decree' of God is the means available to you now. Were you to do everything for the love of God, your life would become a blessed experience of joy and peace. You don't have to love the outer person with all of its distasteful characteristics. But, there is an inescapable spiritual obligation on you to love the inner person.

The inner person is that beautiful being created by God, and by loving this essence you will help their inner spirituality to manifest in the outer. Love is not only harmony and healing for your soul and body, it is healing for all, and you can become a channel for the healing power of love. You must, of course, wholly embrace love and make this holiest of virtues the dominant feature of your life. Love will not only be of the most wonderful personal benefit, it will through you, be of benefit to all who come into contact with you. Love confers human and spiritual perfection on those wise and intelligent enough to embrace it completely.

You should clearly understand that love is not to be found in affection for other individuals or material possessions. There may be persons and things you think you love. Couples at their marriage ceremony declare their love for each other, those who marry in church declare before God and the assembled congregation to love until death. Many marriages end in divorce causing much pain and in many instances the legacy is anger, resentment and hatred. What has happened to their love for each other? The truth is, that people don't fall in or out of love. Love is forever and will last longer than time; time has no relevance to love. You can't say I was in love with my partner, but I now no longer feel any love for him or her. Love cannot be encircled by any human emotion or collective emotions. Certain human emotions can be confused with love; thoughts and feeling of compassion, tenderness and kindness, are frequently confused with love. Thoughts are subject to mood change, one day you can be full of tenderness towards someone, a short time later you feel anger and resentment towards the same individual.

A loving thought is not love; in most cases it is a pleasant feeling of tenderness for someone or something. You should at every opportunity think positive caring thoughts of love, kindness, tenderness and compassion. Better still, you should make these thoughts the parents of good deeds. Such deeds when done without any self-interested motives can be the means to a greater understanding of love. Unselfish giving, when wisely understood, is receiving. Understand clearly that love can't be found in people, thoughts, deeds, or in things. Love is not passion, compassion or kindness, it can't be found in the act of sex, not in genuine concern, not in sympathy, mercy or duty. All of these feelings, emotions and resulting deeds can be a beautiful means of expressing love.

Love is the life energy that sustains everything in the seen and unseen Universes; it sustains the life in you and in your body. If every thought was conceived in love, if every word was spoken in love, if every deed was performed in love, God would send legions of his angels and they feel privileged to be in your company. When you allow love to dominant every word and deed, every cell in your physical and physic body will radiate harmony and health. Let's return again to the New Testament statement, *'The fruits of the spirit are love, joy and peace,'* To experience genuine love God has to be involved in our individual lives; God has to be in our daily experiences. Without God alive and totally relevant in our lives there can be no real love, no actual joy, no lasting peace. Examine your own life as you are presently living it; have you found lasting joy or peace? If not, you now know the reason why; love is the missing link between God and the contentment you seek. For only in divine love can the true meaning of life be understood and only in divine love can we find the true explanation for our existence on planet earth.

Earth is poised on the precipice of global disaster by thoughts of, fear and hate, and by acts of war and other forms of violence. We have tried every human device in an attempt to solve our problems be they personal, national or international, but they don't work. There are thousands of community groups and government sponsored organisations whose function it is to eradicate problems and improve the quality of life. These organisations have experts in all sciences and spend vast sums of money annually, but our personal and global situation continues on a downward spiral.

More and more people accept that our civilisation is terminally ill and are in despair to know what to do to halt the slide towards global disaster. Every human solution tried has so far failed. In truth there is little of value that mankind can offer at this stage of moral insensitivity to end the madness that has engulfed the mass of humanity. The solution is of course, a permanent return to God and His love, divine love being first cause; then we should return to first cause immediately, not only to save our family and community but the whole of mankind.

We all know what must be done if there is to be any meaningful change in the human condition and world circumstances, but we lack the spiritual inclination to react in the only manner that can end the present insanity.

The truth of human existence is that God created each and every one of us to be the vehicle for the expression of His Divine Love and if we would give personal expression to love and the other attributes of God the world would become paradise. Your soul is the means of expressing this love. Never in world history has there been a greater need for a return to God and His love, for if civilisation is to survive there has to a restoration of love and decency in the affairs of mankind.

202

The philosopher Law wrote: *'I appeal to nothing but the state of your own heart and conscience, to prove the necessity of your embracing this mystery of divine love,'*

This world and your existence in it are a preparatory experience so that love may unfold within you. Were you to co-operate with God, His love would manifest in and through you, and you will have as your just reward the secret of all power. In genuine love you will know that your existence is eternal and that your eternal existence is in God. For love will bind you to God forever and ever. Seek guidance from your immortal soul. Mentally ask your soul for help and inspiration for without your soul's spiritual stimulus you will never know the beauty, grandeur and grace of love.

In love, your whole being will be filled with the most wonderful spiritual experiences. You will know the truth of your existence; you will know exactly what you will encounter when you leave planet earth and you will know where and how you will spend the rest of eternity. Yes, in true love you will be filled with the sweet fragrance of eternity. The highest ambition of the intelligent thinker is to become an instrument of God's Divine Love. Before love can manifest, the outer personality has to be cleansed of all negative thinking. All thoughts of hate, fear, anger, resentment and all other destructive thoughts, and their deeds must end.

When we reason from the outer personality, what we believe to be love is nothing more than a transient and sometimes a turbulent reaction to events within personal relationships. The outer personality can and does distort the concept of love. Fanatics and the gullible will kill fellow human beings for what they call 'love' of country. Wars and cruelty are the antithesis of love. Those who call for human sacrifices in the name of love of country or in any cause, are at best fools or worst spiritually illiterate.

Yet love demands sacrifice from each and every one of us. It demands surrender of all fear, all faults, all words, deed and emotions that are insensitive or hurtful to anyone. To experience the new life of love with its accompanied joy and peace, it is first necessary to give up the old life of uncontrolled negative thinking. When you become the spiritual sanctuary of wisdom and love the mighty Truth of God will be revealed to you. The truth of your being is that you have been created by our loving God to love.

Without love you will never know the real you. Ask yourself this simple question. Who am I? You can respond by repeating a name someone gave you at birth, or you could say, I am a human being. But really none of these answers are in the least satisfactory, because they are not answers at all. Love knows all secrets, it understands all things and when you love, as you should, it will reveal the spiritual you in all your divine splendour. You will see the same beauty and splendour in every person; this will fill you with a new understanding of life and human behaviour. You will know love to be the only healing power there is and this power is freely available for all to use. With this knowledge of the power of love do you really want to hold on to your present life with all of its folly, superficiality, frustration, anger, resentment and other forms of mental and emotional pain?

The new life of love will be entirely different from the life wasted chasing after things of this world; the things of the material world do not possess the power or authority to make you the type of individual you would like to be. To be truly happy to live at peace with yourself and all of mankind you must clearly know what stands between you and the peace you desire. Love is the divine protective essence in every human soul, and to gain the protection from all human folly you must allow love to dominate every thought, every word and deed. Love has the power and authority to overcome all conditions, to correct all wrongs, to erase all faults, to end all grievances. In love there is no hate, for anyone, no fear for the future, no recrimination for what is past and gone. Make love the dominant ideal in your life and you will be guided by God Himself to spiritual reality.

The greatest benefit to be gained, from living the life of love, is the glorious reward waiting when the time comes to leave earth. Love is the road that leads directly to Paradise. Paradise is often confused with heaven; very many people believe Paradise and heaven are one and the same, but this is not so.

Jesus said, "My Father's house has many mansions."

These mansions are in fact planes of consciousness or understanding, ranging from first astral plane which is the closest to our earth plane, higher up the spiritual ladder which is the second astral plane, and higher still are other spiritual planes. You and I and everyone who ever lived will experience life in all planes or as Jesus said "mansions." Absolutely no one leaves earth and enters heaven. When, as you must leave your physical body, the closest you can get to heaven is the plane or mansion of Paradise.

When you love unconditionally, love will respond by loving you serenely.

To gain entry to Paradise you must live the life of love. Love is the beautiful price or fee demanded for entry to this divine sanctuary of spiritual peace and tranquillity. Jesus is impaled upon the cross and he promises one of two beings crucified with him, that on that day he would be with him in paradise.

Jesus chooses the word paradise very carefully. How you may ask, could a criminal sentenced to death for his criminal activity gain entry to paradise? The individual concerned had in all probability stolen food to feed his family and for this, was crucified. The first corporal work of charity is to feed the hungry; stealing food to feed your starving family is only a crime if you steal it from others who are starving also.

The good thief had to have lived a loving life and did he not show love for Jesus while both were close to death. When Jesus looked at the good thief he clearly saw the aura surrounding him and knew he was destined for paradise. When you get to paradise you will never again have to reincarnate back on earth. Your earthly experiences will be finished and done with. However, you can't enter paradise unless you have totally embraced the divine essence of love. Love is the only means of understanding God, His creation and our relationship to both.

When, what we call death occurs, you will find yourself in one of three places, or more accurately you will experience all three places. If you have had the intelligence and wisdom to live in loving union with God you will rest in paradise. But, you will briefly journey through the first and second astral planes. In the first astral plane will be found those poor, wretched individuals who, while living on earth, lived the life of hate, crime, violence and who refused to live a life of common decency.

This first astral plane will be a very unpleasant place, indeed for those unfortunate creatures incarcerated there. This place will be dark, bleak and dreary, full of despair and recrimination. Physical death will rob us of all pretence and confront us with reality. Those on this plane will be confronted with the consequences of their crimes committed while in the physical body. They will be allowed a glimpse of paradise, its beauty, peace and tranquillity and this will add to the frustration of those on the first astral plane.

Stripped of all pretence and unable to hide from their evil thoughts, words and deeds perpetrated while on earth they are now experiencing just some of the consequences. And there is more unpleasantness to be endured for when those in this hellish place emerge from it, they will be informed that they must return again to earth in an attempt to cleanse their karmic debt. What these individuals did while on earth, will be done unto them in their next incarnation on earth. What they sowed in their last life on earth, they will reap in their next life.

All of the pain they inflicted upon others will be inflicted upon them. The criminal will be the victim of crime; the child abuser will as a child be abused; the murderer will be murdered. The serial killer who has murdered will be murdered as many times as he or she has killed. Anyone who murders, for instance, four people must return to earth on four future incarnations to be the victim of a murderer. When made aware of their spiritual blindness those in the first astral plane will be filled with bitter regrets against themselves for their folly and stupidity.

Release from this dreadful place will only come when there is true and genuine repentance and an acceptance of the wrongs done. Much of the pain and recrimination will be caused because those in the first astral plane could have, so easily, avoided all of the unpleasantness that they must experience had they embraced unconditional love. And when those individuals emerge from the hell of their own making and return to earth all memory of their dreadful pain and experiences will be eradicated.

Before this happens there will be the dreaded knowledge that unless they unconditionally surrender to divine love, they very well may end up yet again in the first astral plane. The way to avoid all pain and suffering be it here on earth or on the first astral plane is to live a life of love. Embracing unconditional love will allow you to be content in the present and certain of the future this blessed state, which so few have found, is the wonderful consequences that anyone may claim if and when they enter into the holiest temple of love.

What happens to those who have lived decent lives while on earth, you want to know. Those who have lived a life of decency, but who have not committed themselves completely to divine love will not fortunately finish up on the first astral plane, but will be allowed a glimpse of it.

They won't enter paradise, but will find a temporary abode in the second astral plane. As first and for a time this place will be mistaken for heaven. Experiences here will be pleasant and enjoyable. When you leave earth, you leave your physical body behind, but you will still be you, only now you have a finer psychic body. This psychic body will be free of all pain sickness and disease. It will not be a burden to you and you will be pleased to know this body will return to a youthful appearance.

Let's examine the experience to be had. Well the person who had a passion for fishing while on earth will have wonderful rivers brimming with fish at their disposal. Divers will have wonderful clear blue waters in which to enjoy their passion. Gardeners will have the same wonderful experiences, rich soil and perfect growing conditions, which will produce a wide variety of plants, vegetables and flowers. The second astral plane will seem, at first, a wonderful place. It will, for a time, be a place of contentment and will be mistaken for heaven. The second astral plane will at first fulfil the human concept of what heaven should be. However, heaven goes beyond the power of the human mind's ability to conceive, of the true nature, of what heaven really is.

The happiness and contentment of those in the second astral plane will eventually give way to a feeling that there has to be something more than mere enjoyment, peace and contentment. At this point a high spiritual being will appear and confirm that there is more, much more.

This spiritual guide will explain the true nature of the second astral plane and inform those on this plane that they must return to earth because they did not learn the lessons that earth's life is meant to teach. The sad message will be that those who reach the second astral plane must return again to earth. Not only must they return to earth, but also all memory of what has happened since arriving in the second astral plane will be eradicated.

When the guide has finished explaining the situation, an invitation is given to a meeting with other spiritual guides. These guides constitute a 'judgement council' who will, with the active participation of the individual concerned, go over in detail all efforts and experiences on the last incarnation on earth. This council will judge, in detail, the past life; it will be a caring and loving judgement devoid of any condemnation or recrimination.

This adjudication will be a gentle and loving means of helping those who come before the council to understand the soul's need for a further return to earth. It will be made very clear that the soul must triumph over the negative mind, all negative emotions and all human imperfections.

While on earth the individuals must commit themselves completely to love, to truth and to Christ. It's the Christ who is the creative and active principle of the Godhead. This Christ is the loving link between God and we, His children. While you reside in a human body here on planet earth your spiritual salvation depends on having a constant awareness of the presence of Christ within you. This awareness will secure your present and future.

Love is the eternal spiritual power that sustains the cosmos and all things therein and spiritual love will establish its own perfection in the life that is lived in love. When love is totally embraced all imperfection disappears; there can never be anything false in human experiences when love is at the centre of our lives. The Bible informs us that love casts out fear; it will do much more than that. Love has the power and authority of God, and will, for those who take hold of it, make their lives a blessed spiritual experience. There are experiences that no language can convey. Just as words can't convey the reality of love so words can't convey the spiritual experience that only love can produce. But love has to be pure, holy, sanctified and divine. This love of God, His Universal Truth and Christ individualised in every individual is the only means of securing our individual place in eternity. The greatest lesson to be learnt on earth is to surrender completely to Love and be prepared and willing to receive and give spiritual expression to love.

Let's return to the adjudication council and its deliberations, the person appearing before the council will have a very real input into the decisions made concerning future earthly life experiences. The spiritual guides in co-operation with the individual concerned will go over in detail all aspects of the type of efforts made during the last life lived on earth. The decisions made will influence into what type of environment the person will most profit from on return to earth. Decisions such as the type of family and its make-up; will it be a loving caring family? Or will the family be uncaring and unloving? These decisions and others will be jointly be taken before an actual family is chosen. Nothing is left to chance; mothers and fathers get the type of children they deserve. It may be and it sometimes happens that caring and loving parents will be presented with a very difficult child or children to contend with. Such parents need, for their development, to experience the trauma of having to love and care for callous and difficult offspring. The child or children in this situation need, at this stage of their development, the love that will help to overcome their bad behaviour.

No matter what type of situation you encounter it is intended to help you grow into that beautiful person you really want to become. The only method to end further earthly experiences and all that ensues is to end the separation between God and the individual. This separation from God is the cause of all human difficulties and tribulations that has to be endured because of this gap. The individual who allows this gap to endure and develop will have much pain and frustration to endure.

Love flows, in all of its beauty, from Infinite God, and purifies those who are wise enough to partake of it, to enter into it; to bathe in it is to be spiritually renewed in spirit, mind and body. If every word spoken were uttered in love, if every thought was dominated by love, if every deed was an act of love, angels would gather around you to minister unto you and all others so motivated. By becoming aware of the love that exists within every person, by developing this awareness through all means possible, love will be brought to all of mankind. It is a profound spiritual obligation to nurture—this lovely gift of God to us—and to be totally guided by its implications.

Everyone wants to gain entry to heaven; the road that leads there is paved with love. Heaven is not a place you gain entry into. Heaven is a reality to be experienced. Between paradise and the final spiritual destination of Christ Consciousness there are two spiritual planes that must be passed through before final liberation from all limitation is reached. When paradise is reached there is no need for further earthly experiences. Now your journey will be ever upwards towards total union with God. When you leave paradise after having learnt the lessons that only paradise can provide, you will enter the next spiritual plane and when your education is complete you gain entry to the next spiritual plane to continue with lessons to be learnt and the experiences gained there. After the last spiritual plane, you progress to the first plane of cosmic understanding a place of deep and profound loving experiences.

Then on to the second cosmic plane this is the highest and most important mansion spoken of by Jesus. Here your intelligence, love, wisdom, spiritual reasoning and intuition will at last be perfected. From perfection you have come, to perfection you have returned. During your passage through all planes you will be guided and helped by spiritual guides every step of the way. Now you have no need of guides, experiences or learning. You have, at last, reached the state of perfection and now you enter heaven, which is the Divine unlimited Christ Consciousness.

You now know why you should use every fibre of your being to engender love, for love is the Christ of God in you. You must give expression to the presence of God and this expression, if it's to be spiritually effective, has to be love for all of humanity. For to love everyone is to love God, and God will only express Himself in our lives when we cleanse our minds and purify our hearts. Most of us would be thrilled to have God active in our lives, but are not sure how to make this happen. Well here is the only way available, not one of the better ways but the only way. You must live in faith, for the law is, unless you believe, but faith has to be a finished product that has overcome all doubt.

A strong faith will, if acted upon with wisdom and love, produce knowing. Intuitive knowing goes beyond mind, knowledge or intelligence. This intuitive knowing will guide you when you allow wisdom and love to dominate every aspect of your life. With love at the centre of all your thoughts and actions you will, in time, know yourself to be God's Divine child. The greatest mistake made by mankind is that they have mistakenly identified themselves with their physical and mental characteristics. Emotions of all sorts, but particularly the negative ones, prevent love and wisdom from taking hold of our imagination and hearts. If your mind is full of indiscretions there can be no room for understanding, compassion, tenderness, generosity or love. Without these human virtues God will not be active in your life, my life or any other life. The life lived without God must be barren without joy or peace.

The Godless life never provides fulfilment; yes, you will have short periods of cheap excitement and passing thrills, and these feeling provide a temporary relief from the disappointments and disillusions of living a banal existence. Were you to live in love, your life would be without complications of any sort. Realise that Christ dwells within you and your love of the presence of Christ is the means to conquer every human problem. You can, by your awareness of Christ and His love, become a channel for the expression of Christ's love, which is universal and by becoming a channel you will know yourself to be the chosen instrument of God. You see the individual receives the power and authority from the Universal Christ and the great power of Christ is love.

The Christ speaking through Jesus said, "Love one another as I have loved you."

This is without doubt the most important piece of advice ever given. From God you have come, to God you will, at some time, return. The return journey to God can be very long, hazardous, and fraught with many difficulties, or it can be very short, indeed the choice is for you alone to make. Please pay attention to this next statement: 'Do everything for the love of God,' If you give all to God in love, He will respond, by giving you all the power of His Love.

The love of God reveals that the source of all spiritual power is in love itself. Make your body, mind and soul the holy temple of God's love and this love will pour through you, and you will become what you were created for—a spiritual being giving the highest, noblest and loving expression to all of God's attributes,

210

which are Love, Truth, Consciousness and Power. Seek the silent love that dwells within you. Love everyone without exception and you become the loving child of God.

Love puts on no show or display, before men. Love in secret and God will in His loving way reward you openly. Understand clearly that genuine unselfish love is God incarnate and that love cannot fail, but makes everything new. Life means what it indicates, eternal, and infinite, timeless, perpetual and deathless. You are immortal like God; you never had a beginning nor will you ever cease to be. To be what you were meant to be, can only be accomplished by living the life of love. The spirit in you will reveal all secrets to you when love becomes the dominant factor in your life. You cannot live properly unless and until you love God Universal and the Christ individualised in you. You must accept the truth of your being that you live and have you is being in God, you and the Father are one. Love this truth of divine union between humanity and Almighty God. God is Truth. The Christ of God is Truth. Love, which is the real you, is Truth. And Christ speaking through Jesus said, "The Truth shall set you free." You now understand the full implications of the meaning of freedom. Not only will you be freed from the pains that negative thought causes you, but you will be freed from the burden of reincarnating back on earth. This freedom is the greatest freedom of all, no more emotional or physical hurt, no illusion or disillusion, no more failure of any sort. Freedom from anger, resentment, ignorance and fear, this is real freedom and it can only be found in real love. Only love can provide the freedom from the inner turmoil, agitation and chaos that uncontrolled emotions generate. No one is either free or happy who harbours unspoken thoughts of hate, anger or resentment. And don't allow yourself to be fooled into believing that transient thrills or excitement can provide lasting happiness. Thrills and excitement you will experience, but they will not provide the peace or contentment you long for. Let love guide you, let love be your constant companion, let love dominate you and let love determine your every word and deed, that God's plan may be accomplished in and through you.

God is love; to allow your true spiritual identity to manifest you must embrace love and live life according to its dictates. You will not experience true life until you experience true love. God's love is the power used by Him in every act of creation, and mankind is the result of God's love and has to be the true identity of all human races. If God has created mankind in His image and likeness, which is love, then love has to be the real identity of every human being.

All of us have been placed on earth for the purpose of discovering who and what we truly are. When you find genuine love, that love which surpasses all human understanding, you will know who and what you really are and the whole of nature will be at your command. To know yourself, as you are known by God means you have successfully accomplished your earthly mission and Paradise beckons.

Until you fully embrace the divine essence of love nothing in your life, or circumstances, will change or have any real meaning or worth. Nothing in your individual life can be different until love enters into your life, then everything will be different. At this moment in time you cannot be sure that your life will change in the manner suggested and you wonder can it really be true. Well I can't convince you, I can only encourage you. In an attempt at further encouragement, I suggest you examine your life until now. Is it all that you would have liked it to be?

Have you found lasting joy, peace or contentment?

Or have you been the victim to heartache and pain born of discontentment, fear and uncertainty. If you have endured these conditions, you will probably have tried every human remedy and all such remedies are doomed to failure. Diversion or perversion is no remedy, alcohol is no remedy, drugs are no remedy and renewed sexual partners offer no lasting relief. The accumulation of wealth, the status of social acceptability, fame or notoriety, cannot provide you with what you long for. If you were to live by love alone, your life would be a continuous experience of profound contentment. In genuine love you will live without anxiety, worry or fear. Love will dispel all anxiety and the pressures that modern living imposes on all. While we continue to live in ignorance of the power of love, this ignorance will be the impenetrable barrier between lasting happiness and ourselves. Not only this, but you are now beginning to understand that only love will propel us forward to our ultimate spiritual destination. Love is a haven in our distressed world and is the means of attaining heaven when, as we all must leave planet earth.

Love and trust in God. For only in love of God can you grow into the light of eternal life. Acknowledge yourself as spiritual light and loving energy and learn to trust the Lord our God that he may claim back what is rightfully His. From God you have come and to Him you will eventually return; love will shorten the return journey to God. From perfection to perfection and the road of return you now know.

Thank your loving Father that he has made these things known to you and give thanks every day that you may know more and more. God is ever-present love and to claim your spiritual inheritance in full you must become love itself.

Love is the holiest right of the soul, the crowning glory of man's noblest thoughts and activities. If every thought was conceived in love, if every word was spoken in love, and every act was an act of love God would send his angels to surround you and they would feel privileged to be in your company.

In love you will think the purest thoughts, your every action will be virtue in motion; every word spoken in love will be full of understanding and genuine regard for the well-being of all of humanity. You can become the type of person being described if your desire is strong enough. The means of escape from the insanity that is today's world is to take hold of the truth of your being. It is Almighty God Himself who lives in you and you must become aware of His presence and this awareness must manifest as love for all creation, everyone and everything; no one or anything can be excluded.

For love is the power that has created all things seen and unseen and love attracts everything to it. It is only when we totally embrace love, only when we allow love complete expression through us and only when we fully accept that love is the uniting bond between ourselves and God, that we can gain a crystal-clear understanding of spiritual realities. And only when we acquire this degree of spiritual understanding can we hope to become complete human beings.

Spiritual love when adopted and given expression by any individual is truth in human manifestation, and if you live in love, knowing that God Himself is watching over you, and His love is constantly pouring into your soul, and this endless supply of love makes you the complete being, both human and spiritual. Love, which is kindness to all, understanding of everything, tenderness in all situations, compassionate always; with these virtues continually practiced your humanity will be perfected. When you allow yourself to become the highest expression of humanity by your genuine care for others, by compassion and mercy, then and only then, do you begin your journey ever upwards, towards conscious union with Christ Consciousness. When you know the path to God you will delight in making others aware of the way. This you will do through your expression, at all times, of your love, by kindness, understanding and generosity. By this type of example you have much to contribute.

Accept that it is God who dwells in your heart and there dwells the power of God when you love. God will manifest in you when you fully realise your oneness with Him and all of life's problems will be brought to a permanent end. However, this realisation will not manifest in you or through you until you allow love complete expression in every aspect of your day-by-day living. God in His infinite love has as the highest expression of Divine love created all of humanity in His image and likeness and the explanation for the present sad condition of today's world is that not enough individuals are giving expression to this likeness. Now you know that love is the expression of God Almighty and that love is the real you. Allow this magnificent Truth to influence every thought, word and deed that your future will be the pleasant experience that you would like it to be. Should you decide on this course of action, not only will your future be pleasant, but also your future in other planes of consciousness will be assured. Love is the means chosen by God for His Divine expression of His concern for every single individual and if this be true, then love has to be our true means of expressing our gratitude to God. For God's way has to be the only way forward for the salvation of mankind and God's way is the only hope of individual and world redemption. Love, when wisely understood, is the eternal, omnipresent, omnipotent and omniscient God, and His glorious life lives in all of us right now.

Truly the truth is that God and mankind are one. It cannot possibly be otherwise. Jesus knew this great truth when he uttered these glorious words, "The Father and I are one." Truth, to be the Truth has to be universal; if it's not universal then it cannot be the Truth. Jesus spoke for all; He knew that God and we, His children, are as one—the great universal whole united by love.

"Open your eyes, and the whole world is full of God." (Jacob Boehme)

Keep these thoughts at the centre of all your worldly activities, that you may be guided by God's love to do what is right in all circumstances. When you become aware, continually aware, that it is God Himself who lives in you, then love shall manifest in and through you to make your existence on earth a blessed experience. If you are wise and intelligent enough to allow love to the guiding principle, all of God's other attributes find expression in you also. His truth, wisdom and healing power will be at your command and you will be of positive benefit to all of humanity in ways that at this time you cannot imagine. Love is the key to God's treasure store and this treasure is the means of deliverance from all human problems and is the key to paradise. It's love that unites man to God, and only through love can we be with God, for God is love and when the individual accepts the proposition that love is the only means of unity and responds accordingly then, God will respond by making His attributes freely available to any person who loves totally, completely and unconditionally.

You will never find love outside of your true self; you won't ever find it in the ordinary daily activities of life. You must search beyond the superficial outer personal self; the outer personality is your individual reactions to external events and human conditions. You are the individualisation of the Spirit that is God and you live and have your being in His Infinite Mind. When you fully and finally take hold of this truth your mind and heart will flood with Divine love and only in this Divine love can the spiritual you, which is the real inner you, manifest. Love has much to teach. It will reveal all spiritual knowledge, all wisdom and truth and the personality who is prepared to live according to the law of love will live the life of absolute and everlasting bliss. Your immortal soul has not forgotten that it was created by God, and has been with God always. Have you ever given serious consideration to soul? Soul to the overwhelming majority of people is a mystery, an unknowing something. Most people believe that it has something to do with God, but are ignorant of its purpose or function. The function of the soul is to serve the individual; the soul is the cosmic essence of God in every individual and is therefore freely available as a source of inspiration. The wise will seek, in love, for soul's inspiration, and the soul will respond positively to the sincere seeker after truth, this is the function of the soul and it must respond favourably to any individual who is totally committed to love.

Your soul will reveal all that is to be known when you live in love.

Love is the holiest right of the soul and the soul will only reveal its knowledge and truth to those who place love at the centre of every human thought, emotion or condition. Soul's knowledge is only available to those who have gained, through love, the wisdom and intelligence to use the power of soul-knowledge for the benefit of all of mankind. You have the free choice to embrace either spiritual love or, as many people have accepted, a human counterfeit love. Human love is largely based on some form of contract. If someone is tender to you, your response is tenderness and you mistake your feeling, thinking tenderness is love. When this tenderness fades, so does your counterfeit love. What you felt was a passing human emotion and genuine love has nothing to do with emotion, only to the extent that you can make another person aware of your genuine love by loving tender emotions. But emotions no matter how loving, tender, kind or considerate are not genuine love; spiritual love surpasses all human understanding and cannot be experienced by any physical faculty.

God is your lifeline to His glorious love, and His love is, in return, your lifeline to God. God and love are inseparable; if you claim to be a loving person and God is not at the centre of your life, then you deceive yourself. Love is constantly seeking expression in and through every individual. If you are not, in all circumstances, expressing compassion and understanding you will never understand true and genuine love. However, we should not seek love for personal benefit alone; allow love to stream through your soul to all of mankind. By reaching into your immortal soul in search of God's love, you become a channel for the distribution of love to all, and then you become a true Son of God. To consciously become a true Son of God is the reason for your individual existence. When you love, know that it is God Himself who is expressing the love you feel, and that the Spirit of God is manifesting through your soul and consciousness.

The love of God dwells in every living soul and all life throughout the Cosmos is the direct result of God's love. By giving expression to love you give expression to all that is noble, holy and divine in nature. By knowing that God is love, you, His child, must also be love, and it is through your understanding of your real identity, which is love, that you come to the realisation of yourself and God as being one. Your relationship to God and humanity can only be clearly understood when you fully live the life of love and as you become aware of the in-dwelling presence of love. You help to bring love into the world and every member of the human race.

To love the world and everyone and everything therein you are fulfilling your obligation to God and in so doing you secure the present and take care of the future. Love is the only means of purifying the heart, and the heart when purified gives expression to all that noble in human nature. God has created you in His image and likeness and love is the only means at your disposal to allow the image and likeness of God to manifest in the outer physical being. For the outer to become as the inner, you must, be willing to receive and give love.

To become the complete human being, to become capable of all that you are capable of becoming, you must live in true and genuine love for only in love is there any spiritual growth and you will, in love, grow into the complete spiritual understanding of your immortal self. This understanding can only take place when love and peace are present.

Dante wrote, *'he deeper contentment which every man seeks can surely be found,'*

Unquestionably this deepest contentment can be found and the only means of doing so is in love. Your search for love will be greatly assisted by eradicating what you know to be wrong in your life. By eliminating the bad you are adding to the good. This is wisdom in action.

Mankind seeks power in all manner of ways; wars are often the means chosen to gain power. Violence against the weak is used to gain power; fear is another method used to exercise authority. Cruelty is probably the most gruesome method of exercising power. The power of fear, violence, economic deprivation and cruelty is coercion in which force and duress are used to instil fear and compliance.

The most potent force and power are to be found only in love. Love is the spiritual power that has created all things and is the only permanent power and authority in the whole of the universe. The power of love, unlike worldly power, will benefit those who live in love through all eternity. Love is more powerful than violence and will cleanse the individual of all negative thoughts, emotions and inclinations. This cleansing of the personality is supremely important. There can be no spiritual advancement until we end the mental nightmare of thoughts dominated by hate, fear, anxiety, frustration, envy, greed, jealousy and other similar destructive thoughts. The personality you have constructed upon these thoughts and their corresponding emotions are not the real you. You are too great to be confined within the thought process. If your thoughts, desires and inclinations have become a dungeon into which you have imprisoned yourself, turn to love and you will regain your natural composure. Love will not only free you from the mental torture that are negative thoughts, but will lead you to sanity and salvation. Our present civilisation is in grave danger of collapse because of the psychic conditions surrounding mankind. These negative psychic conditions grow ever stronger because of the insanity of violence, fear and hate generated by wrong thinking. There is a school of thought that predicts humanity will endure a cataclysmic experience and this school of thought is gaining more and more acceptability because of the dreadful state of mankind. Greed is rampant; drugs and alcohol are ruining more and more lives; sexual perversion has further plighted this civilisation and murder is increasing day by day. Child abuse, neglect and abandonment continue unabated. Our learned psychologists could, I'm sure, write long and complicated treatises on the solution for our moral malaise. The solution to our dreadful predicament is really quite simple—theoretically at least. Love is the solution and just about everyone would agree with this preposition, but all too few are prepared to apply the only remedy that is guaranteed to save humanity from the dreadful fate that surely awaits.

However, people will argue that unconditional love is, for them, impossible. The truth is love requires no effort, is natural and spontaneous; it does, however, require a purified heart and a noble mind for its manifestation. Love cannot be taught; you won't learn to love by reading books or attending lectures, but you can, and hopefully are, gaining a clearer understanding of the power and authority of love, its relationship to God Universal, the presence of Christ within you and your relationship and duty to all of humanity. God is all Life seen and unseen. He is perfect love, and as we were created by Him then perfect love is your foundation and true identity. Your deliverance depends on the acceptance of this spiritual reality. Give devout thanks to God that He has made your true identity known unto you. How many millions have left earth ignorant of this truth and who have had to return here, much against their will, to go through the whole sad experience yet again? Yes, life on earth for countless millions is at best very sad experience and for all too many, life is a continuous nightmare.

Genocide, ethnic cleansing, child abuse, sexual perversion and hooliganism are all daily evidence that our social structures are crumbling. Cruelty and crudeness have triumphed over decency and compassion; kindness has given way to savagery and hatred. You, however, can become a saviour of mankind, if you decide to fully embrace the Divine Essence of Love. Jesus came to earth with the great message of hope and salvation. He said, "Love one another as I have loved you." Jesus knew that love was not only the means of personal salvation, but is the only means of protecting humanity from ignorance and folly and inevitable disaster. When love exists, there is perpetual healing of body, mind and soul, because there is no disease that love can't cure, but the patient has to embrace love completely. To be healed you must work in harmony with God's Law and love is, as we now know the fulfilment of the law. Love unites all to God, and with God all things are possible. The body changes through the conscious awareness of God's love active in your life, and this awareness and the acceptance of love will revitalise every cell of the body, perfecting the circulation of blood to every organ and perfect health. The Kingdom of Heaven spoken of by Jesus is a kingdom of many things: peace, joy, light and understanding. However, it is above everything else a kingdom of love and love is the passport you must possess to enter Heaven. You cannot purchase this passport with cash, worldly authority or by mere human achievements. You require a sincere and abiding love of God and mankind, a love that knows no bounds, that is strong enough to overcome all obstacles and surmount every barrier. Until the heart is full of love, love cannot express itself. By reaching out to all in love, you reach that which is real within you and by reaching out to all in love, God will touch you in His very special way. Your life here on earth will be lived in harmony, peace, joy and contentment and your future in eternity will be secured. Jesus warned us that unless we loved one another we could not enter the Kingdom of Heaven, for this kingdom is one of love. Don't be concerned about your future, by the love you expressed in the here and now, your present, and future experiences are taken care of. While mankind continues along the path of self-destruction through crimes of brutality and genocide, by pollution of the air we breathe, the water we drink and the food we eat, there is, however, a safe haven of tranquillity, a sanctuary of peace and a harbour of safety in love. Refuse to stay any longer in the madhouse that is today's troubled, bloodstained world. Seek refuge in the world of sanity, peace and the deepest contentment by living the life of love.

Consecrate your whole being to God and the Christ in you will express Divine Love in and through you. Recognise completely that you exist in the Universal Mind of God and the Universal Mind fills all space, is all intelligence, all wisdom and all knowledge. All of the power of the Universal Mind is available to you when you recognise that God has created you and you were created to manifest spiritual greatness. Your liberation depends entirely on your acceptance that God, the Creator, and you His creation are one. You live now, and always have done, in God, and He lives now as He always has done in you. The real you is the loving, spiritual and physical expression of God Almighty.

People are seeking miracles to prove the existence of God. Each and every individual is living proof of the existence of God and this miracle will manifest when we love, as we should. People, who claim to believe in God, complain that God should impose His will on every situation. What they mean is that God is not active enough in human affairs. Well, God is not a 'cleaning lady' with a mop and bucket who will clean up our human follies. God in His love for us gave us the truly wonderful gift of free-will. We misuse this beautiful gift to cause the problems we want God to resolve.

Mankind in its folly and ignorance abuses everything that it comes into contact with. This abuse causes mental, emotional and even physical pain and when the pain becomes unbearable, we turn to God that He may deliver us from our self-created problems. How childish and immature we are, God in His love has bequeathed to all of His children Divine power and authority. All that God has is ours, we only have to believe and respond with unconditional love. We must learn to seek deliverance from all our cares, woes, pains and misery by allowing love to control every aspect of our lives. Freedom will enter when ignorance has been replaced with love, compassion and spiritual understanding. Allow these virtues to enter into your consciousness and love will flow, continuously, through you and will benefit all of humanity.

To the same degree that you express love you express life; love is directly related to life and life is directly related to love. Those who attempt to live without love experience only pain, fear, frustration, and finally failure and the price of failure is a return to earth in another attempt to get it right. It matters not what ails you, love is the solution and is freely available to all. You must clearly understand that love is very demanding. It demands total loyalty, complete compliance, obedience and recognition of its power and authority. Love demands that we become honest in our dealing with all we come into contact with; it demands that we do not cause offence or fear. Love demands that we do not cause or condone violence. Love demands that we put a stop to all negative thoughts and emotions. Love demands that we forgive all who have sinned against us no matter how grave and serious the deed. Love demands that we all become the true sons and daughters of God. Love demands, most emphatically, that we love. Love demands that the heart and mind is kept pure so that life can express itself in all its glory.

Love is not an indefinable something, but is a vital and tangible Divine Energy, without which nothing could exist. This Divine Energy vibrates at a level that is undetectable by any of our physical senses and no mere machine, made by man, can detect it either. Only when we have purified our thoughts and human emotions, only when the human mind has reached the heights of purity and nobility can we hope to make spiritual contact with this perfect Divine Energy that is love. And when we make ourselves ready, this Divine Energy that is of God and is in fact, God, is ours to command. Jesus used the power of this energy in some of His healings. This is not the time to go into any great details of the use of this Divine Energy by Jesus for healing, but in the New Testament account of some of His healing, it states that, *'Jesus looked upon them with pity,'* In fact, pity had nothing to do with healing. The truth is that Jesus looked upon them with love. Or, more accurately still, Jesus was, through His eyes, directing this Divine Energy into the individual and curing their disease. Those who do not understand the spiritual law involved, call these healings by Jesus, miracles. But to Jesus and other spiritual masters, healing is the natural result of the power of Divine Love. What Jesus did, He accomplished because He loved divinely. You may do what Jesus did, but only when the love in you becomes Spiritual.

The Divine stream of Spiritual Love will flow into your purified heart when every beat of your heart is lovingly devoted to God. Love, when fully embraced, will allow you to fully understand the true loving nature of God. Live in faith believing, knowing and listening and when you allow wisdom and love to guide, you will know that God and you are one, united for eternity in love. The light of love will reveal the Father in all His power, glory and splendour to be resident in you and every other person. If only we would cleanse our moral window spiritually clean, we would witness the true splendour of life. People would be seen for what they truly are, spiritual and eternal like their creator. Love, being God, is the unseen Spiritual Energy that energises everything seen and unseen throughout the whole of creation. The only substantial reality is love and only those who live totally in love can experience Spiritual Reality. The pain and suffering that humanity has inflicted upon itself, is caused because of the insistence that a meaningful life can be constructed upon the foundation of human nature alone.

Without God, Christ, Truth and Love, humanity will blunder from disaster to disaster. Things happen in our life that causes anger, pain and bewilderment because of the low level of our psychological awareness. No matter how hard people try to change their lives nothing much happens. It would seem that intellectual understanding, of itself, cannot produce the desired and required change. Pious resolutions or saintly vows of amendment cannot of themselves bring any lasting improvement. Only by raising the level of psychological awareness can any real and permanent change take place. The only way of raising this awareness is by totally embracing the Divine Essence of love. Total surrender to love will mean you losing your personal life. This thought may upset you, at first, but honestly what has your personal life meant to you? Has it been a life full of superficial activities, mere distractions from the anxiety brought on by the nagging notion that there has to be more to life than your present thoughts and activities?

Don't be afraid of losing your present life; by losing your personal life you gain Universal Life. The Universal Life is one of lasting love, joy, peace, contentment and happiness. This life will be totally different from anything connected to your personal life experiences. In the Universal Life you will live in harmony with nature and mankind and in this loving harmony there is spiritual growth and understanding. All human imperfection and ignorance will be wiped away, to be replaced with divine knowledge and understanding. The Truth will be revealed in you and you will be freed from the world of illusion, imitation and limitation. Love will awaken you to a clear understanding of spiritual consciousness. Because there can be no stationary condition in spiritual understanding, growth is assured. Jesus said, "I've only to ask and legions will be sent to help me." These same, unseen spiritual legions will be ever ready to respond to all requests for help and assistance, either for you personally or for others you wish to help. Let love reside in you, the love of God, Christ, truth and mankind and all of the unseen spiritual forces are yours to call upon.

Love is brought into operation in our individual lives by aspiration, perception and inspiration.

Aspiration must be deeply profound and has to be heart-inspired. Repeat many times every day, *"Almighty God you my beloved father and I are one, for which I lovingly thank you. Amen."* Unless heart, soul and mind are the driving force of inspiration, love in all its beauty and grandeur will not be achieved, because it cannot manifest. You cannot play games with love; it will only respond to total honesty and absolute sincerity. When you master honesty and sincerity and when your aspiration has become your strongest desire then, and only then, will love transport you to a state of bliss that you can't at this time begin to imagine. Acknowledge God as the master architect, since it's He who sustains you when you acclaim God as being the creator and sustainer of your life in and out of the physical body and accept that whatever your problems are, God and His Spiritual Love will provide everlasting healing, harmony and peace.

Your troubles, whatever they may be, will end when you accept yourself as the beloved child of God. In love God becomes your partner and every barrier is removed and the way forward will be made known. The Journey to Paradise will be a journey of love and self-discovery; you will know yourself to be the perfect expression of the perfect Life Principle. For love will cast out all that is contrary to your true spiritual identity. In spiritual reality you are God's Holy Temple, it is God who lives in you; your soul is the Temple of the living God.

When you live the life of spiritual love you become the Temple of light, the perfect dwelling place for Almighty God. And your soul will radiate, to all mankind, love, wisdom and healing power; your light won't be seen with the physical eye, but it will shine on the whole of humanity. Spiritual light has never been more important, because the dark side of human nature is casting a long, lengthening and lasting shadow over civilisation itself. The future well-being of all of humanity is at stake and unless this moral darkness has spiritual light shed upon it, this darkness will eventually seriously obstruct common decency, compassion and understanding.

The antidote to this eventuality is to shine the spiritual light of genuine love on the moral darkness. Love, when properly understood, will be clearly identifiable as being the only means of eradicating all human problems and imperfections.

Love in all of its splendour is always freely available to any individual who is sincere in the quest for a life that has real meaning and worth, the truly wise and intelligent labour for eternity. Most individuals are concerned about today and tomorrow and never give serious consideration to where and how they will spend eternity? The present and future are taken care of throughout eternity by the adoption of love; this is the means of lasting happiness for all time.

It's all so wonderfully simple and easy to comprehend; spiritual love equals an eternity of profound peace and utter bliss in the company of God and high spiritual beings. Our finite human minds cannot conceive of the things that God has in store for those who live the life of spiritual love.

To end all trials, tears and tribulations we must liberate our souls from the tyranny of the unrealised personality. In love there is no limit to individual potential, all possibilities are inherent in our spiritual nature. There is, locked up, within all of us powerful spiritual forces, but power is denied us because of the damage we would surely do to ourselves and others without love to protect and guide. Love will open our spiritual eyes and ears. When this happens, we will see Creation as it truly is; we will hear God say, *"Well done my faithful children."*

Don't search for love in the physical world of form and phenomena; you won't find it anywhere, but deep within your spiritual heart and soul. And when you have found how to love you will have found the know how to live. There can be no meaningful or satisfactory life outside of love. People go through life seeking thrills and excitement as the means of achieving happiness; no one has ever found lasting peace, contentment and happiness in the external world of human activity. If you were to gain all the honours that the world has to offer; were you lavished with wealth untold; were you to have the admiration of all humanity, it could not make you happy. Only in a true and devout love of God and His children can happiness, peace and lasting contentment and health be found.

You now know that the real benefit of love begins when soul and consciousness leave the physical body at transition. Only through spiritual understanding will you know that your future in eternity is guaranteed. And spiritual understanding can only be obtained by love and service. In love the body is made strong. In love the mind is at peace. In love the soul proclaims the presence of God. If you allow your thoughts, emotions and deeds to be the end result of love, you will become conscious that the perfect life principle is manifesting through you. For love is the only means of infusing spirituality into human nature. God will communicate directly with you if you express the deepest and most profound love for Him and all of humanity. Do everything for love and you will be rewarded with a Divine Revelation of God's faultless Presence but don't expect this to happen unless you live your life in total service to the love of God and all His children. When you love God above everything, remembering that only this love of God can purify the heart, then you will experience lasting peace, profound joy and utter contentment. Love of God and for one another is the highest form of wisdom and those intelligent enough to seek union with God give expression to supreme wisdom. To go through each day, dedicated to do everything for the love of God, is the highest form of wisdom in action. A passive or static condition does not exist in genuine love.

Love, being spiritual energy, is ever active and all those who seek to bathe in this pool of spiritual energy must be prepared to become an active worker in God's vineyard. What type of activity will be required you may well ask? You will be expected to engage in activities that will exalt the whole of mankind. How you want to know, can I do such wonderful things for mankind? Well it really is very simple. Let's examine again what the problems are and then with wisdom, intelligence and your new knowledge decide what part you can play in saving mankind. The saving of mankind is a sacred, divine obligation for each and every one of us. Of course, we as individuals must first take steps to save ourselves. We can with wisdom, as we seek personal salvation, consciously help mankind also.

Mankind is living in a desert of human illusion. Human thoughts and reactions are mainly due to fear, hate, anger, doubt, ignorance and worry. Mankind, because of the morass of spiritual ignorance, can't rise above the crude imprisonment of the mass mind. Countless millions of minds are imprisoned in the dungeon of ignorance and illusion. Is it any wonder that our world is in turmoil, that corruption of all sorts is rampant and that violence in the home, in our society and between nations is everywhere evidenced! But all is not lost. We carry the solution around within us. This solution you now know and can use, not only for yourself but also for all of humanity. By embracing genuine love, by living to its dictates, you help in a very positive manner all of mankind. The ability to overcome negative conditions resides in the power of positive thinking. The most positive thoughts are these, 'The Father and I are one. I am the life,' God has created me to become the living expression of His Divine Love. This is of course true of everyone. God is no respecter of persons. God's love is universal and we are all equal in His perfect sight. Clearly see the Presence of God in every person! Know that love is the expression of God and is superior to all of human activity. By your ability to see God in all of mankind, by your willingness to become an active agent for the expression of love, you do exalt yourself and all of mankind. Make the power and authority of love known by your loving example.

People go about blundering from one crisis to the next because of their spiritual blindness and lack of soul's guidance. Your power and ability to help mankind is established when you genuinely love. By your unselfish love you become a shining example to all those who come into contact with you. Don't hesitate to give out your secret but give it in compassionate modesty. Love makes you worthy of giving advice because you can now offer deliverance from human folly and misery. By your loving thoughts, words and deeds, when given intelligent direction, you help elevate all of humanity.

What mankind needs now is nourishment of spirit. And mankind has to be made aware that humanity is sustained and maintained by the loving power of God alone. God is omnipresent and eternal and you are one with Him. There is no separation and to become consciously aware of this union of love, between you and God, is your salvation. To become an inspired soul, be aware of the living presence of God within you as love. This Presence of Love will bring an end to all personal problems and will bestow on you the power to heal in many situations. If you embrace completely God, Christ and love then the perfect life will find expression in and through you, making you the perfect person.

Yes, human perfection is possible to all whose thoughts, words and deeds are charged with love and a continual awareness of the presence of God within. And your thoughts of love can and will be used by spiritual beings, who will work with you to bring healing to all of mankind. If you worship God, who dwells in your soul and you continue to be aware of His presence within you and your worship is of devout love you will attain human perfection. The realisation of God's Divine Love for you is the only means of protecting yourself from all sorts of adversity. In genuine love you will be divinely and serenely protected. God Himself will be your protector and with Him on your side you are completely safe. The tabernacle of God is a tabernacle of safety and love, and is the means of gaining admission to God's inner Kingdom of Heaven. Know that your spiritual heart is the holy tabernacle in which God resides. Become aware of God's presence and say, God loves me, guides me, protects me and heals me, for which I am lovingly thankful!

You know now that God does love you; you know you are guided and protected by God and if you have faith and love for God, He will heal you. Be aware of His presence and lovingly say, *"Father you are my shepherd; there is nothing I shall want."* Immediately give thanks. *"Almighty God I lovingly thank you."*

You have been told in many different ways of the importance of love and of the power of love. Hopefully you are now convinced of the utter necessity of embracing the Divine essence of love. You also now know that love is 'the kingdom of heaven within' proclaimed by Jesus. You now understand that love of God and mankind is supreme wisdom in action. Understand clearly that love of God is the beatitude of mankind. For mankind can only be saved by understanding that love is the way to divine understanding.

Love Meditation

Behind the façade of your individuality, which in turn is your reaction to worldly experiences, exists the real you. You will be pleased to know that the real you is a beautiful spiritual being of love and peace. How, you ask, do I liberate the real from the outer personality? This liberation is the reason for your existence in a physical body. You now have the reason for your earthly existence and you now know how to make your life one of peace, joy, contentment and happiness. Your immediate task is to accept the need to master the art of loving more and more. With loving awareness of the in-dwelling presence of Christ this awareness becomes the spiritual nourishment for soul, spirit, mind and body. During this loving awareness you are very close to God, close enough for God to whisper His intention for you. As you listen for the sound of the silent word of love become aware of the breath of God entering your body, and as you breathe out, offer love to everyone and everything in the cosmos. And know that on breathing out that the love you express for all in creation becomes, a spiritualised energy that is used by high spiritual beings for healing and helping mankind. You can, you now know, become an agent of Almighty God's spiritual plans for humanity. The method you now know. Love is the way of personal and humanities' redemption and liberation. Yet another meditation you might consider is to offer God love and gratitude on behalf of humanity for whom and what God is. In the same circumstance as love meditation breathe in and mentally say 'love', and as you breathe out mentally say 'thank you,' Before you start this meditation pray thus: *"Father of all, on behalf of all your children I lovingly thank you for who and what you are and for having created us in your image and likeness. Thank you."*

You might consider this second meditation to begin immediately after your loving meditation. To thank God on behalf of all His children is a very powerful spiritual exercise and will reap for you rich spiritual rewards.

A mighty prayer: *"Lord God you and I are one, the reason being that you are the only living Being, the only Creator, and you have created me—and all of humanity—out of your perfect spiritual substance in your spiritual image and likeness. God you are the Perfect Being. You cannot therefore, create imperfectly. All of your divine attributes you have bequeathed to me and I am lovingly grateful."*

Lord God I am; I Am Who I Am. I am the life of Universal Love. I am the life of divine consciousness. I am the life of inspired intelligence. I am the life of all-inclusive wisdom. I am the life of profound peace. I am the life of healing ability. Remember, if you live the life of love, you will love life. Real love means joy, peace, contentment and spiritual fulfilment forever and ever. Amen.

He called for my will, and I resigned it to His call

But He returned me His own,
In token of His love
The Story

Chapter 10
The Ten Commandments

These personal statements of beliefs are definitely not intended to be an alternative to the Commandments present by God to the prophet Moses on Mount Sinai and bequeathed to all of humanity.

1. **God** is the only eternal reality. His attributes as described in the Bible are:
   i. Omnipotent (all-powerful),
   ii. Omnipresent (everywhere present),
   iii. Omniscient (all good). God can't be understood by human intelligence alone; the individual, whoever they maybe, but who do not know themselves, should not be surprised that they don't understand God.
2. **Mankind possesses** a higher faculty greater and higher than mere intelligence, namely institution, but this must be called into manifestation by frequent prayer of truth. Such as 'You my beloved Father and I are one,' Remember God is omnipresent there is not a millimetre of space in the whole of the Cosmos that is not God occupied. Truly you and the Father are one when the individual accepts this spiritual union and behaves accordingly that person treads the road that leads directly to the gates of paradise and beyond.
3. **Love** is unfailing. It will of itself correct all fault and deliver the weary traveller to profound peace that can only be experienced by those who love, totally, completely and unconditionally. The Bible in three beautiful words gives a truly remarkable definition of God. It proclaims 'God is Love'; therefore, love has to be the most potent power in the universe. Love is infallible and will eliminate all faults and correct all

human imperfections forever. When love is fully accepted and given unlimited expression, the person who has the spiritual wisdom to act accordingly will personally experience the crowning glory of spiritual liberation from all bondage and limitation. Love without eyes sees all, love without ears hears all, and love without mind knows all.

4. **If every thought was conceived in love,** if every word was spoken in love, and every deed was performed as an act of love, God would send legions of His angels to surround you and they would feel privileged to be in your company.

5. **Truth:** The quest for truth has to be sought diligently, for in love and truth there is liberation from emotional pain, frustration, fear, and folly; unless truth is established and put to right use there can be no spiritual evolution. Truth being the highest spiritual authority bestows on the person that achieves truth, all spiritual power and he or she becomes in reality the embodiment of the living God. The truth is forever the same; truth cannot be found outside of self. You and God are One. God fills all space. Each and every individual is the physical and spiritual manifestation of TRUTH.

6. **Obligations:** The disciples approached Jesus with this request, "Master teach us how to pray." Jesus taught them what we Christians call 'THE LORD'S PRAYER,' The first two are of supreme importance, 'OUR FATHER,' When Christians repeat these two words, they are proclaiming God universal that there is one God and one universal family of God. Every member of humanity is the beautiful offspring of Almighty God. This spiritual proposition should be diligently studied, scrutinised, investigated, and probed. The message itself is clear enough. We are all spiritually related. This places an obligation on each and every one of us to care and cherish every member of humanity. It's for the individual to decide how to discharge this spiritual obligation and none of us can escape this responsibility.

7. **Aspiration:** You should aspire to become that beautiful person that you know that you can be and know you should be. Yes, Willie Shakespeare was on to something extremely important when he wrote *'To be or not to be, that is the question,'* Aspire to know and comprehend the hidden spiritual resources that exist in your soul. God created you out of His perfect spiritual substance and God can't create imperfectly. You and

230

the Father are one. The acceptance of this truth will lead you onwards and upwards to become that beautiful person that you want to be and know that you can be.

8. **Life**: Why is it do you suppose that you have been given life? What obligations, if any, does life demand from each and every individual? If we refuse to countenance the reasons for life on planet earth where and how will we spend eternity? What penalties, if any, will be imposed on those who refuse or ignore this spiritual duty? Our lives are burdened by our insistence on procuring positions of power and authority or the possession of material goods in the vain hope that position or things will confer peace and contentment on our lives. The only thing that has the authority to confer happiness is a contented mind; the only means of establishing a contented mind is to rid the mind of all self-destructive negative thought, such as hate, anger, greed, envy, and jealousy, and resentment, and replaced with thoughts of love, compassion and clear understanding.

9. **Intelligence**: The finite mind of mankind has serious limitations; if we decide to travel the spiritual path human intelligence will not of itself deliver us from the clutches of human folly. There exists in every individual the spiritual power and authority of God and is always available to anyone seeking redemption from ignorance and human foolishness. To fully comprehend life and our obligations to it we should seek to know what our purpose on planet Earth is meant to achieve and how the achievement can be accomplished? We should therefore seek guidance from our spiritual soul, which is of God and from God; this spiritual gift we have to our cost ignored.

10. **Prayer** is inevitably thought off as being a means of securing a favour or favours from God; prayer should be a loving sentiment of gratitude to God for all the wonderful gifts bequeathed to us. Prayer is meant to be a quiet conscious union between the aspirant and God. God dwells within every person; pray to the in-dwelling Presence that is always present; accept that prayer is the solution. When you pray, be aware of the presence and with faith make your request; listen to your unspoken word and when you hear so also does God. God is not afar-off dwelling in some remote area in the Cosmos. The spiritual truth is that we live, move and have our being in Him.

11. **Compassion,** when wisely understood and practiced is a very beautiful means of becoming a person of spiritual consequence. Concern that provokes sympathy and loving support for those in need of emotional help and assistance, particularly those who live in destitution in the third world, will lead the compassionate individual directly to the gates of Paradise. Their lives will become a very pleasant experience, like a walk along the beach on a late spring evening.

12. **Repentance:** There can be no spiritual advancement until there is atonement for past follies; possibly the greatest folly of all was indifference of the spiritual and satisfaction with the mundane activities.

Chasing after a reputation that will only further egotistical ambitions, in a futile effort to be admired and to default on our spiritual obligation to God and self is folly at an extravagant level. There is one great certainty accepted by all of humanity which is the event called death. In truth, there is no death for the soul, it will survive into eternity. The wise and intelligent will labour for eternity while fulfilling their worldly obligations.

Conclusion: These commandments are meant to be of some spiritual benefit to those seeking to know and understand what life is all about. There are a number of questions that every intelligent person should ask of themselves, (1) Why am I living on planet Earth in a physical body of corruptible matter? Is there a spiritual dimension to my life? If so what relevance or meaning should I understand concerning spirituality? What will happen if anything, when I die?

Where and how will I spend eternity?

I want to quote from Ralph Waldo Emerson, probably the greatest mystical thinker that America has produced.

"If you always do what you have always done, you will always get what you have always got."

Jesus said: "Of myself I can do nothing it's the Father WHO EVER REMAINS within me he does the work." Jesus was able to perform miracles because he was always consciously aware of the presence of God existing within him. To me this statement from Jesus is the greatest spiritual advice ever made known.

To those seeking healing I offer the following advice, ask God once and once only for healing; ask in faith (Which is only a continuous constructive thought held immovably in the purified mind). When you've made your request give expression to this continuous prayer of gratitude.

Pray thus, "Almighty God, I lovingly thank you that my physical wellbeing is now as perfect as is your Universal Spiritual Love that you have bequeathed to me. Again, Lord God with love and devotion I lovingly thank you. Make every word become alive with the awareness of the Presence of God alive within you."

When Moses went to Mount Sinai and received the Ten Commandments, he ask God, "Who shall I sent me," and the response was *"I AM, WHO AM."* The name of the nameless one is "I am, who am." Reverse the name of God (Who Am I Am). So the identification of every person is 'Who am I am,' We were all created by God in His image and likeness.

Prayer: Any individual may use the name of God in the personal pronoun by saying, who am, I am, the life of universal consciousness bequeathed by God to me and all of humanity for which I am lovingly and sincerely grateful.

Who am, I am, is the life of universal love bequeathed by God to me and all of humanity, for which I am loving and sincerely grateful.

Who am, I am, the life of universal truth which is as proclaimed by Jesus. "I and the Father are one." Truth is Universal as it applies to every individual and not to any particular person. Each and every individual is the Divine manifestation of truth which is that God dwells in everyone and everything in all of His Creation.

Lord God I lovingly and sincerely thank you for bequeathing the truth to all of humanity.

"Who am I am the life of spiritual intelligence that you have bequeathed to me and all of humanity for which I lovingly and sincerely thank you.

"Who am I am the life of universal wisdom bequeathed by you to me and all of humanity for which I lovingly and sincerely thank you.

"Who am I am the life of spiritual compassion bequeathed by you to me and all of humanity for which I lovingly and sincerely thank you. Amen."

A prayer that should be said every day with deep devotion and an awareness of the presence of God who dwells in every atom, cell of every person.

"Lord God to you this day I dedicate every beat of my heart; every breath I breathe, each thought, spoken word, step I take, deed I perform. I offer all to you

this day as an expression of my loving gratitude for all that you have bequeathed to me and all of humanity."

Interruption from the spiritual narrative.

Chapter 11

A Dying Leper at the Taj Mahal in Agra, India

In the second week of my first visit to India in the year of our Lord 2001 I decided to visit the world heritage site, the Taj Mahal close to the city of Agra.

Having travelled from Delhi in an overcrowded train that was uncomfortable, hot and slow, I finally arrived in Agra, only to be immediately surrounded by a hoard of rickshaw owners touting and pestering me to use their taxi to take me to the Taj. Upon arrival at the Taj I marvelled at the splendour of this wonderful edifice. I spent a couple of hours meandering through this marvellous edifice left and decided to go for a walk alongside the Taj Mahal where I came upon a garden restaurant and decided to have a light lunch. Having satisfied my hunger I paid for my meal and headed to my village destination, when I almost immediately observed what I thought was the dead body of a youngish man. I thought to myself—*not again*—the day previous I came across a dead body of an old homeless street woman on the street outside the New Delhi Railway Station. The police maintain a twenty-four-hour presence at the station entrance, which was only twenty-five meters from the police cabin I reported the presence of the dead female to the police on guard and he informed me in a very off-handed manner that he would deal with the matter later. As he was standing not engaged with any other duty, I requested that he report the matter to the appropriate authority. He shrugged his shoulder and walked off in a calculated act of displeasure. I went after him, volunteered my name and requested his name and rank; at this he became very annoyed and told me it was not my business to asked him questions, to which I retaliated that my oldest son was the principle secretary to the minister of Foreign Affairs in the Irish Government and if the presence of the old street woman was not reported quickly, I would ring my son and the matter would be reported to his superiors. I repeated my request for his name and rank;

he relented and reported the information volunteered by me. I assured the officer I would stay by the body until it was removed, which happened within fifteen minutes.

In India there is a fear or respect of superior authority and it was out of fear that my request was conceded to. So you can imagine my apprehension at the thought of finding another dead body. When I reached the person lying prone on the footpath it was immediately obvious the man was a leper; a substantial section of his left foot had rotted and remainder of the foot was oozing a pinkish fluid. His right hand was also severely affected, much of his was rotted away, and the hand was oozing a pinkish fluid; the stench from his rotting flesh suggested that both hands and feet were gangrenous. Upon close inspection he was asleep but very much alive his chest which moved methodically as he breathed slowly. I shook him gently and after several agonising seconds and to my relief he opened his eyes. I attempted to verbally communicate with this leper, but to no avail as he spoke no English and I spoke no Hindi. There was no one in the vicinity so I decided to return to the garden restaurant and purchased a small meal assuring the owner I would return with his cup and plate. Having paid for the meal I returned to the leper and had to help him to sit-up so that he could eat the meal; during many visits to India I've had to endure heart-breaking experiences, and this particular episode remains by far the most painful. It was patiently obvious that this leper was only days from certain death and here he was lying on a footpath without any medical intervention; he was every callously abandoned by those who could have helped, but didn't. As the leper was slowly eating the café owner appeared. I immediately verbally castigated him wrongly thinking he was concerned about his utensils. Before he could speak, I repeated my promise to return with cup, plate to his café; he collected his belongings and requested that when it was convenient to call and talk with him. Several minutes later, in a state of deep depression, I returned to the café and the owner had placed on the counter the money I paid for the leper's meal. When offered the refund I ardently refused to accept it and offered to leave a sum of money to pay for a meal for the next six weeks. He requested that I accept the refund; he told me because of my intervention on behalf of the dying leper he felt shame [his word] and promised to provide one meal per day for the leper. I sincerely thanked him and asked why this unfortunate young man was lying alone and dying? I asked what I could do to help, and to my amazement he informed the leper who was laying at the gate of Mahatma Gandhi Leper Colony. On hearing this, I entered the leper colony and there was a committee meeting taking place under a leafy tree; my appearance, which was totally unexpected caused some surprise. I asked was there an English speaker in the committee It transpired that all five members spoke good English. The secretary who was a well-educated individual spoke perfect English; I informed them of something that they were already aware off, that a leper close to death was lying outside on the footpath; they confirmed that they were aware of the situation. I asked why the leper was not admitted into the colony and was informed they had no accommodation to offer.

I retaliated by offering to provide a large tent and to pay a rent for the space of the tent and give the committee $200 for the provision of meals the offer was firmly rejected on the pretence that their constitution did not permit this sort of suggestion. I was dejected before I entered the colony; this casual indifference to a desperately ill man was, to me, nothing short of cruelty. My feelings and anger was made abundantly clear. I rounded on the committee and told them that the man dying on the footpath was after all a victim of leprosy and deserved a more compassionate response to my request for assistance for a fellow human being. I told the committee that they should feel a deep sense of shame and their refusal to help this stricken individual was heartless, cruel and totally unreasonable.

It became all too obvious that I was trying to discuss with a summer insect on the subject of ice—a waste of time. How in the name of compassion and common decency could this lack of concern and sympathy for a seriously ill and near-death fellow leper be happening; thankfully, I never encountered a similar again.

As I was leaving the leper colony, almost as an afterthought. I asked how much money was required to build the tiny houses that prevailed throughout the colony and was informed that a leper house could be provided for £1000. I informed the committee that if I ever returned to India, I would provide the money to build a new house; of course when I made this promise I had no intention of ever returning to India.

Three days after I arrived home. I was in my office uploading images from my camera that I captured while travailing in India, and I became upset at the plight of those who have been smitten by the dreadful disease of leprosy. Tears were streaming from my eyes. At that moment my wife entered my home office with a cup of coffee, and immediately became aware that I was in some distress.

My condition prompted my wife to ask what was wrong with me; my response was that I informed her that I was returning to India to bring some little measure of relief to those living stunted lives in abject destitution.

I have been to India some sixteen times and have provided the finance to build seventy-three houses for lepers, a mixed gender orphanage, five schools in different districts in India, have worked with the destitute from Nepal in the east to Mexico in the west; I'm very much aware that what I've done any person could do.

Action with Effect is a tiny registered charity number NIC-103339 and is the only charity that works with lepers, orphans, and street children in the subcontinent of India.

All members are unpaid volunteers, giving of their time without any remuneration.

Therefore, every penny we receive goes to the destitute.

Eamon Melaugh giving first aid to a homeless boy who has a catheter inserted into his bladder through his penis.

Action with Effect exists to offer some measure of relief from ravages of cruel, unrelenting poverty and to provide some measure of hope for the destitute, marginalised, untouchable lepers, orphans, and homeless street children in India.

Any activity that promotes hope amongst the grouping mentioned must be at the core of everything we do. In the planning and implementation of everything we undertake we should to the fullest extent encourage the participation of those who are marginalised, shunned, and in many cases despised by Indian society.

It's all too obvious that destitution will never be eradicated by N.G.Os, as it would necessitate the involvement of the collective developed and prosperous countries who have the financial resources but lack the moral will to end the sickening spectre of starvation, disease, and daily deaths counted in the tens of thousands every single day.

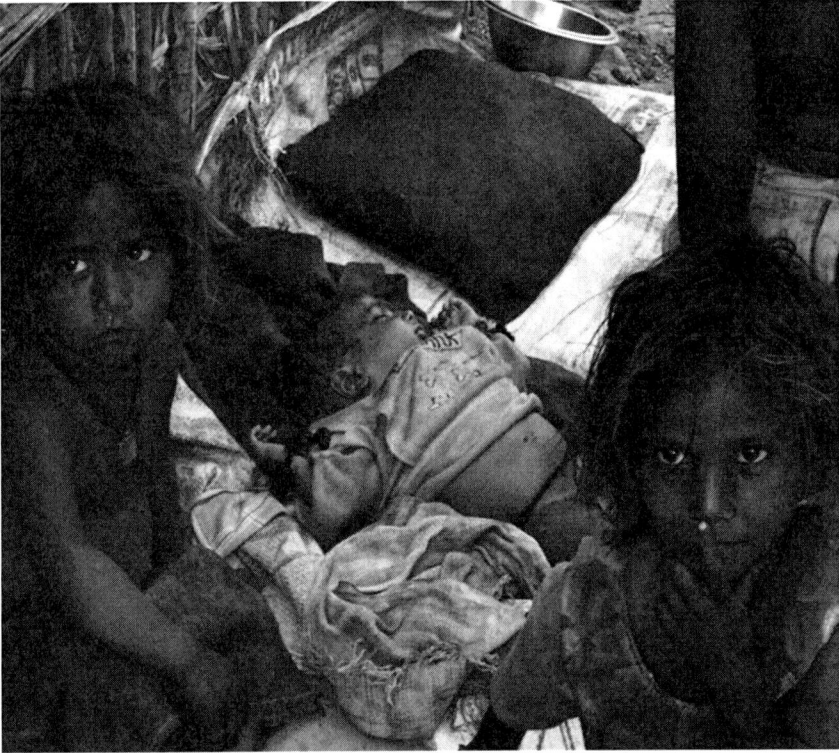

The photo is of a destitute untouchable family of five.

There are millions of destitute families living in abject squalor and no one seems to care. Action with Effect cares but we desperately need financial support to continue our involvement with the homeless destitute.

The combined concentration of two groupings could end the ravages of death from painful disease the inevitable consequences of malnutrition; there are no reliable statistics of the number of daily deaths from starvation. The best information available suggests that 50.000 of which 26.000 are totally innocent children, die every day. World governments spend $ ten billion every day on the procurement of armaments designed to slaughter and maim fellow human beings. One day's armaments budget could feed the hungry for in excess of a year; the EEC common agriculture policy is cruel lunacy paying farmers billion of £££ not to grow food while thousands of destitute are condemned to a slow lingering painful death for lack of basic food.

Our world leaders are in the main totally and actively indifferent to the squalor of their self-imposed importance. At best they stand accused of gross moral indecency and squalid ineptitude, living worthless lives of affluence and in difference; their only concern is the magnitude of their self-importance.

In the first quarter of the 21Century two billion are malnourished 870 million are on the verge of starvation.

The two groupings referred to as having the financial capacity to end the unrelenting pain and deaths of the destitute are, (1) the collective labour and trade unions of the developed world, (2) the combined and concentrated effort of the Christian churches. The world-wide Christian churches could and should set aside one Sunday each year for the relief of world hunger. On the designated Sunday all monies collected should be set aside for the relief of hunger; all monies to be spent exclusively on the destitute. Young Christians between the ages of 19-24 could be sent in a hands-on operation to setup feeding stations, to purchase food, to cook and distribute the food.

I have written a lengthy letter to the Pope who has made some comments concerning the destitute. I posted the letter years ago; since then, as yet, there has been no response, not even an acknowledgment.

To be honest I never entertained any hope of awakening the moral conscience of mother church.

The indifference of the world-wide Christian community is staggering for this reason; the most popular prayer in churchanity is the lord's prayer, whose first two words are, *"Our Father."* These_words proclaim one God and one Family of God. To repeat this prayer and be indifferent to the suffering and daily deaths of tens of thousands of destitute children is spiritual hypocrisy of the worst type. Personally I accept the starving children as my children and my responsibility demands from me a compassionate response. I have worked at an individual level for twenty years in six different countries. In 1995 I founded

Action with Effect, a tiny Irish based 'third world ' charity registration number XR 88946. Visit our website, actionwitheffect.org, for confirmation.

I now appeal to the Unions of the world to raise their sight to look with compassion on those who will never be afforded the dignity of a meaningful occupation to stave off hunger, disease, and premature deaths of their families.

Compassion is one of the greatest virtues known to mankind, but virtue has to be nurtured and given intelligent direction. FOR SURE NO PERSON WILL EVER COME TO ANY HARM IN THE PERSUIT OF COMPASSION.

I call upon the British Trade Union Movement to take a leading role in galvanising a world-wide compassion crusade to eradicate from the face of planet earth the scourge of all deaths from starvation.

As previously stated, Action with Effect is a genuine charity. All members are unpaid volunteers and give of their time and talents for the sake of compassion. Every pound we receive goes in full to the destitute that we are privileged to serve; when volunteers go to India they pay all expenses from their personal finances.

Our intention is to open a school for the most deprived children in the world, the children of leper parents. The only passport out of life-long destitution is education, there is no other route.

Eamon Melaugh, founding member of Action with Effect.

Please visit our website for confirmation of our status and evidence of the work we are privileged to be involved with.

We do not differentiate on the basis or creed, colour, culture, or gender all are the children of the one god.

www.actionwitheffect.org. We will with consummate gratitude and accept any size of donation.

Eamon Melaugh: Love without eyes sees all, without ears hears all, without mind knows all.

If the tens of thousands of children who die every day were white Christians there would be a cataclysmic explosion of outrage and immediate compassionate action would be implemented to end the suffering of Christian children. My question to so-called Christians is this, why the total indifference? Are not all children equal in the sight of God? Every child is the most beautiful thing in all of creation and should be treated with dignity and respect.

The Power of Prayer

The story is told of an American infantry combat regiment that fought many battles during the course of the Second World War and gained a reputation for being ruthless and daring. In one engagement the regiment suffered seventy-four percent causalities, the highest number of any engagement during the course of the war.

The American European Army Command decided because of the decimation of the regiment to order a period of rest, recuperation and replacement. A new commanding officer was installed and at the first regimental parade on the completion of his speech he informed his troops that every day no matter what the circumstances there would be no exception. All members of the regiment would come together to recite the 21st psalm. The result was that the regiment suffered no fatalities during any of the following engagements during the course of the war; there were on occasions no fatal wounding of individuals of the regiment.

Was the lack of fatalities the result of providence or was there divine intervention? It would stretch the imagination beyond credibility to accept that chance alone was responsible for the dramatic change on the fortune of this regiment. You can be sure that those who prayed daily to be spared death on a battle field would have prayed with great intensity and sincerity.

Psalm 23

'The Lord is my shepherd; there is nothing I shall want.

He makes me to lie down in green pastures, he leads me to still waters; he restores my soul.

He guides me in the path of rightness for His name's sake.

Even though I walk through the valley of the shadow of death I will fear no evil for you are with me: your rod and staff they comfort me.

You prepare a table before me in the presence of mine enemies.

You anoint my head with oil; my cup overflows.

Surely goodness and love will follow me all the days of my life and I will dwell in the house of the lord forever,' Eamon Melaugh.